BRONX BRAT

ALVIN BILLINGS

Copyright © 2019 by Alvin Billings

All rights reserved.

No part of this book may be reproduced in any form or by any electronic or mechanical means, including information storage and retrieval systems, without written permission from the author, except for the use of brief quotations in a book review.

*Dedicated to the Memory
of my Dear Friend and fellow Bronxite
Joseph Del Bourgo
who passed away on Jan. 10, 2017
after 55 years of friendship
and to the Memory of my sisters
Gloria and Carol
who died far too young,
leaving behind grieving parents
and two grieving brothers.*

Ode to the Bronx
Yet I will look upon thy face again,
My own romantic Bronx, and it will be
A face more pleasant than the face of men.
Thy waves are old companions, I shall see
A well-remembered form in each old tree,
And hear a voice long loved in thy wild minstrelsy.

Joseph Rodman Drake, *early 19th century*

Contents

Preface	xi
1. Memories of the 'Old Block'	1
2. Jenny, My Stickball Sweetheart	5
3. Bernie's Parents Marry	11
4. Bernie's Earliest Birthdays	15
5. Anschluss: Precursor to World War II	23
6. Bernie's Family	31
7. Baby Sister Gloria	47
8. Bernie Turns Five	55
9. Little Bernie Learns of War	63
10. A Young Friend Dies	69
11. Starting School in the West Bronx	75
12. Grandpa, My Hero	85
13. The Twins are Born	93
14. 1943: Wartime Riot in Harlem	99
15. First and Second Grade: Knowing Too Much	107
16. The Twins: Early Years	115
17. A Quiet Retreat to the Library	121
18. Bernie's Dad Tries to Buy a Taxicab	127
19. The Family Gathers at Grandpa's	133
20. Grandpa Goes To Heaven	143
21. The Great Blizzard of 1947	151
22. Dad in Danger	159
23. Baseball and the Circus	165
24. Mom Gets Jealous	171
25. Let's Pretend and Let's Play	181
26. Exploring the Bronx	191
27. Manhattan Adventures	199
28. Palisades Park Beckons the Bronx	207

29. Atlantic City Trip Interrupted: Aunt Dolly Elopes	217
30. Truman, Israel and Junior Smuggler Bernie	227
31. The Melting Pot	233
32. Our Dogs: "Beauty the Second" and "Lucky"	237
33. Bar Mitzvah Preparations	247
34. Sixth Grade at PS 11: School for Smarts	255
35. Macombs Junior High	265
36. Gloria Comes of Age	277
37. Seagate in the Sand	283
38. Coney Island	291
39. DeWitt Clinton High School	299
40. Transfer to Theodore Roosevelt Evening High School	313
41. Discovering Girls	321
42. Wedding Bells Ring for Gloria	329
43. The Crippling Car Crash	337
44. Carol's Music: Triumph & Finale	343
45. Fond Memory	353
Epilogue	355
Acknowledgments	357

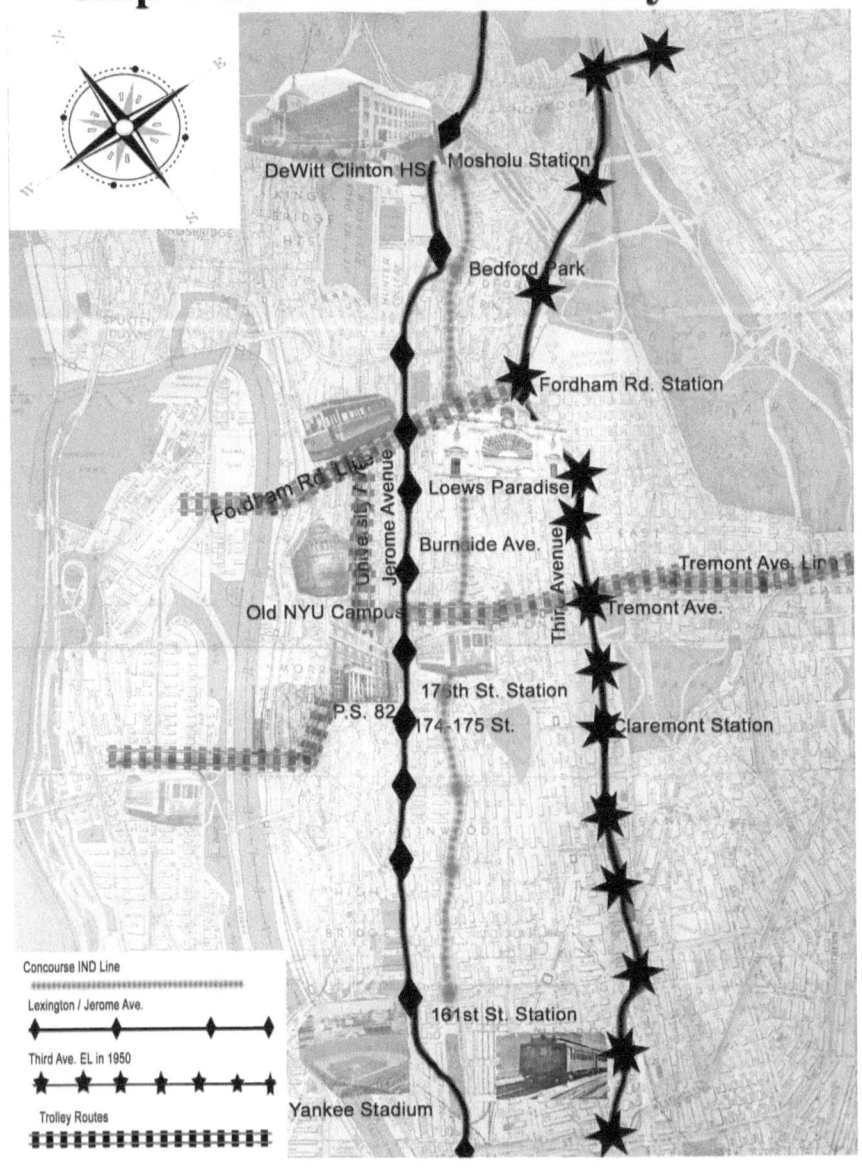

Preface

This is the story of Bernie Seiden, a precocious boy growing up in the Bronx of the 1940s and '50s. It was a far different Bronx than the Borough eulogized by poet Joseph Rodman Drake in his ode: *To my own romantic Bronx,* lyrically set in the pastoral Bronx of the early 19th Century. While mainly based on memories and experiences of the author, this book is an adaptation of these events, with some character names changed to protect their privacy.

Bernie's Bronx was urban and gritty. There were many dark-fronted older apartment houses looming amongst a scattering of newer art-deco buildings, and mottled greenish public parks bordered by cracking asphalt paths.

Bernie's tale begins with his paternal grandfather Adolph Seiden, who died six weeks before Bernie was born. In 19th century Germany, Adolph was once a respectable old-time Jewish name to bestow on boys. But family tradition to name a baby to honor a deceased grandparent was abruptly broken by the Seiden family's first-born child Bernie. Jewish babies born in the 1930s were NOT named Adolph for obvious reasons!

Bernie's story continues with the close, bonding relationships with his father and maternal grandfather—paternalistic, retired businessman Moritz Ralutzky. These positive adult male relationships helped balance his emotional difficulties with his mother. She was a caring person, but excitable and frequently antagonistic in dealing with her children and relatives. Dad was often henpecked into silence and withdrawal from her.

Bernie's childhood was mostly a lonely one, There were often few other children to play with. He first had a pair of early pre-kindergarten playmates, twins Harry and Sammy. That relationship was wiped out by the sudden death of Sammy at age four. Harry's mourning parents quickly moved out of the neighborhood because of the bitter memory. Five years went by before Bernie had another close friend, beyond just an occasional playmate, who was not silly or shallow, as many other Bronx kids were. That new friend was Randolph (Randy) Jones, a bright black boy—son of the superintendent in the apartment house across the street.

Struggling to emotionally overcome the deaths of both a beloved uncle and his Grandpa during his seventh year, Bernie began a complex journey towards adulthood as both bratty schoolboy, caring older brother to siblings, and precocious child.

At war with God, his parents, the school system and sometimes other neighborhood kids, Bernie did not grow up easily, but he DID manage to grow up! Now, let him tell his own story, and we will also relate the tale of the people and events that shaped his young life. Some of these stories later were told to Bernie in his adult years by older surviving relatives.

1

Memories of the 'Old Block'

*T*here it was. A prim 54-point gilded signboard font displayed on a bright sunny spring day in the window of my neighborhood Queens Pharmacy—UNDER NEW MANAGEMENT: Stefan Kaczynski, R.PH and Martin Kaczynski, R.PH. Registered Pharmacists. *Familiar names*, I mused briefly ... then remembered in a flash ... *they were my childhood enemies from over a half-century ago!* I was now seventy-five years old—an age when a surprising chance encounter with someone not seen in many years can trigger old memories.

The plain old dignified "Johnson's Drugs" sign had disappeared from the storefront window. Pausing, I read the new sign in wonderment ... *it's easy to greet a childhood friend not seen in decades, but how do you greet a childhood enemy?*

I thought to myself ... *Stefan Kaczynski. Hmmm. Is this the bully 'Steve' I knew and hated in my old West Bronx neighborhood? It's too coincidental. I cannot believe my eyes—there couldn't be two Steve Kaczynski's practicing as pharmacists in Queens, with partner-brothers named Martin!* But there it was—on the store sign. I paused, briefly trying to rationalize this coincidence of past names in my mind. Instead, with a brief shrug, I strolled into the drugstore.

While old man Johnson had still owned the pharmacy, I sometimes bought shaving cream and razors there, but had never seen the Kaczynski brothers behind the counter before. Mr. Johnson or his clerks waited on me sometimes, without any name recognition.

Steve greeted me routinely at the counter. "Can I help you?"

"Hello, Steve." I smiled at him, offering a firm handshake and a touch of recognition. "Congratulations. Lots of luck with the store! Nice new sign you have outside … should draw in some good business." Steve accepted the handshake gingerly, eyeing him in puzzlement. Hesitatingly, he asked, "Do I know you, Mr …?" His voice trailed off. I was surprised that he did not remember me and left.

A few days later, I walked into the store again to see both brothers. Steve greeted me at the counter without personal recognition. "Can I help you?" I answered quietly. "Don't you remember me, Steve? I am Bernie Seiden, your childhood enemy from the West Bronx." Steve looked startled, and raised his eyebrows with a look as if he were confronted by a process server. Just then, his younger brother-partner Marty walked in, eyes squinting past the counter at me in a glimmer of recognition. Marty still looked like Steve's younger brother, but they were now grown and graying professionals.

"Bernie?? Oh yeah, Bernie from the West Bronx … Macombs Road."

Steve winced. Marty, always the friendlier brother, broke out in an adult simulation of the gap-toothed grin he had flashed as a kid. He was still tall and skinny, but the braces on his teeth were long since gone.

"Oh yeah ... Bernie," Steve murmured vaguely. "Nice to see you again. Excuse me, I have some prescriptions to fill." He hurried off with a discomfited look on his face.

Now it was Marty's turn to get uncomfortable. With a final light sarcasm he said, "It's often more interesting to meet childhood enemies than childhood friends," Marty Kaczynski then excused himself to wait on other customers. I pondered resignedly, *I guess Steve doesn't like being reminded of his bully-boy days, when he was the terror of the block.* I left the pharmacy and never returned there again. My wife continued to shop there, since the Kaczynski brothers did not know her. After being snubbed by the reformed bully brothers, and other childhood memories both pleasant and otherwise, I became motivated to write this book about my childhood years, and about family, friends and enemies in the old-time Bronx as it was in the 1940s and '50s.

2

Jenny, My Stickball Sweetheart

*I*t was a bright cloudless early summer afternoon back in 1950, about a month before the Korean War started. A few miles south of Macombs Road, in Yankee Stadium, young rookie outfielder Mickey Mantle was trying to fill the shoes of an aging and ailing Joe DiMaggio, increasingly hobbled by a heel-spur in the final phase of his fifteen-season career as the star centerfielder of the New York Yankees.

'Joltin' Joe was painfully playing out his next-to-last major league baseball season that year. But on most Bronx blocks, stickball was king of the street games, not baseball with its greater window-shattering potential. For a fifteen-cent pink rubber 'Spaldeen' ball and an old broomstick, every boy lived the dream of someday going to bat for the New York Yankees.

My memories today flash back to recall Steve, the 'Kaczynski Kid', star stickball player of the West Bronx, who had almost made it to the baseball majors. A New York Yankees scout spotted and signed him as a Taft high school graduate. In the next two years, he only got as far as triple-A minor league ball in the Yankee farm chain. But he did not 'make the cut' for the Yankees in spring training in his third year. Instead, Steve returned to Fairleigh Dickinson University in New Jersey to study pharmacy. His brother Marty graduated two years later. Many years afterwards, Steve and Marty opened a retail drugstore in Bayside, Queens—my home neighborhood today.

* * *

CRACKKK! The broomstick bat whipped around in a semicircular arc. Steve hit the ball squarely. It soared over the delivery truck facing up the West 175th Street block and gained altitude rapidly as it arced over six-story apartment houses, then across Macombs Road to land on the far side. Outfielder Johnny Westin started back after it, but gave up after a few strides. "Heyyyy, a home run!" screamed the 175th Streeters as Kaczynski circled the bases. "Geez, it's over the roof," groaned the Macombs Road team. The teams often lost several Spaldeens per game—to traffic, frisky dogs and sewer gratings. Only Steve could lose balls to the rooftops and beyond. The losing team traditionally chipped in and paid for any balls lost in play.

It was a big inter-block stickball match on a Saturday in early June 1952, Macombs Road (the 'Macombers') vs. 175th Street (the 'Streeters'). There were no pitchers, but each batter tossed a ball upwards and could either hit it in mid-air or on the first bounce. The bases were marked in yellow chalk by the team captains, twenty paces apart. We played bare-handed, with some parents and passers-by briefly stopping by as an occasional audience. Catches and fumbles in the field alternated along our asphalt-paved street 'stadium.' Spinning balls hitting the ground often took weird bounces from the cracks or pebbles in the roadway. A sidewalk catch or bounce was a 'foul out' and the gutter was fair territory.

There were usually no umpires because nobody wanted to risk getting beaten up over a disputed call. The team captains argued, and if they didn't agree, then a coin toss settled the call on a disputed play. The home field for my team was on West 175th Street which had a mild one-block uphill slope between Grand Avenue and Macombs Road. First and second bases were marked before the game in chalk by the team captains, and home plate was a sewer manhole cover.

Players dodged traffic with lookouts posted at either end of the block to warn of oncoming traffic. Shrilled lookout cries of "Cars!", "Trucks", "Cops", or "Lady with a baby carriage!" stopped the game until they passed by. Local cops usually did not stop stickball games unless players were fighting or broke a window.

In contempt for the Macombers, their opponents (the Streeters) took Steve Kaczynsky, their star player, out of the game and substituted a girl for him. They were leading 3–0 at the time in the sixth inning. The Macombers were mortified. They had only eked out three base hits so far in the game. *Girls? GIRLS?? Playing against guys???* Even one girl was too much of a put-down to the team's boyish sports egos, some of the local boys thought, and then asked aloud, "what are girls doing, butting in on boy's sports? They have their own games! Hopscotch and Jump Rope!" Roller Skating, with clamped skates slipped over shoes and skate keys strung around necks, was one of the few sports equally shared by boys and girls in the Bronx. A few others and I were more quietly accepting of girls joining in our games, if they played well. In this game, I was the lookout for cops and cars while roaming the sidelines and walking up the block.

Jenny Selkirk entered the game as a Streeter substitute in the sixth inning, after their left fielder tripped and sprained his ankle. The Macombers laughed loudly when she stepped up to the plate with a runner on second and none out. I quietly admired her guts for getting into the game, but said nothing until she stepped up to bat. On her first swing, she lined a double to right field, which bounced off a Buick and scored the runner from second base. The laughing stopped. I cheered.

Jenny at bat

Jenny came to bat again in the ninth inning. With some half-hearted bravado, the Macombers captain called out "Betcha can't do it again!" She did even better. Jenny smashed a bases-loaded home run into deep right field. By our playing rules, a ball hit past the street corner 'on the fly' was an automatic home run, so that outfielders would not risk their lives chasing it into cross-street traffic.

Jenny jogged around the bases, ponytail flying, grinning and waving to all. The Streeters went on to win that game, 5-3. She was a tall and attractive twelve-year-old girl athlete, new to the neighborhood, and not a tomboy! She was not yet budding with signs of early womanhood, but her chestnut hair bobbed as she ran. She was lean-figured and moved with a fawn-like grace. I was smitten. My adolescent male hormones raged when I looked at her.

She was my first puppy-love—all pony-tailed and perky. With a feline quickness and enviable agility, she was the only neighborhood girl playing stickball with the boys on the block. Her pivoting style in double-plays earned her the nickname 'Spinning Jenny'.

Jenny did not throw balls with the awkward stiff-armed push-and-pivot stance and swing typical of girls her age. She rarely struck out, aiming her swing at the Spaldeen with a leveled batting stance. Her short, accurate swings of the broomstick bat sent hits to right, center or left fields. Wherever she aimed the ball, that's where it usually went.

I watched her play in stickball games against some other Bronx teams in the following weeks, once walking as far as Kingsbridge Road, two miles away. Jenny recognized me but only smiled and briefly said hello. Later I overheard the Kingsbridge first baseman say sarcastically, "Someone should check inside her pants to make sure she's a girl."

The other boys guffawed, but I responded angrily, screaming, "How dare you talk about a girl like that!", slugging him with a swift left to the gut and a right hook to the jaw. Joey went down, then got up with a bloody lip and scrambled off quickly.

Jenny strolled over to where I stood glowering. She said haughtily, "I didn't need you for that. I was about to slug him myself." Someone giggling on the sidelines called out, "Yeah, she will fight your battles for you any day," In a surly mood, I snarled back at them, "I don't need a girl to fight for me!"

Walking away from Jenny and the game, I felt crestfallen and emotionally crushed. Since young chivalry was now dead in the Bronx, if it had ever lived there at all, my puppy love for Jenny quickly died away in disappointment.

In the next few weeks, I made myself busy elsewhere with other sports, such as handball and punch ball. I never wanted to see Jenny play stickball again, so I stopped playing for the next several months. Handball was played on one bounce off an apartment building against one opponent or sometimes as doubles—two against two. The game was played within paving line sidewalk boundaries for 21 points. It was also played in playgrounds with a full-sized marked court. These street sports suited my then-soured adolescent mind as a consolation for the loss of Jenny. *No teams, and no girls ever again for me*, I vowed silently.

Several months later, Jenny and her parents moved from the neighborhood and disappeared from my life. Then I regained my emotional equilibrium and began to play stickball again.

In the Korean War era, (1950-53) most Bronx boys and girls did not begin dating until around age sixteen (*or so their parents believed!*). Romance, or its lesser cousin, 'going steady', was not supposed to happen until senior year of high school, at the earliest.

3

Bernie's Parents Marry

A dozen years before Jenny and stickball entered his young life, Bernie became the first-born child of David and Rose Seiden. They had married in 1935 at the Concourse Center of Israel, a conservative Bronx synagogue, after a two-year courtship.

Bernie's maternal grandparents sighed when Dad finally proposed to Mom. At last, a man had come to take unwed Rosie off their hands! One less mouth to feed, and well-worth the small dowry paid to her bridegroom-to-be. Was he a *"good catch"*? Not in professional or financial status. He was a cab driver. But he earned a living, which was more than many other men of higher education and life status were doing in the mid-1930s!

Dad's mother bluntly discouraged his occasional girlfriends, but she finally yielded to Dad's sister Claire, and brother Bill in their arguments that she was depriving my father of an opportunity for a married life of his own. It was ironic that his brother and sister extolled the virtues of marriage for Dad, since Aunt

Claire was divorced and childless and bachelor Uncle Bill had never married!

When they wed, Dad was 35 and Mom was 28—well past the usual marrying age in the Bronx Jewish community. An unmarried woman of 28 was deemed to be an *'alteh moid'* (old maid). It was considered a family disgrace if no substantial Jewish man wanted to marry her.

1935: Wedding of Bernie's parents

Aunt Claire was trim-figured, sophisticated and fascinating to Bernie. Her divorce made her a somewhat scandalous figure in the insular neighborhood of the middle-class Bronx. Feelings towards her were mixed with a tinge of envy by local women at her glamour and independence from any man. In an age when most women were stay-at-home housewives, and much of American male-dominated society strongly endorsed a female subordinate role, Claire parlayed her marketing degree into an executive position as a fashion buyer for Saks Fifth Avenue. She earned over two hundred dollars per five-day week, more than triple the money Dad made in a six-day week as a taxicab driver. Claire was caring to Dad, her brother, and to Bernie, her favored nephew.

Uncle Bill was a shadowy figure who rarely visited with his brother's family. Bernie only met him twice during his childhood years. He lived in a fancy westside Manhattan bachelor apartment, and owned a shoe store. For whatever reason, he kept a distance from the rest of his family. Perhaps it was the 'status' thing? He was a college graduate, and may have been ashamed of his brother being an uneducated taxi driver.

4

Bernie's Earliest Birthdays

*B*ernie was born on April 9, 1938 in the crumbling old grim grayish brownstone fortress of old Bronx Hospital on Franklin Avenue.

Old Bronx Hospital

Mom went into labor around 5 a.m. that day. Dad called his garage to take the day off from his taxicab. He knew it would be a long day in the delivery room, so off they drove to Bronx Hospital while Mom's contractions were still coming five minutes apart.

It was a cold gray spring morning, and the early mists chilled the streets for the few who were up and around at that hour. Bernie's Dad was joined an hour later by Grandma and Grandpa in the waiting room. He paced the worn carpet in the maternity waiting room for over five hours until the doctor came out to tell him that Bernie was born without complications.

Grandpa chatted softly with Dad while Grandma sat quietly on the sofa, not interrupting. As always, Grandpa, the patriarch, did much of the talking and did not ask for a woman's input. However, he did accept the parental choice of the neutral name Bernard for the newborn child. And that is how baby Bernie entered the world. His earliest conscious memory was of Aunt Irma, his 'not-Mom.'

In November, 1938 I was seven months old ... too young to form word thoughts or coherent images .... I remember sensing a hazy, dream-like brightness glowing ahead and being carried by Mom swaddled in a soft cotton blanket. A not-Mom lady sat next to her. We were riding on an elevated subway train.

Looking out the window, I felt peaceful, but disturbed at the tense way in which Mom held me. Reaching out to not-Mom for rescue, I wailed loudly. Mom handed me to not-Mom Aunt Irma, and her vibes soothed me.

Then the scene faded out like a dream ending. This image

stayed with Bernie for many years until he was old enough to ask Aunt Irma about the details of the infant experience and she confirmed his infant remembrance.

Understanding of words and images expanded rapidly in the early years of Bernie's development from babyhood into boyhood. Each birthday party marked a milestone in mental and emotional development. The third birthday was the first one to come into sharp focus of his memory. Bernie still played with age-appropriate toys, but in an imaginative, more grown-up way.

In later years, Bernie tried to remember his earliest birthdays, recalling ... *I do not remember my first birthday. That was a party for my parents and family to celebrate. I am sure I enjoyed it, too, since I have seen the pictures of myself eating cake with my face instead of mouth as a happy smiling baby. For my second birthday, I remember being aware that everyone was singing and laughing. I had on a party hat and was making silly faces at everyone. I could not yet separate fantasy from reality and the Bronx was the whole world to me, bright and shiny and exciting. I played with real doggies and with pretend doggies that were big and fluffy and talked to me.*

Now Bernie began to associate words with images and could remember things and events and what was good and bad ... These were his first steps towards thinking and experiencing in this world. He was still far too young to be aware of the beginnings of World War II raging far beyond the borders of the Bronx.

Sister Gloria was born three years later in April, 1941 and became the new baby of the family. Bernie overheard many young Bronx boys say that they believed girls were trouble for them, and sisters were the biggest trouble of all!

There was a cozy little third birthday party for Bernie at

home with his Mom and Dad, and Grandpa and Grandma. The apartment foyer was decorated with colored twisting streamers. He counted the candles, then announced his own surprise ... that he could count up to twenty! The family was duly impressed with this.

Bernie at Bronx Park, 1941

Presents were opened and Bernie thanked his parents for the toy fire engine with real battery-operated siren and flashing lights. From Grandma and Grandpa came a set of Lincoln Logs —a wooden mini-log set of interlocking parts wrapped inside a cardboard tube. The logs were used to construct model houses and forts.

After the party, Grandpa offered to show Bernie how to use the logs, and they sat down together to play with them.

His Dad helped out also with Lincoln Log lessons, and within a few more play sessions the next week, Bernie became proficient and started building model log cabins, lighthouses, towers and forts. Grandpa soon taught him the "Alphabet Song", sung to the same tune as "Twinkle, Twinkle, Little Star".

A, B, C, D, E, F, G
H, I, J, K, L, M, N, O, P
Q, R, S, T, U, V
W, X, Y and Z
Now I know my ABCs
Next time, won't you sing with me?

Then Grandpa went beyond the ABCs . . . well beyond!

Sensing a higher comprehension level in his grandson, on one bright Tuesday morning in May, he pulled out of a bureau drawer a file of pictures and advertisements. And, from the kitchen, Grandpa retrieved an apple.

"Bernie," he began. "Everything we see and do can have a picture that shows what it is. This is a picture of an apple." Bernie nodded solemnly. "But there is also a writing word for 'apple'." Grandpa then wrote the word 'apple' on a blank piece of paper. Then he pointed to each letter separately and pronounced them … "A.P.P.L.E. These are the letters of the word, APPLE.

Now we do the B ..." After the C and D, Grandpa told him, "Now you do these alphabet letters for me." Bernie dutifully copied these four first letters of the alphabet and went on over the next several weeks to progress through the alphabet, adding four more letters to his repertoire each time.

Grandpa tested Bernie by mixing up the order of the letters, and his grandson quickly identified each letter every time and wrote it out. When Bernie had acquired several dozen written words in his writing and reading vocabulary, he was able to read the *Golden Books* without interruption or mistake or coaching.

From the *Golden Books*, Bernie moved on to read *Grimm's Fairy Tales* and the *Merry Adventures of Robin Hood*. In his kindergarten year he discovered geography in an old, worn *Rand McNally World Atlas* while at the dentist's office. A fascinated Bernie pored over the pages and maps in color. There was also a constellation map displaying the stars in the Northern and Southern hemispheres with all the imaginary images of mythology that populate the sky.

The dental nurse noticed Bernie's nose buried in the Atlas and whispered curiously to his Mom, "is he really reading the atlas?" Mom replied, "yes, he is! He knows all the countries too!" The nurse declared, "this atlas is torn and worn. It was going to be thrown out anyway...." She paused.

"Bernie, how would you like to have it?" Bernie was thrilled. "Oh wow! My own atlas! It's old, and doesn't show the Anschluss, but that's OK. I will tape the torn pages and fix it up real good!" Mom and the nurse both looked blank. Mom asked, "Bernie, what is the Anschluss??" She never read newspapers or talked about the War.

Bernie explained. "The Anschluss" was the joining of Austria with Germany on the day I was born. Grandpa told me about it. The Austrians were a small nation that lost their big kingdom in

Europe after the first World War. They saw their joining with Germany as a way of sharing in the new German power.

It was only years later, after the defeat of the German Third Reich, that Austria claimed that they were Hitler's first national victim.

5

Anschluss: Precursor to World War II

Six hours east, and some four thousand miles away from the less-than-bucolic Bronx of the mid-20th century, was Vienna, the city of 365 Catholic churches, one for each day of the year. It had been the glorious past capital of the Austro-Hungarian Empire, spanning much of Central and Southern Europe in the mid-nineteenth and early twentieth centuries under the longest-reigning Habsburg Emperor Franz Josef I (1848-1916). But on April 9, 1938, it was the setting for the Anschluss—a joining of Austria and Germany into a new Greater Germany flexing its military muscles across a cowering Europe and in full view of an alarmed America.

This former imperial capital was also the center of a realm of splendid culture, marble palaces and Viennese waltzes. All this magnificence collapsed in 1918 after the First World War, leaving behind in its surviving central core area a much smaller Austria—a major defeated empire nation shrunk down into the size of a small province. For comparison, one can imagine if the territory of the United States were shrunk down to the size of New England by a conquering enemy.

On this day, gray-clad *Wehrmacht* infantry and armored battalions roared through the wide boulevard lanes of the *Ringstrasse* as the Austrian crowds cheered and waved, chanting the Nazi slogan, *Sieg Heil* (Hail to Victory!), the Hitler 'salute'. Some Jewish Austrians, who were following then-current events, may have had premonitions of the grim fate that awaited them. *Der Fuehrer*, a native-born Austrian, after a triumphant train ride through the Austrian countryside, had returned home to lead his birth-land into the Third Reich.

On April 9th, through cheering crowds strewing flowers in his path, Hitler was greeted in the late afternoon by Cardinal Innitzer, Primate of the Catholic Church in Austria. The Cardinal stood on the City Hall steps of Vienna, bedecked in his full scarlet robes with red *biretta* and flared golden pectoral cross to welcome Hitler to Austria.

Innitzer was flanked by two black-robed nuns, who joined him in brandishing the stiff-armed Nazi salute to Hitler while the assembled crowd roared approvingly. A few Viennese Christians and all Austrian Jews did not join the cheering. They remained discreetly silent and out of sight for their own and their family's safety.

The next day, on April 10th, a national plebiscite approved the joining of these two nations under Adolph Hitler by a 99 ¾% majority in a balloting held under the direct gaze of the *Gestapo* at open polling tables all across Austria.

On that brisk, cold late Central European springtime afternoon, Nazi flags by the thousands were fluttering in the stiff spring breeze as Hitler mounted the steps of the *Rathaus*, (City Hall), to receive the accolade of the Anschluss. A chill wind blew through the streets of Vienna, but few noticed it. The feeble

Weimar Republic had crumbled into dust, succeeded by a ruthless Fascist German, now German-Austrian regime that would soon plunge Europe into World War II.

Citing religious themes in the oratorical style of a Bishop being consecrated, Hitler invoked God's will to support his accession to supreme power over Germany and Austria.

"First of all, this land is a German land, and its people are German! Here the Reich once established its Ostmark. The Reich's people moved here and throughout the centuries fulfilled their duties in the Ostmark of the Reich. Not only did they remain German, they became what one might term bearers of the shield for Germany.

Secondly, this land cannot exist without the Reich for any period of time. What are 84,000 square kilometers today? What are six and a half million people? No one takes notice of them. Here, too, the realization applies that each German tribe by itself can be destroyed easily but once all tribes stand united they are invincible. Reality has proven that this land with these six and a half million people cannot exist in seclusion. This tiny country is incapable of solving the problems of its 300 thousand unemployed and hundreds of thousands of dispossessed. And this proves that so small a country is not a viable unit. The greatest evidence yet for the lack of all prerequisites for life lies with the development of birth and mortality statistics. No one can deny that this is the country with the lowest birth rates and the highest mortality rates.

Third, this Volk (people) never wanted to be separated from the Reich. The instant that its mission as leader of the peoples of the Reich was rendered obsolete, the voice of its blood spoke out. After the 1918 collapse, German-Austria desired to return to the Reich immediately. The democratic world prevented the Anschluss of German-Austria. Now the Volk has turned against this world. As the banner of National Socialism rose in Germany, the people here as well began to increasingly look to this symbol. In their hearts, hundreds of thousands pledged their allegiance secretly. Then came the time when this Volk suffered abuse at the hands of a group that could claim neither numerical superiority nor moral supremacy to justify its leading position.

Fourth, all I can say to those still not content: it is my homeland! I fought as a decent German soldier, and once this war was over, I went on a pilgrimage through Germany, and I won this country for me, this country so dear and lovely. When Germany was in despair, I was so proud to be German. I fought and struggled for this Volk, and I won its trust. I have wasted my best years in this struggle! This Reich has become so dear to me. It should come as no surprise that I yearned to integrate my own homeland in this dearest of Reichs.

Fifth, all I have to say to those who still remain untouched: I stand here today because I fancy that I can do better than Herr Schuschnigg! (Last Austrian chancellor before the Anschluss) *I believe that it was also God's will that from here a boy was to be sent into the Reich, allowed to mature, and elevated to become the nation's Fuhrer, thus enabling him to reintegrate his homeland into the Reich. There is a divine will, and all we are is its instruments.*

When Herr Schuschnigg broke his word on March 9, at that very instant I felt that Providence had called upon me. And all that happened in the next three days could only have come about because Providence willed and desired it. In three days the Lord struck them down! And it was imparted upon me to reintegrate my homeland into the Reich on the very day of its betrayal.

When one day we shall be no more, then the coming generations shall be able to look back with pride upon this day, the day on which a great Volk affirmed the German community. In the past, millions of German men shed their blood for this Reich. How merciful a fate to be allowed to create this Reich today without any suffering! Now, rise, German Volk, subscribe to it, hold it tightly in your hands! I wish to thank Him who allowed me to return to my homeland so that I could return it to my German Reich! May every German realize the importance of the hour tomorrow, assess it and then bow his head in reverence before the will of the Almighty who has wrought this miracle in all of us within these past few weeks! Sieg Heil!"

"Sieg Heil! Sieg Heil!" The Viennese screamed this mantra for all the world to hear, as they cheered wildly. Their new 'Messiah' had returned, bearing a *Hackenkreutz*—the swastika. The 'Thousand Year Third Reich', which was to only last a dozen years in all, now began to cast a sinister dark shadow by flaunting its goose-step image across Europe.

The United States also saw the Anschluss on its Pathé movie newsreels, but most people only felt it as a remote and distant threat—a whole ocean away from American shores on the day baby Bernie was born in the Bronx, about four thousand two hundred miles away from Vienna, Austria.

Western civilization was about to plunge into world war with Germany and its allies. Grandpa knew of it, but Bernie's parents did not fully understand what was happening in Europe.

Absorbed in their mundane affairs of maintaining a modest-size Bronx apartment and raising a family, Bernie's parents, like many other American families, were not directly affected at first by the new fascist militancies of Germany and Italy in Europe.

Meanwhile back in the still-peaceful pre-war Bronx, Bernie's Dad drove his taxicab, his Mom ran the Seiden home, and Uncle Dave ran the civilian section of the Brooklyn Navy Yard as an appointed administrator. His job was very 'hush-hush' and he was not allowed to discuss military issues or current events with anyone who lacked top-secret clearance.

Bernie was still too young to realize it then, but 1941 became a big year in the Bronx and everywhere else in the war-torn world. His world existed on three levels—firstly the fantasy realm of a bright and curious three-and-a-half-year-old American boy; secondly, the dimly-understood land of the real-world far away from the Bronx where big events were happening and read about in the newspapers and heard on the radio; and finally, the immediate Bronx world of family and school in which Bernie lived every day. The Nazis were at the height of their military power in 1941, building up to a climax on December 7, 1941, when Pearl Harbor was attacked by Imperial Japan, a Nazi ally. Hitler then declared war on the United States.

After the attack on Pearl Harbor, the United States entered the global struggle against the Axis powers. American industry geared up for wartime production. The classic luxurious Lincoln Continental had stopped production a few days past Pearl Harbor, after producing only several dozen 1942 Lincolns—which are rare collectors' items today. Ford retooled its assembly lines in six weeks to produce tanks, armored cars and military trucks, which began to roll out by the end of January, 1942. This happened in record-breaking time.

Unemployed workers from all across the country flocked into

military production factories that began large-scale hiring for the first time in over a decade. America had finally shaken off the extended Great Depression of 1929-39 by ramping up its armaments and supplying the British and allies in the Second World War.

Franklin D. Roosevelt ('FDR') began his historic third White House term of office in Washington, DC on January 20, 1941. Closer to home, Tom Dewey was Governor of New York State, Fiorello LaGuardia was Mayor of New York City, and Ed Flynn, a local Tammany Hall political boss, close friend and advisor to FDR, ruled the formidable Democratic Party machine of the Bronx.

Ed Flynn had been a long-time confidante of Franklin Delano Roosevelt since the time of FDR's governorship of New York (January 1929 -December 1932). Flynn was not the typical stereotype of a local political boss. He was a graduate of Fordham Law School, politically savvy and not corrupt. He was a 'fixer', power broker and patronage dispenser in the typical old Tammany Hall tradition, but as a Bronxite, he was not a member of Manhattan-based Tammany Hall itself. During the war years, he was an influential voice of the Bronx behind the scenes in Washington DC, and was often invited to dinner at the White House with Franklin and Eleanor Roosevelt.

The looming military shadow of overseas events went over the heads of most younger American children, as they went about their daily play and school studies, innocently learning their ABCs while the battles raged far away. But the war did not pass completely over Bernie's tousled top. He read the magazines and newspapers, saw the Movietone newsreels and discussed current events with Grandpa. At age four, Bernie began to emerge from cocooned babyhood into early boyhood as a lonely, high-IQ, high-tempered, and high-strung Bronx Brat.

6

Bernie's Family

Many years later, Aunt Irma told Bernie about the family history from the decades before he was born. Irma paid no heed to Mom's generally negative opinions of her own relatives—the Ralutzkys—Bernie's other maternal aunts and uncles, or the relatives on Bernie's paternal side of the family—the Seidens. Mom's father, Grandpa Morris Ralutzky, was tall, slightly stooped, fierce-eyed and white maned with some facial resemblance to the great maestro, Arturo Toscanini, late conductor of the NBC Symphony orchestra.

A white handlebar mustache framed his lower face, balanced by flowing grayish hair capped with a gold-trimmed black yarmulke. Grandpa often wore white or gray Coolidge-style, round-collared shirts and striped ties, offsetting his dark-toned business suit. His bearing was aristocratic, commanding instant respect from friends, family and strangers alike. As an elderly man in his mid-seventies, his gait was still firm, his stride purposeful. He was about seventy years old when Bernie was born as the first child of Rosie, his youngest daughter, the last of his thirteen children—a change-of life baby born to Grandma at age 45. Grandpa was wealthy, as Bernie's Mom was born in a hospital with doctors and nurses, instead of midwives in attendance.

Bernie's family—Back row: Mom, Dad and Bernie
Front row: Gloria, Mark and Carol

Bernie's grandparents lived in a three-room flat a few blocks west of his parents' apartment on Crotona Park South. Grandpa came to fetch him, starting at age three, but by the following year, he was walking alone on the three-block route to Grandpa's place. Mom was only too glad to hand him off to Grandpa to gain herself a few hours of peace from Bernie's demanding attention.

Crotona Park had the largest swimming pool in the Bronx. It was beautiful, but rowdy teens had started to infiltrate there, so Bernie was only allowed to go when the whole family went for the day. The verdant foliage of 28 tree species is nestled within the park's 127 acres, included oaks, magnolias and maples. Hundreds of stately elms ringed Indian Lake in the central section of the park. Rental row boats plied the calm greenish-blue lake waters. On their walks together in Crotona Park, Grandpa and Bernie usually headed north toward the late-Victorian garden and marble fountain facing Tremont Avenue. Along the curving park paths, they paused to rest on the wood-slatted wrought-iron benches with rounded filigreed armrests Their walks went up to the sweeping staircase facing Tremont Avenue leading up to the old Borough Hall office building. They noticed the birds and squirrels on the way, and smiled at neighborhood residents who cast crumbs to those little creatures.

Crotona Park Fountain

Bernie's Grandpa was the big story-teller to his visiting grandchildren, and Aunt Irma filled the gaps in Grandpa's tales of family history and boyhood in Russia to a fascinated Bernie. Grandpa's stories were also of the war-torn world of the early twentieth century after he emigrated with his parents to America. The other grandchildren, Bernie's cousins, were older—well past story-telling age, and with looser bonds to Grandpa because of their greater distance from his home.

Unlike Bernie's Grandpa or Uncle Dave, Uncle Eddie had never owned a business. Dave, the oldest son, went to college, but Eddie chose trade school instead and became a mechanic. Dave was Eddie's bitter rival within the family. Eddie had always avoided Dave when they met, but Bernie never noticed this adult snubbing amidst the tranquil Sabbath family dinners that assembled at Grandpa's apartment on Friday nights.

Dave was of medium height, trim build, bouncing in his athletic gait and hearty in manner. Still spry and ten years older than Bernie's Dad, his brother-in-law, he often teased Dad about his pot belly, which came from many years behind the taxicab wheel. Dave sometimes challenged him to race a 50-yard dash, while spotting him a 10-yard head start. Dad never took him up on this challenge. Periodically, Aunt Margaret would tartly remind Dave of his age and scold him for 'showing off' his physical prowess and recklessness.

Uncle Eddie was short, balding, slightly stooped and hollow-cheeked. He could laugh one minute and be very serious the next. He carried candy treats in his pockets for visiting nieces and nephews. Eddie also told Bernie family stories which were more interesting than stylized kindergarten tales such as *Little Red Riding Hood*, *Goldilocks and the Three Bears*, and the *Three Little Pigs*.

Bernie's Mom gladly passed on parental bedtime story-telling tasks to his Dad, because she could not get into the play-acting skills that a good story-teller often needs to relate to young children. His Dad play-acted the stories as best as he could, but had no real knack for it. Never did he catch on to Bernie's pretense of being a wide-eyed little boy hearing these adventures over and over again, ending the story session with a hug and kiss and a "Thank you, Daddy." By age seven, to the relief of his parents, Bernie had taken over the bedtime story task for Gloria and the twins.

Of the various feuds that loomed over Bernie's family relationships, the hostility between Uncle Eddie and Uncle Dave was the most bitter. A close second to this quarrel was the even longer-lasting hostility between Mom and Aunt Irma. Eddie vs. Dave began in the early years of World War II. Dave's manufacturing business of assembling precision pharmaceutical and scientific scales was withering away as it became more difficult to import scale parts and other precision instruments from Switzerland to America due to the Depression. The pharmaceutical industry was overtly anti-semitic, so Dave changed his family name from Rylutzky to Douglas for 'business reasons'.

Dave was a highly skilled business manager and machinery production expert, as Grandpa, his father, had been for Henry Ford as a plant superintendent in the boom years of the 1920s. Eddie was laid off from his hardware store job in Brooklyn early in the war years and, being proudly independent, did not ask Dave for any help in getting another job. Instead, Eddie applied for and was hired as a Brooklyn Navy Yard mechanic on his own credentials.

During the Second World War, Dave obtained a government appointment as Deputy Superintendent in charge of non-military staff at the Brooklyn Navy Yard, answerable only to the Superintendent, the Admirals and the War Department. No one in the family ever knew exactly how Dave obtained that high-level job. Perhaps it came from Dave's Masonic connections, kept hidden from the family and the public.

Uncle Dave was a Freemason, accustomed to keeping ceremonial and organizational secrets. As a big Navy 'Yard boss', Dave did not know that the Yard had hired his brother because the name, Edward Rylutzky, was buried in the personnel list among many other temporary employees.

Three years later, when post-war layoffs began, Eddie's name was on a layoff list signed by Dave. For the rest of his life, Eddie remained convinced that the firing had been deliberate. In later years, Dave told Bernie that Eddie was on the layoff list, but he had not noticed it among the many names on the list. Eddie remained unforgiving of his brother for the rest of his life.

Bernie's aunts and uncles gathered, with the family feuders ignoring each other, but not their spouses, at the grandparents' Sabbath table almost every Friday afternoon before sundown. Each white linen place setting displayed Hebraic-lettered plates and bowls alongside swirled-pattern embossed silverware laid upon matching folded napkins.

Grandma began her Sabbath meal preparations on Wednesday morning by polishing silver and pressing linen tablecloths and napkins, with some help from Bernie's aunts. The chicken was bought at the butcher shop on Thursday morning and the dinner preparations for Friday night began the same afternoon.

Grandpa sat at the head of the table wrapped in his *talis* (ritual shawl). Grandma was on his left, and Uncle Dave, as the oldest living son, on his right. The gleaming table silverware, silver cups and candlesticks were freshly polished each week. Long tapered candles were inserted in the two silver candlesticks and lit for Sabbath by Grandma as she covered her eyes and silently gave the first blessing …

"Baruch atah Adonai Eloheinu melech ha'olam asher kidishana b'mitz votav vitzvanu l'had'lik neir shel Shabbat... Amen." (translation) *"Blessed art Thou, O Lord our God, King of the universe Who has sanctified us with His commandments and commanded us to kindle the lights of Sabbath."*

Grandma then uncovered her eyes, waving her hands over the candles to welcome the Sabbath. Then the Kiddush blessing was chanted by Grandpa while holding the poured Kiddush wine in its embossed silver ritual cup, facing the table.

"Baruch atah Adonai Eloheinu melech ha'olam. Borei p'ri hagafen. Amen." (translation) *"Blessed art Thou, O Lord our God, King of the Universe Who created the fruit of the vine."*

Before Grandma rose to serve the Sabbath meal, still hot from the kitchen, the family performed the ritual of 'Washing of the Hands'. A wash bowl was passed around for each adult and child to dip, recite the blessing and then dry the hands.

"Baruch atah Adonai Eloheinu melech ha'olam. Asher kidishanu b'mitz votav v'tzivanu al n'tilat yadayim." (translation) *"Blessed art Thou, O Lord our God, King of the Universe. Who has sanctified us with His Commandments and commanded us on the washing of hands."*

The Sabbath table was set just as it was set in the time of Grandpa's father and grandfather before him in Russia—when the Sabbath silver and other precious objects were hidden in the barn for protection against the Cossacks when they rampaged through the town periodically.

The house lights were dimmed just before Friday sunset, not to be touched again until Saturday night when Shabbat ended.

Nobody dared ask Grandpa who else was coming to his table for Shabbat or threatening not to come that week if 'so-and-so' came. All ongoing family quarrels were stopped for the Shabbat, and then resumed again during the following week.

Aunt Irma was the next youngest child of Bernie's grandparents—one-and-a-half years older than Mom. Both sisters were loudly aggressive, with Irma's booming voice reinforced by her beefy body and stout lungs. Aunt Irma's lips were in a perpetual pout, and she only smiled to her nieces and nephews, not her sisters and brothers, except for Aunt Dolly, with whom she shared a mutual interest in horserace betting. Irma's former husband, Saul, escaped Irma's verbal tyranny by divorce. Aunt Irma told Bernie the divorce happened when he was a baby—too young to remember Uncle Saul.

Bernie's Dad usually accepted with a good grace his regular husbandly henpecking from his wife and the periodic criticism from his sister-in-law Irma in the intervals between family fights when they were temporarily on speaking and visiting terms.

Bernie once overheard Aunt Irma in Grandma's kitchen, loudly criticizing the cooking of Bernie's Mom. "Rosie," she said, "To make a family Sabbath meal you should do it strictly in kosher tradition with no shortcuts." Mom protested back sharply, "Irma, please criticize less and help more!" Grandma stepped in between the warring sisters. "*Oy, meine kinder!* Enough already! Kosher is kosher. Rosie is doing it right."

Irma wanted to continue her own education into high school—the ninth through the twelfth grades. But Bernie's Mom had no interest in any further education after the eighth grade. Grandpa the patriarch, ever a traditionalist, also felt that higher education was wasted on girls, and refused to pay for Irma's high school.

In the early days of the twentieth century, there were often tuition fees for public high school, plus books and supplies, the way college costs are structured today. The high school diploma of yesteryear was as academically advanced for a job credential as college is in today's high tech world. Irma shrugged off the parental refusal, and then she 'needled' herself into a millinery career to pay for her nighttime high school studies.

'Tough cookie' that she was, Irma gained the respect of her co-workers by actually slugging a male anti-union goon sent by the bosses to break up a union rally! She was elected as union shop steward of the ILGWU as a result of her successful fisticuffs. Grandpa then prevailed upon Irma to arrange a millinery job for Rosie. Irma grudgingly agreed, fearing that her sister might embarrass her on the job. Since Rosie was unmarried, without a prospective husband in sight to support her, she needed to get a job instead.

Much to Irma's relief, Bernie's Mom became a skillful

milliner, and did not take advantage of Irma's union leadership position. However, Irma continued to resent the pressure from her parents that led her to take Rosie into the millinery shop. Long after they had married, left the business world and had children, the squabbling sisters continued to fight, punctuated only by occasional short-lived intervals of peace centered on a family event such as childbirth, wedding, Bar Mitzvah or funeral.

Grandma usually took the side of Bernie's Mom in her quarrels with Aunt Irma. To Grandma, her 'little Rosie' was a 'change-of-life' final child and the spoiled baby darling of the family. In the early twentieth century, 'change-of-life' pregnancies were rare and risky. The mortality and birth defect rates for surviving infants of birth mothers past forty were much higher than today.

Mom's big problem, from her parents' point of view, was that she was 26 years old and still unmarried! This was long past the usual marrying age for women in the pre-war Bronx community of about a half million Jews. What a family 'disgrace' it was if no substantial Jewish man wanted to marry her! Then Bernie's Dad came into her life. A peace-loving man of modest means, they 'kept company' for almost two years before getting engaged.

Grandpa and Grandma were anxious to marry off Bernie's Mom, but Dad was far from their ideal choice of a bridegroom. He was a taxicab driver, far below the education level that Grandpa had hoped for in a suitor for his daughter's hand in marriage. However, since Mom was well beyond the usual marrying age for Jewish daughters, Grandpa reluctantly accepted him as a suitor of last resort.

Bred in upper-middle class European Jewish traditions, Grandpa would have preferred a professional man as a prospective son-in-law. Bernie's Mom had once dated a doctor, who met her at a dance. Once. He never called her again. That time, Aunt

Irma, who usually relished any excuse to criticize her sister, refrained from commenting about a boyfriend ditching her. This usually happened after one or two dates ending with a stern 'good-night' glance from Grandpa when Bernie's Mom came home.

Bernie's Dad was short, stocky and a balding bachelor of thirty-five when he met Mom. A jokester in English and Yiddish, his jests wore the ancient beard that his rotund face lacked. One of his oft-told riddles was "what do you say if the Pope gets in your taxicab during the High Holy Days?" The 'punch line' was "Good *yuntif*, Pontiff." *(translation: "Happy Holiday to the Pope").*

The family was reminded years later of Dad's old joke when Pope John Paul II arrived in New York City for a visit on Yom Kippur, 1995. The Jewish communities of New York City, then over a million strong, were a little offended by the unfortunate papal choice of arrival dates.

Irma bit her tongue and joined the family game of trying to 'fix up' Bernie's Mom with a man who could last more than one or two dates with her. A prickly personality and her stubbornness chased most prospective boyfriends away—the ones she dated before Dad came into her life. But he was not deterred from dating her by parents or personality.

Bernie's Dad was called 'Dovid' by Jewish men who knew him casually, in keeping with his dovish tendencies, but he was 'Danny' to Bernie's Mom and those friends and family who knew him best. Dad stayed within Mom's dating orbit, and meekly began his lifetime habit of being bossed around by her. In later years, after belittling him repeatedly, she would then turn around and bemoan the fact that he didn't act like a 'man' *(whatever that was supposed to mean!).*

A frequent typical macho image of the 'American Family Father' extolled in the 1940s was for the father to 'wear the pants' in the family, making decisions and ordering the 'woman of the house' around, politely but firmly. Bernie saw this role played out by many of his friend's fathers in his growing years.

Bernie's Dad was the opposite of this patriarchal stereotype of suitors when he called on Mom's parents to seek her hand in marriage on a late summer Sunday afternoon in 1934.

"Mr. Ralutzky, I am asking your consent to marry Rosie." Bernie's Dad fidgeted and harrumphed uncomfortably as he sat at the oaken dining room table with Grandpa. Bernie's Mom was the last of Grandpa's children still living at home. According to the traditions of that time, she still needed Grandpa's consent to marry.

The two sitting men, Grandpa and his prospective son-in-law, were surrounded by memorabilia of the family's proud past mounted on worn mahogany-paneled walls. Only awards and plaques from his bitter Ford years were missing. They had been sold off for scrap.

Bernie's Dad held his breath and waited for his future father-in-law's response. It seemed to him, in that moment, that the family ancestors, including a Polish early 19th century Grand Rabbi of Lvov, were scowling down disapprovingly from their sepia-tinted photographs mounted in silver filigree frames.

"Dovid," Grandpa replied. "These are hard times. If you marry Rosie, how will you make a living? How will you support your children?"

"I drive a taxicab. That job is more than a lot of other people have now."

"Yes, but is it enough to raise a family on? The dowry will be small."

"Times will get better. Roosevelt is turning this country around now."

Bernie's Grandpa winced at Dad's economic forecast and

must have thought: *not bad for a man who mainly reads the funnies' and the Sports section of the New York Daily News!*

Bernie's Grandpa knew this from what he observed in his future son-in-law while waiting patiently for Rosie to get dressed for their date. He squirmed uncomfortably in a double-breasted suit 'off the rack' that almost fit him. Bernie's Mom had advised him, sensibly, to wear a suit similar to Grandpa's own style for their meeting. But she did not check the fitting first.

Discomfort in a suit was a lifelong habit of Bernie's Dad that friends and family knew from the few formal occasions in his life that required his 'dress up'. However, Grandpa's tailoring had also known better days. His stiff rounded shirt collars and cutaway tailoring dated from his executive days at Ford in the 1920s. So Grandpa did not judge Bernie's Dad by his simple clothing.

Bernie's Dad was not an educated man. His schooling stopped after the eighth grade, since high school education was not mandatory in the early 20th century. But with a good heart and beaming smile, he was widely liked by friends and family. Many college graduates sold apples on the streets in the thirties, but at least Dad had a job. He worked steadily as a cab driver, sometimes waiting an hour between fares in an era when the meter started at a quarter and most city cab fares were under a dollar a ride with a dime tip.

Rabbis and families often disagreed on levels of ritual observance in family life, but mostly believed that a woman of 26 was an *alteh moid* ('old maid'). It was considered a family disgrace if no substantial Jewish man offered marriage to a young lady after dating her at least several times.

Dad's family was also unhappy at his betrothal. Their depression-fueled attitude was: *Oy! Our breadwinner is getting married! That's the last money we will ever see from him!* Dad appeased them somewhat by giving his widowed mother half of the two thousand-dollar dowry after the wedding. In later years, Bernie dimly remembered his paternal grandma as a sweet-but-senile old lady in a Bronx nursing home whom the family rarely visited.

Dad had supported his mother and put his younger sister Claire and brother Bill through college on a cab driver's pay. For this ill-rewarded generosity of Dad to his family, Mom stayed resentful of them for the rest of her life. She rarely and grudgingly visited sometimes with Dad's side of the family for the sake of her children.

But there was also Bernie's Aunt Claire to be reckoned with. She was Dad's glamorous younger sister who stylishly drove up to the Bronx in her big Buick Roadmaster, flaunting it at the neighbors. Furthermore, Aunt Claire was (scandal of scandals in the forties!)… divorced!

Bernie's family was typically middle class. Grandpa's successful management career became a model that later inspired Bernie's own future in the business world.

Grandpa had sighed when Bernie's Dad proposed in 1934. At last, a man had come to take unwed Rosie off their hands! One less mouth to feed, and well worth the small dowry paid to her bridegroom-to-be. Was he a good catch? Not in professional or financial status. But at least he earned a living in those bleak Depression-era years.

Dad's mother bluntly discouraged his occasional girlfriends, but finally yielded to Uncle Bill and Aunt Claire's arguments that she was depriving him of a married life of his own. It was ironic that they extolled the virtues of marriage since Aunt Claire was divorced, and bachelor Uncle Bill had never married! Their attitude had suddenly changed after they graduated from college and no longer needed Dad's small stipend to help support them.

Aunt Claire was trim-figured, sophisticated and fascinating—

like a Bronx version of Bette Davis. She had no children, divorced her husband before Bernie was born and never remarried. There was some family envy at Claire's glamour and independence from any man.

Uncle Bill was a shadowy figure whom Bernie only met twice in his childhood. He lived in a fancy Westside Manhattan bachelor pad, and we were told that he owned several shoe stores. For whatever reasons, he kept a distance from the rest of Bernie's family. Perhaps it was the 'status' thing, and college grad Bill was ashamed of his brother being an uneducated cabdriver. But he had not been ashamed for Dad to have paid his college expenses!

Under the marriage *chuppah* (canopy) at Temple Israel on the Grand Concourse in the Bronx, Dovid Seiden and Rosie Ralutzky were joined by the rabbi in Holy Matrimony on a bright summer day in June 1935. It was one of the few holy moments in Bernie's family for many years to come.

Bernie's Family—From left to right—Mom, Gloria (age 11), Mark and Carol (age 8), Bernie (age 14), Dad

7

Baby Sister Gloria

In 1941, the biggest event for me was the springtime birth of Gloria, my freckle-faced, pug-nosed, red-headed new baby sister. Grandpa had begun to tell me about the World War, but he related it in a filtered story-telling mode, and it did not really register in my conscious reality until Pearl Harbor.

Dad and Mom both smiled indulgently when I declared that Gloria was 'my baby'. But it was a nice laugh by parents laughing with me and not at me, in appreciation for my devotion to baby Gloria. I was now trusted by Mom to walk unescorted to Grandpa's apartment four blocks away, and to push Gloria's stroller when walking with Mom or Dad.

This was not a 'one big happy young family' scenario, however. I began to sense that there was primarily a one-way physical affection between Mom and Dad. To Mom, he was like a big hugging bear, playfully trying to embrace her from behind, often in the kitchen when she was busy with meal preparation. She fended him off, not harshly, but firmly without so much as a

"Later, not now!" to him. He cheerfully shrugged off this rebuff, and was not discouraged from trying again and again. I do not ever remember her returning his affection visibly in those early years. At best sometimes, Mom would grudgingly accept a peck on the cheek from Dad accompanied by a facial grimace.

Mom kissed or hugged me sometimes, and I responded dutifully. Baby Gloria sensed Mom's basic negative vibes and avoided affection with her most of the time. We were both affectionate with Dad, however. And Mom had a streak of jealousy in her that occasionally flared up over his being closer to us children than she could ever be.

Dad read the *New York Daily News,* a large picture tabloid newspaper, and shared it with me. But I wanted more current events and less scandal than the *Daily News* covered. Grandpa told me that their editorials ranted, and then explained what ranting was (loud, vulgar and bombastic language). He also said that mixed in with the rants was some good, tough truthful reporting.

The *Daily News* kept publishing its three-cents worth of daily rants. However despite its often crude and vulgar style, the *Daily News* has won several Pulitzer Prizes over the years. I asked Dad to buy the *New York Times* instead, but he made excuses that "The Times costs a nickel." Today, in retrospect, I think that perhaps the real reason he didn't buy the *Times* was that their sophisticated writing style was beyond his understanding.

Eight months later, a few days after Pearl Harbor, I stood in our narrow apartment foyer, bundled up and ready to brave the December chill to stroll outside with my baby sister. Pouting, I asked: "Mommy, why can't I take Gloria outside in the stroller today?"

"Because it's too cold for her. Go outside yourself and play now."

I protested. "But Grandpa lets me wheel her around and take care of her." Mom sighed. "Yes, but only when Grandpa or Grandma is watching you."

'No' was 'no', so I stalked out the door and downstairs, crossing the street onto the empty gray sidewalk bordering Crotona Park East, while sulking and being consoled by the bracing chill of wintry December. Mom had this manner of positive certainty about her that was impossible to argue with, whether she spoke of matters that she knew about, such as home and the children, or other matters on which she was not well-informed. When a 'sore spot' in dialogue was touched upon, her voice quickly rose to a shrill scream. When she started screaming and yelling, Dad was quick to appease her. I was less willing to do so, but reluctantly yielded to her forceful adult authority in order to avoid a spanking.

Even as a precocious, stubborn, somewhat bratty and strong-willed kid, there was a soft side to me too—a nurturing side. Unlike many young boys, then and now, I did not feel that babies were icky pests to be avoided.

In those pre-Dr. Spock days, mothers often forced their older kids to mind the younger ones, thus sowing the seeds for future Freudian sibling rivalry and resentments. When I was naughty, Mom grounded me from playing with or helping to take care of Gloria for a day or two as punishment.

Mom knew that I enjoyed caring for Gloria and telling her nursery tales, as she grew out of babyhood and began to talk when she was two years old. Each time I told her a favored nursery story a little bit differently, Gloria frowned and asked me to return to the original text.

Gloria never tired of any nursery story repetition. If Mom or Dad tried to tell her a sleepy-time story, she went 'on strike' unless I took over the tale, sitting next to her crib with the storybook.

By the time she was three, "Little Red Riding Hood" was Gloria's special story favorite. Since the first time she heard it, she always came up with new curious questions about the tale. Each time I read it to her, it was transformed into a dramatized 'big brother storytelling scenario.'

Clearing my throat, I began, "Once upon a time, there was a Big Bad Wolf." Gloria interrupted. "Why was the Wolf bad? Isn't the Wolf only a big doggie? Doggies are nice and wag their tails at you." She had never experienced a nasty dog before, only cute little local pets—puppies and kittens belonging to neighbors, and sometimes a stray street mutt who would run away when anyone came near. The few big dogs in the neighborhood were mostly retrievers and collies who loved adults and kids alike.

"Gloria," I began, "Wolves are not doggies. They are like cousins to doggies. You know some of your cousins are nice, and some are not so nice."

"Yeah. Cousin Ronnie pulls my hair. He's not nice." She made a face. "Doggies can bite!" I said. "But wolves bite more, that's why they are bad. They bite so hard, they can eat you all up." "Ooh!" She made big eyes, imagining their big teeth chewing on her.

I explained, "Wolves live in the woods and are afraid of people. Dogs live with people, and are not afraid of them unless they are mean. They know people feed and take care of them." I continued the story. Soon, she nodded off to sleep and I tiptoed out.

At age five, I often trotted off to Grandpa's for our regular *New York Times* 'newspaper session'. Proud of crossing streets unaided, I politely declined occasional street-crossing assistance offers from kindly adults passing by.

Bronx boys and girls were taught to beware of strangers, then as now, but rare were the kidnappings, rapes and murders of children that scream across today's news headlines. I felt no fear and took childish pleasure in shocking grownups with surprising adult-like responses to their 'cute kiddy' overtures to me.

Strolling across Crotona Avenue at the southeast corner of the park one fine spring day in 1943, I passed by a stout middle-aged lady at the curb who smiled and sweetly offered, "Can I help you across the street, little boy?" I did not feel polite toward the world that day, brooding over being denied the privilege of caring for Gloria as a punishment for some near-forgotten offense from several hours earlier that day.

In a simulated treble imitation of a grown-up voice, I declared, "Thanks, but it isn't necessary. I'm not a kid. I am a circus midget." *She believed it!* To the sound of stammered "excuse me's", she scurried across the street.

I "ha-ha'ed" all the way to Grandpa's and mused, *Should I tell him what happened at the Crotona Avenue corner? No, I better not. Grandpa will scold and lecture me on truth-telling.* My ears tingled at the very thought of what Grandpa would say if he heard about the disrespectful Crotona 'midget' act.

Grandpa hugged me a hearty "Hello'" at his door before starting our stroll. The woodsy scent of cologne hinted of leather and lavender mingled with the sweetish scent of imported Egyptian tobacco wafting through his foyer.

Smoking was then considered by society to be a widespread manly habit, but Grandpa himself did not smoke and forbad his family to indulge in tobacco while under his roof. To Grandpa, a woman seen smoking in public was a particular disgrace.

Curiously I asked, "Grandpa, why is smoking bad for women and children, but okay for men?" He harrumphed, "Aromatic tobacco leaves are manly, but are too strong for women and children. They are less harmful than cheap regular cigarettes, if not too many are smoked."

"How many are too many'?

"More than three or four a day causes a cough."

"Grandpa, did you ever smoke?"

"Yes, when I was younger. But my doctor stopped me when I developed asthma. I was in the tobacco importing business many years ago, so my smoking was for business reasons. Who would have bought my cigarettes or pouch tobacco, if I avoided them?"

He gestured with his brown-stained right hand. "This little hand-rolling machine in the corner is all that is left of the old tobacco business, so I must continue grinding away with this to make a living." Then he strongly warned me against smoking, and I promised him never to smoke in my life. That promise has always been kept.

Then we strolled for our usual walk, but headed in a different direction this time, going west towards Third Avenue where the rickety old 'El' rattled by overhead with its rattan seats and nickel fare. My train questions were eagerly shared with Grandpa as the dark-stained gingerbread scrollwork of the Claremont Parkway Station street overpass loomed above us.

"Grandpa", I asked abruptly, "is the Third Avenue 'el' as old as you are?" He smiled ruefully. "Yes. The 'el' is about my age. The Ninth Avenue line was the first 'el', born in 1868, the same year I was born in Russia. The Third Avenue 'el' opened ten years later. I rode on the Third Avenue line as a young school boy, after my parents came to America from Russia and settled in the Bronx."

I asked curiously, "why did they come to America?"

"Because Cossacks were murdering Jews and the Tsar secretly encouraged them to kill us and loot our villages."

The 'El' loomed ahead in its shabby gabled splendor as we

approached the 174th Street station. I was fascinated by trains and travel. I pasted clippings of sleekly designed trains and planes from magazines and newspapers into scrapbooks. This was the beginning of a lifelong love of adventure that carried me far beyond the subway, the 'El', or the New York Central train racing up nearby Park Avenue to Westchester and beyond. I boyishly dreamed, *maybe I will travel up north someday on the New York Central—all the way up to Canada when I get older!*

Grandpa abruptly changed the subject as we neared the station. Arriving at the grimy gummed stairs leading up to the northbound platform of the 'El', we began climbing up to the screechy floorboards of the northbound platform heading to Fordham Road.

He continued. "The 'el' had steam locomotives pulling the train along single tracks in its earliest days. Pot-bellied coal stoves warmed the five-car wood-lined trains. The electric rail lines were built years later." Glancing at the train agent's booth, Grandpa whispered, "You can shrink down a little and slide under the turnstile. You go in free if you are under six years old."

I ducked under the crossbar, and Grandpa went through with a nickel dropped into the slot of the wooden cross-beams. *Ka-chunk*, the turnstile clanged, a part-bell and part-gong like sound, reverberating in the musty station as it ground around a quarter-turn to admit Grandpa to the train station.

That clanking would scare Gloria now, I thought. But I resolved to share my riding experience on the Third Avenue 'El' someday with her when she was older. Each new trip with Grandpa became a special adventure to cherish and remember. After a short ride, we arrived at the Fordham Road station about fifteen minutes later and stepped across the street to the six-story oblong concrete and brown brick landmark Sears Roebuck store. Black pot-bellied stoves, similar to old-time railroad stoves, were on sale that day, and Grandpa showed me how they worked. For fire safety reasons, the store used fake coal to demonstrate the stoves.

My own life became too busy with boyhood adventure, Golden Book readings and school, to notice that Mom's belly was growing again in the spring of 1943. Some of my friends had expectant Moms, but it was a mystery to them how a baby could grow inside a mother's belly. The younger ones still mostly believed in the 'babies are delivered by the stork' myth.

I recall, in those early years, that other pregnant Moms in the neighborhood had neighbors and friends as networks to supplement friends and family supportive networks. They frequently visited each other, babysat for each other's children, and held a baby shower to mark the 'blessed event'. Mom had few family and friends that would visit and help her during her pregnancies. If she mentioned this lack of family presence at all, she would say they were 'stuck-up'. But actually, it was her paranoia, quick temper and combativeness that scared them away most of the time.

Mom and Dad would not discuss the baby-to-come with me, and Grandpa was unusually silent on this subject also. He gruffly told me it was up to Mom to tell me about it if she wanted to do so. She did not say anything about the baby until her sixth month approached, and then she tried to give me the lame excuse that it was brought by the stork. I laughed and pretended to believe it. I knew at least, that the baby was in her belly. Then she told me that there were two babies coming. Twins!

8

Bernie Turns Five

My fifth birthday was exciting—the first one with neighborhood children and little sister Gloria invited, not just adult friends and relatives of Mom and Dad and their children. I played nicely with them, but sometimes used big words too complex for other young children to understand.

I proudly showed off to my playmates the reading and writing skills learned from Grandpa. But Mom had more to show off on birthday party day than anyone else there. It was her belly! She was seven months pregnant with twins when the five candles were lit. For once, Mom relented from her go-it-alone home tasking attitude, and allowed Dad to help her with party preparations. Multi-colored streamers and decorations, centered on the foyer chandelier, rose up around the foyer walls, tacked into place by Dad perched on a stepladder.

From well-meaning adult relatives and friends, I received toys and book presents intended for older children. Grandpa advised the grown-ups in the family that baby books would not be appropriate because I would be bored by them. It was a typical children's party—balloons, cake and ice cream, a few friends from school, their parents, my grandparents and Uncle Eddie, who had a very special present for me. I knew it would be special because Uncle Eddie came all the way from central Brooklyn to visit us. To a little Bronx boy, Brooklyn seemed as far away as China.

The biggest present came from Uncle Eddie, wrapped in a large flat box. There was no ribbon or bow, but the wrapping was thick dark green lightly striped construction paper. It looked heavy and felt through the wrapping like a metal case. Then the big moment came. I unwrapped to the beat of an imaginary drum roll at the sight of a square-cornered hinged red metal case.

Only serious toys came in a metal case! The beam, gear and wheel-laced logo gave away its contents immediately. It was a deluxe Gilbert Erector Set, with its own registered serial number, and hundreds of gears, girders and an electric motor.

"Thank you, thank you, thank you, Uncle Eddie!" I cried and hugged him. The rest of the party was an anticlimactic blur. I could hardly wait to get to my room and try out the Erector set. The assortment of other childish toys and games that well-meaning friends' parents had gotten for me was anti-climactic, but received with polite thanks. There was even a teddy bear! I resolved to put that away and give it Gloria next year.

The tiny print warned it was for ages twelve and up. I pretended not to notice that. Because of the age proficiency gap, none of my young friends could join in playing with the Erector set. This was a dilemma, because older Bronx boys did not want to hang out with a younger kid—especially a very bright one.

Friends in my age group were good for street games sometimes, but that was the usual extent of their interaction with me. So I devised the idea of dividing the 25-pound Erector set into the complex part with gears and motor hidden away in a separate box, and the basic construction parts of beams and bolts, girders and wheels, lights and switches kept in the original red-painted steel box to be shared with other playmates.

The party continued on routinely. The mothers had picked the gifts, and did not realize they were too childish for me. I would have liked to get a world globe or science toy like a gyroscope or junior space rocket kit, but instead got roller skates and simple board games.

Grandpa and Uncle Dave made up for the 'little boy' gifts by giving me teenage level books. Grandpa gave me a set of the World Book encyclopedia, and Uncle Dave gave me a set of the works of Mark Twain. If any adults there glanced my way, they did not notice that these works were apparently too advanced for my age, or they kept discreetly silent.

Uncle Eddie was itching for an excuse to recapture his boyhood and do an Erector set project to guide and encourage me. But he did not supersede or override my own creative instincts. I had to wait and cherish the infrequent opportunities to get together with him every two months or so. He was one of my most favorite uncles. Not just because of the presents, but because he both loved me and respected my intellect.

In my formative years, Dad instilled in me his personal example of gentility towards the opposite sex. After long, earnest discussions with him about the female gender, I gained a positive attitude toward girls from him.

Fathers were supposed to 'wear the pants in the family' in those days and teach their sons how to grow up as tough manly 'John Wayne' types. Blue-collar rough-and-ready laboring fathers were often deeply enmeshed in the masculine image that society expected them to be and implant machismo in their sons at a tender age.

For that matter, the real-life John Wayne was not like the

stereotype macho image from his movie roles. He was an honor student in high school, studied Latin, and his own personal hero was Winston Churchill. John Wayne personified the stereotyped American western frontier hero, often playing cowboys, cavalrymen, tough guys and unconquerable loners. My anti-macho Dad was different and special. He deeply believed in respecting women as the other 'better half' of the human race, even if some of them did not necessarily deserve it. These were among the many reasons that his family loved and cherished him so much.

As a blue-collar worker in the Depression thirties, then later as a New York City taxicab driver, Dad only went as far as the eighth grade in public school, then took brief jobs as a stock clerk and delivery man in the job-scarce thirties. After these job sources dried up, Dad drove a cab for the remaining forty years of his working life.

By the time of entering kindergarten, I had advanced from Golden books to a fourth-grade reading level and beyond with heroic adventure stories such as *Tom Sawyer*, *Huckleberry Finn*, *King Arthur's Knights of the Round Table* and *Robin Hood and His Merry Men* in Sherwood Forest.

Most neighborhood kids near my age had no interest in current events. They ridiculed me as a 'smart ass' for trying to involve them in adult-level dialogue. I soon stopped trying.

During the infrequent visiting opportunities when I tried to engage my aunts and uncles in adult discussions, they just smiled indulgently and brushed me off. So Grandpa remained as my primary source of sharing happenings of the adult world in the early 1940s.

At age five, by reading newspapers and magazines, I became aware of the events of World War II, raging in Europe and Asia, as the allies stopped the advance of the Axis armies in 1942.

Grandpa interpreted the *New York Times* and current events for me on a near-adult level—telling me as much as I could absorb.

In earnest tones, Grandpa explained weighty *Times* words and concepts to me. He saved the *Times* each day for my next visit. Dad only read the sports pages and comics of the *Daily News*. He was a big Yankee baseball fan, and his enthusiasm rubbed off on me. I hungered for more news and less sports and scandal than the Daily News provided. Grandpa filled my mind with reading, writing and simplified explanations of current events and politics. Meanwhile, Grandma filled my belly with fresh-baked homemade cookies.

Grandma was a graying stout lady of middling height with rounded, but smallish features. Whenever my parents and I visited, she bustled about with her chores, too busy to emerge from the kitchen to chat.

Finally, worn out by seemingly endless years of cooking, cleaning and raising thirteen children, Grandma succumbed to a heart attack and died at age sixty-eight when I was six years old. After Grandma's funeral, Grandpa withdrew and became a semi-recluse, visited sometimes by my parents and me. Gone now were the family gatherings of aunts, uncles and cousins with grandparents. The curtains remained drawn in his apartment, and sunlight seldom was seen anymore in his living room. But I believe that our walks together provided him some respite from the gloom of his empty apartment.

I never knew my other Grandfather—Dad's father—who passed away six weeks before I was born. All I knew of him was what Aunt Claire told me—that in the early years of the twentieth century, he had a small dry goods store on the Lower East Side of Manhattan and worked long hours, six days a week, to feed his family.

Dad's mother, my other grandma, lived on until I was fifteen.

I remember her as being very aged and somewhat senile. We visited her every month in a Bronx nursing home, and sometimes she had difficulty in recognizing all of us. But she usually knew that I was her grandson.

Mom rarely came with us to see her mother-in-law. It was usually Dad, Gloria and myself who made the trip to the senior home. Grandma could get into a wheelchair with the assistance of an aide who usually took at least fifteen minutes to respond to a call for patient assistance.

One bright, beautiful spring morning, Dad and I went to visit Grandma while Gloria stayed home to go to a friend's party. As we were trudging up the hill from the bus stop to the nursing home, I asked Dad about Mom's absence.

"Daddy, how come Mom doesn't come with us to visit Grandma? "

He hesitated. "Well, Mom and Grandma don't get along too well."

"Why? Grandma is always nice to us. Isn't she nice to Mom, too?"

Dad answered lamely, "Yes, but Mom doesn't like hospitals." He shrugged and changed the subject. Sensing his discomfort, we got onto a safer topic ... should we bring Grandma some cookies or soft caramels for a treat? A few years later, when I became old enough to be more aware of adult interactions, I asked Aunt Irma about this coolness by Mom towards Grandma. She laid it straight on the line to me with her typical bluntness.

"Your Dad's mother opposed his marriage to your mother because he became the family breadwinner to her after his father retired in poor health from working in his dry goods store. She discouraged or chased away his earlier girlfriends with various excuses. Finally, he cut loose from his mother's apron strings in 1935 when he married your mother after a two-year courtship."

"Your Dad was living on a cab driver's pay, but supported his family and paid for his two sisters and brother to go to college. They graduated, got good jobs and then forgot about their 'poorer brother' who had helped their careers get started. Mom was particularly peeved at your Uncle Bill for not getting your Dad into shoe sales, which would have given him a better income than cab driving."

I started a scrapbook of military pictures and clippings from newspapers and magazines. Not the wreckage and devastation of cities—I was attracted by the machines of war—the tanks, the planes, the ships and the artillery. These images were no worse than the images of everyday mayhem that kids were exposed to in Popeye and Donald Duck cartoons and war toys sold in every department store and local toy shop.

When children, mostly boys—but with a few girls too—played war in the Bronx, it included shouts of "bang-bang, you're dead!" Often it was 'cowboys and Indians' of the Wild West, not the soldiers of World War II. Then the 'victim' gets up and the kids continue on to play another game.

Sometimes, just for fun, I also played 'bang bang, you're dead' with some young friends on the block. Unlike other five-year-olds, I lived and experienced both the childhood fantasy world and the real world, and could separate the two worlds in my perceptions. I knew that real animals could not talk, wear human clothes and act as furry humans living in houses and having human and heroic adventures in the way they were shown in Walt Disney cartoons and comic books.

But I sometimes enjoyed pretending that Mickey Mouse and other cartoon characters were real. And I began to notice that adults around me liked me better when I hid my adult side and acted like a typical normal boy of my age.

9

Little Bernie Learns of War

*P*earl Harbor screamed "War!" in public headlines all around the world, as America joined the battle against the Axis two weeks before Christmas, 1941. A few days later, Canada also declared war on the Axis. Bernie's pre-kindergarten war perceptions dawned dimly at first then grew to greater awareness when he began kindergarten in January, 1943. He knew there was fighting and bombing and dying going on 'over there' in Europe and the Pacific, but could not fully grasp death as a real image or a real happening.

Bernie had experienced death briefly by having once seen a dead dog lying in the street—messy and smelling bad. But that was only the singular death of a local stray animal, not big body counts in media of human tragedies reported from far away places. There were stories and pictures of burning and wreckage-strewn cities in Europe, which Bernie 'sneak-peeked' at *Life Magazine* war pictures in the library while the desk librarian was busy and not noticing a child browsing in the adult section.

Bernie discussed war and violence with his Grandpa, after

promising not to tell anyone else that Grandpa had shown pictures and read articles to him about the World War. Slowly, Bernie began to grasp the full horror of the reality of war.

Grandpa had never served in the Russian military. His family had fled Cossack carnage and the twenty-five year mandatory conscriptions of Jewish men into the Tsar's army while he was still a teenage boy.

The Ralutzky family sought refuge in America from a heavy wave of anti-Jewish violence in Russia set off by the murder of Tsar Alexander the Second in St. Petersburg by three anarchist assassins in 1881. One of the assassins was rumored to be half-Jewish. This became an excuse to wrongfully blame the entire Russian Jewish population for the royal assassination. Wild stories flew and anti-semitic pogroms erupted in cities and towns across Russia.

Thousands of Jews were beaten or killed; many Jewish homes and businesses were burned or wrecked, and over a hundred thousand Jews fled Czarist Russia to seek freedom in America from persecution and pogroms.

Thirty years later in the United States, as the First World War began, Grandpa and his brothers became established and prosperous American citizens, scattered across America. Grandpa's siblings had lived and died estranged from the rest of Bernie's maternal forebears because they had kept their traditional Orthodox Jewish lifestyle and did not fully interact with modern American community life or understand its ways.

All this happened long before Bernie was born, and he was told about it decades later by his maternal relatives—the *mishpocha*. That's the Yiddish word for 'clan'—relatives by birth or marriage—aunts, uncles, cousins, and in-laws.

Bernie's Dad was too young to serve when America entered the First World War and too old, at age forty, to be drafted into the Second World War. The military draft began in the United States in September, 1940, passing Congress by only one vote. So there was only his Grandpa, and later Aunt Irma, available in Bernie's life as knowledgeable sources of war news, current events and family ancestors.

Other adults and teachers in Bernie's life felt that any discussion of war was unfit for young children's ears, so they also avoided the topic with him. When Bernie spoke to his playmates, he soon discovered that only a few were even aware of the War, so he stopped trying to talk about it with them. The few politically aware playmates came from families that had sent off their older brothers to war as enlistees or draftees.

One late wintry day in March 1943, Bernie sprang a verbal surprise question on Grandpa. "What is a counteroffensive?" he asked, after seeing the word in a Daily News headline. "NAZI COUNTEROFFENSIVE HALTED NEAR KHARKOV." The *Daily News* war article referred to the final German victory on the Eastern front in Russia before the Red Army resumed its slow grinding march westward towards Berlin.

Bernie's rapidly expanding reading skills took in much world and local news, but often he gave it a childish interpretation. So many new and strange words to be reading about! *Nazis, Wehrmacht, Panzers, the Soviet Union and Blitzkrieg.*

Grandpa responded. "The German army attacked eastwards through Poland towards Russia," explained Grandpa patiently. "Now the Soviet army, also called the Red Army, is pushing back westwards towards Berlin." He paused for emphasis.

"The Germans are wicked people who are making war against the rest of the world. Many people think the Russians are just as bad as the Germans are, but they are now fighting on our side as allies and friends against the Nazis."

"Grandpa, why are we friends with the Russians if they are as bad as the Nazis?"

"We need Russian help to win this war. They need our help, also. Maybe we will become friends with them after the war—maybe not."

Bernie pondered his Grandpa's wisdom as he continued. "War is not like when children play with toy soldiers, forts and cities, or go 'bang-bang you're dead' with other boys. Then you get up off the floor, or set up your military pieces again for the next game."

Grandpa continued on, gesturing for emphasis: "War is for real. It's not a game. It's about killing and being killed. When that happens, you never get up again." Bernie nodded. "War is the worst kind of death. It kills a lot of people who did nothing wrong." "I know the word for that", Bernie piped up. "The word is 'innocent'."

Grandpa nodded 'yes' and sighed. "For the Jewish people in Europe, this war now is the worst of all wars ever fought. The Nazis began killing Jews six years before the world war started in 1939. Our people were in the wrong countries at the wrong time, unarmed and exposed, where they could easily be grabbed and sent to concentration camps.

The Jewish people had lived in Europe for many centuries, surviving many persecutions, with a few periods of peace in between when a benevolent king reigned. But the Nazis were more systematic and continuous in their killings than the brutal pogroms and riots that had flared up briefly, and then faded away in the centuries of Russian Czarist rule from medieval times up until the beginning of the 20th century. First Germany, then Austria, then Czechoslovakia were occupied by the Nazis when they invaded these countries and took power. Jews were often killed wherever the Nazis went, and the survivors became slaves."

Bernie asked, "Grandpa, why do the Germans hate us so much?" He responded, "You will understand this more when you get older. But for now, I will tell you that the Germans are blaming us Jews for anything that has ever gone wrong in Germany, and for their losing the First World War, so that they don't have to face up to blaming themselves."

"Oh, I get it now! It's like when Harry does something wrong, then blames Sammy for it, and Sammy gets punished."

That's the way Grandpa and Bernie often talked—on adult topics with a naive analogy sometimes added in by Grandpa to bring the dialog down to Bernie's comprehension level. Bernie was referring to Harry and Sammy Levinsky, his preschool friends in the Crotona Park neighborhood. There were only three sets of twin children in the whole neighborhood; the other two twin pairs were all much older than Bernie, and not friendly with him.

Bernie's Grandpa smiled at the example of misbehaving twins Harry and Sammy. "Not exactly, but…" He paused, momentarily at a loss to explain the horrors of the Third Reich and World War II to a very bright little boy.

This subject came up again a few months later in a parent-teacher conference between Bernie's kindergarten teacher, Miss Oppenberg and Grandpa. He justified Bernie's intelligence to her by declaring, "Intelligence in children is God's gift … not to be questioned."

Grandpa had taught Bernie much about life and the big wide world out there beyond the Bronx in his pre-school years, but arthritis now slowed him down to fewer and shorter neighborhood strolls, pausing for breath on almost every block.

When Bernie's parents moved to an apartment on Macombs Road in the West Bronx in 1943, Grandpa rented a small flat down the block, to stay near his children and grandchildren.

Grandpa's talking and walking sessions with Bernie around the neighborhood diminished gradually into sitting sessions in Grandpa's apartment.

Sometimes Bernie helped with his Grandpa's home-based tobacco manufacturing business as they sat around a small wooden work table, together churning out hand-rolled Egyptian cigarettes on a hand-cranked tobacco leaf wrapping machine.

Bernie never smoked when he got older, because Grandpa had sternly warned him against that and gave up his own smoking habit years earlier on doctor's orders. However, Bernie did enjoy the sweet smell of Grandpa's aromatic pipe tobacco wafting through the air.

Grandpa eked out a meager living during the war years by selling hand-rolled cigarettes to local Bronx neighborhood customers. This was the last remaining fragment of his formerly prosperous imported tobacco company. The long vengeful arm of Henry Ford's business connections had reached out to block Grandpa from getting another good job after he left his management position with the Ford Company. Grandpa was left with his pride, some stocks which lost most of their value in the 1929 Crash and a few thousand dollars in savings. Then Grandpa's bank closed down, and hard times descended on Bernie's family and millions of other families whose jobs and assets were wiped out in the decade-long recession that followed the crash..

10

A Young Friend Dies

Spring was shouting its warming splendor under bright sunny skies, as robins sang and squirrels scampered about in early April 1943, but my neighbors and parents were whispering in the streets and hallways of Macombs Road that day. I knew that adults often whispered when they were trying to hide bad news from kids. But I sensed that something was wrong at my brownstone apartment house—very, very wrong!

No kids were playing outside on our street. Neighbors buzzed about in clusters near our building stoop, brightening up momentarily with a "Hello, Bernie" bravado as I trotted by. My ears picked up a distant wail from upstairs—was *it a cat*? I listened more closely. It was a woman crying—not a voice that I knew. Hastily scooting out of our walk-in apartment, Mom snatched me back from the street by the arm. I protested.

"Mom, I want to go outside to play with Harry and Sammy. Why can't I go?" Mom frowned. "Because Harry is still sick today. He didn't get any better since yesterday."

I had not seen or played with Harry in nearly a week. Harry

and Sammy were twins, bright and lively boys—the only twins on our block. Sammy was kept inside also, for fear he would tell other children that Doctor Weinberg was coming to see Harry every day and the Rabbi was saying prayers for him.

"Then why can't I play with Sammy? He ain't sick, is he?"

She abruptly responded. "You can't go out now because I said so, that's why."

As usual, Mom's superior adult motherly force backed up her inferior argument. I went inside, pouting and very reluctantly. Mom was determined to shield me from the awful truth of mortality. My playmate Harry became very ill for several days with pneumonia, and then suddenly I was forbidden to ask about him anymore.

I only knew he was sick in bed—I did not know how sick, or that in that pre-antibiotic era, children and adults often succumbed to infectious illnesses now easily curable in today's world. Later that day, hallway and street whispers near Harry's door grew more hushed. Some wiser parents traditionally explain death to their children, often in simple and beautiful terms such as 'returning to God' or 'going to heaven'. Many more parents, less wise, do not discuss death at all with their young ones. That was the general child rearing style in those days—to 'keep things from the kids'. But we youngsters often knew intuitively what was going on anyway. Babysitting arrangements were hastily made by my parents so that they could attend the funeral. Gloria and I were sent off to Grandpa for the day.

After Harry's funeral, Mom and Dad came home and told me half-heartedly that "Harry went away to Heaven, and he won't be back." I looked properly sorrowful, and then went off to read my books until Sammy could return and play. I had no other close friends to turn to for consolation except for the twins. I decided to wait until Sammy was let out to play again. Then I planned to pump him about how Harry went to Heaven. *He'd know*, I thought. *They couldn't keep it a secret for long from Sammy!* But when I next saw him several days later, Sammy couldn't tell me much. He was quiet, but calm. His Mom had forbidden him to talk about Harry's death.

Grandpa was my intimate source of wisdom, so on my next visit, I asked him the ultimate question:

"Grandpa, please tell me about death. What's it like when people die? Does anyone come back from death, or are they just gone and nobody talks about them anymore?" In our grandpa-to-grandson talks, he always told me frankly about the world 'like it is'. We often discussed the Holocaust and the World War and local politics, among other topics. Harry's funeral was one of the few times I ever saw him hesitate on a touchy subject with me …DEATH.

Grandpa rubbed his grizzled chin as he continued explaining death to me.

"Bernie, God calls all living things back to Him when their time in this world is done. Some are called sooner, some are called later. Some live long lives and are called very late. But all are called someday, and all must go. We do not know how God chooses, but we have faith that God protects us and is with us even after death.

It is only our bodies that die. Our souls live on in Heaven with God. It is like a dream, but you do not wake up from it. You travel by thinking about it and go places without moving your body. You do not have to eat, but if you think of eating, a plate appears for you from your thoughts. It is not physical, so if you drop the plate, it cannot break unless you want it to."

I puzzled over this. "Will Harry still get ice cream and chocolate in Heaven?" Grandpa laughed. "I don't know. The Torah does not speak of this. But since the dead are with God and have no more physical bodies, they may get spiritual ice cream for their souls." *Trying to imagine this, I envisioned Harry licking a spiritual strawberry ice cream cone. It did not drip and he did not get any on his face.* That was my first encounter with human death. Of course, by local Bronx custom excluding the very young, I was not allowed to go to the funeral.

Then I carefully crayoned in a black-bordered handmade condolence card with a smiling photo that I had of Harry. Then I tiptoed out and sneaked it under his apartment door.

Shortly after the funeral, Sammy's mom left her mourning group *(Shiva)* and rang our doorbell. When my Mom answered it, Sammy's mom asked, "Where's Bernie?" and showed Mom the card. Then they both shook their heads in amazement and hugged me. The card read:

Harry has gone to heaven, and left us all behind.
I write this to remember him, my little friend so kind.
Death is like sleep, but without waking—that's what I'm told
Harry died as a little boy, and now will never grow old.

I was invited over for an hour to visit Sammy and sit *Shiva* with the adult mourners, a nearly unprecedented privilege for a young boy in those days. In Hebrew, Shiva literally translates from Hebrew as 'seven', the number of days of intense mourning to be observed—seven days minus the Sabbath day.

Before going to the *Shiva*, I dressed up in my little dark brown suit, and Dad pinned a small bowtie on my shirt because regular hand-knotted ties were too long for me. I was accepted by the adult mourners, and sat with Sammy—the only other young child at the *Shiva*. I hardly touched any of the cookies or cake served by the ladies of the family.

Sammy stayed quiet. No games, no jokes—we talked of school and what we wanted to remember about Harry. In accordance with tradition, the mirrors were covered, and two of Sammy's aunts did the food preparation. However, I was too young to be counted for the minyan of ten men, including bar mitzvah boys, who were required to recite the *Kaddish*, the mourner's prayer. The nine men waited and talked quietly until a tenth man came and joined us.

The Rabbi was not there to forbid my presence, so I tried to act as grown-up as possible. But then I came back to my apartment later and privately cried in my room and became a little child again. Still in short pants but long in thoughts, I began to vaguely try to conceptualize what death was all about.

Mortality tales were just newspaper, magazine and radio stories to me. Kids my age played 'bang-bang, you're dead!' then got up again to play their next game. Movie cartoons showed creatures falling off cliffs, or with pianos landing on their heads, but these make-believe 'victims' only saw stars, made a brief hole in the ground where they landed, or they got a few lumps that usually healed in the next few frames.

I had already seen dead animals in the park sometimes—pigeons, cats and squirrels, all stiff or squishy. And that's all I saw of death personally. I did not cry because they were not my pets. Animals didn't have funerals in the mid-20th century working-class Bronx, but people did.

Harry's death made mortality an issue that impacted me personally, more in puzzlement than in grieving. One of my twin playmates was now gone. I missed Harry's laughing silliness, Sammy was a little more serious-minded. He was inspired by my reading to him to try reading also.

He picked it up slowly and deliberately. Sammy had not even wanted to try, saying with a smirk, "That's what mommies and daddies are for—to read to us. When I grow up, then I will read and write." But I finally persuaded Sammy that it was fun and he should do it. I hoped that God would send Harry back to school in Heaven.

11

Starting School in the West Bronx

From the crumbling aged streets of the Crotona Park area, Bernie's parents relocated to the hilly West Bronx in early 1943. Grandpa recommended this move to give Bernie a better schooling environment in PS 82, even though his grandparents in the East Bronx would now be more distant from him. In the 1940s, East Bronx schools were deteriorating from overcrowding as families from the teeming tenements of Manhattan moved north into middle-class East Bronx declining neighborhoods.

The new apartment was on Macombs Road, a mile-long winding street rising from the elevated subway station at 170th Street and Jerome Avenue to University Avenue. It was a sunken street-level two-bedroom basement flat with windows just above the sidewalk at street level.

Bernie had one bedroom, while baby Gloria slept in a crib near her parents in the other bedroom. Stretched out on his bed, Bernie could see the walking feet and ankles of passers-by and tried to imagine what they looked like above foot level. Sometimes he ran to the door to check and see if he was right. There was no scientific analysis here, just a young boy's imagination at work.

The ceilings were crisscrossed by painted pipes leading through the walls to the basement boiler room. They sometimes flaked paint chips onto the linoleum-covered floors in the winter when the walls were heated by the pipes. The living room was graced by an overstuffed medium beige sofa and two matching chairs—all covered in darker beige corduroy slipcovers. The walls were decorated with some cheap Woolworth's rural landscape reprints in chipped gilded frames.

The narrow elongated apartment foyer doubled as a dining room. Since only a small kitchen table with four seats fit into the foyer, the family usually ate in two shifts—children first, and then parents separately. Only when the family had company were extra chairs and a table extended into the living room to accommodate up to eight family and guests all eating together.

World War II was in its fourth year when Bernie's family moved to the West Bronx. The Allied Forces had stopped the advances of the Axis powers in the Atlantic and Pacific regions, but had not yet turned the tide of battle. Bernie followed the shifting lines of battle with cutout maps, paste-up soldiers, tanks and airplanes, and pushpin bulletin board battlefields with arrows and battle lines updated daily. This was much more fun to him than coloring books or board games. He did sense that the World War had fighting with real blood and battles. Or … as real as his imagination could render them.

Bernie sometimes invited other older kids over to play war games on a map board of Europe. "No, no, dumbhead!" he once cried out to a playmate who had placed his headquarters markers on the wrong side of the board. "Rommel is a German General, not British." His playmates did not understand war logistics or battle frontlines. Bernie read the daily papers and listened to Grandpa's talk of a troubled world at war, with only a partial but gradually increasing understanding.

Blood and bombings, dismembered bodies lying in the fire-swept rubble of ruined cities as survivors searched for scraps to eat among the garbage—this was all beyond his childish comprehension and Bronx boyhood experience. Only the children of the bombed-out cities, the occupied cities, the terrorized cities of Europe and Asia knew real war from their own exposure and were not children anymore by the knowing of it.

"Bernie, hurry up! Time to go to school." Mom's sharp voice cut through the closed bedroom door. It was the dawn of his first day in kindergarten, and he was all excited about it.

School! School! To learn from real teachers about the world which he only knew secondhand from books. Classroom lectures and discussions—that's what Bernie expected to happen there. His idealistic hopes came from reading about higher grade schools, so he was not prepared for the new reality of play/learning that awaited him in kindergarten. Bernie felt very grown-up by going to school. Then, in the spring of 1943, he entered the kindergarten at PS 82.

"*Wow!*" he thought, "*a day away from Mom at school!*" Off they went, Mom and Grandpa and Bernie, walking up Macombs Road hill to the red brick school facing diagonally onto University Avenue. As they walked towards the school, Bernie behaved nicely for once and took Mom's hand quietly without pulling away.

Bernie's birth certificate and filled-out inoculation forms were tucked into his Grandpa's worn brown leather briefcase—a relic from his general manager years at Ford Motor Company. A half-hour later, Bernie was in Miss Oppenberg's kindergarten classroom with twenty other five-year old kids. Some were tearful, some happy, some puzzled and waiting for the teacher to guide them in this new play and study adventure called 'school'.

Bernie was disappointed. There was very little reading done by students in this kindergarten class—just a few words recited from picture books. The children were immersed in game playing, arts and crafts activities, singing and social interactions. Bernie's own out-of-school education had rapidly advanced under his Grandpa's tutelage, moving up from 'Dick and Jane' alphabet readers into *Golden Books* and the newspapers.

Grandpa cautioned Bernie not to show off his reading skills in class, to avoid resentment by the other children. He told Bernie's parents of pressure on teachers from principals and school boards to 'conform to the norm'. That's the way it was back then, even in the earliest grades, except for a few special schools which were far away and difficult to qualify for admission. In his elementary school years, Bernie did not make any close friends. The spectral shadow of remembered Harry dying at age four darkened over him when he sometimes began to meet other little children.

It was easier for Bernie to become friends with books than with young boys or girls. Book characters did not die permanently. If any were killed in a story, all he had to do was turn back the pages to resurrect them.

Grandpa attended the school parent-teacher conferences with Mom, since Dad was too tired after a day in the taxicab to go to school on 'parent nights'. Many kindergarten parents did not know that Miss Oppenberg was a German Jew, not a German Nazi! Their eyes narrowed in suspicion when they met her and heard her accent. In the war years, with a teacher shortage on, foreign accents did not disqualify teachers from classroom jobs.

Some kids called Miss Oppenberg 'heinie' and 'kraut' behind her back—mimicking those words from their bigoted parents.

However, she was an excellent teacher, a refugee from Nazi Germany, the country that invented kindergarten. Shortly after Bernie's kindergarten year, Miss Oppenberg left PS 82. Rumors from older kids claimed she was forced out by bigoted parental pressures. But no one really knew why she left. Early in the 20th century, there was much anti-foreigner sentiment coming from immigrants "off the boat' just a generation or two earlier.

At first, Bernie pretended to be a normal kindergarten kid, in order not to cause any classroom commotion. Miss Oppenberg was strict, but was sensitive to student's personalities as she perceived them. She was faithful to her duty of starting kids on their first steps along the education road, and gave the class basic school behavior rules to follow.

The rules were 'No shouting or crying, raise your hand and wait until called by the teacher, pay attention in class, and be clean'. Bernie's 'play and learn' pretense began at the first classroom Tinkertoy session the next day. In kindergarten, work and play were interchangeable and almost the same.

Miss Oppenberg kept an eye out for all happenings in her classroom.

"Here, Robert, blow your nose. Sheila, raise your hand if you vant to say something." She then busied herself around the room, settling the class into their seats. Later, requesting time to discuss Bernie, Miss Oppenberg slipped into Principal Celia Stevens office and closed the oaken door behind her. "Hmm. There is something strange about dat Bernie kid," she said. "I need to discuss him mit you. I can't kvite put my finger on it, but his play seems zo purposeful. He is pretending to pretend. He's not really into construction toys or building blocks".

"Pretending to pretend?" said the Principal quizzically. "That's a new one on me."

"New vun on me too." Miss Oppenberg shrugged.

Miss Stevens continued. "He's either very bright or emotionally disturbed. Maybe both. Keep an eye on him and tell me at the end of the week how he is doing."

Back in the classroom, Miss Oppenberg kept wondering about Bernie the rest of the week. She observed him working on one of the Tinkertoy construction sets amidst the giggles of her kindergarten class. The other children were uninhibited, but beginning to learn school behavior, with many missteps along the way.

A smile broke out on her face. *Yes, Bernie Seiden can be a playful little kid after all,* she thought. *Brain or no brain ...*

"Vork quietly now," she reproved them, heading towards Bernie. "Vat are you making, Bernie? You handle der Tinkertoy parts vell."

"I can't explain it to you."

"Vell, try."

"It's a big word that I read in my grandpa's books."

"Vat's the big word?"

"Tesseract."

She felt a chill needling down her spine. *Gott im himmel! Das ist ein wunderkind?! This child is constructing tesseracts at age five? Impossible! Or ... is it?*

Chokingly, she asked, "Bernie, do you know vat a tesseract is? Tell me, please."

"Yes, Miss Oppenberg. A tesseract is a four-dimensional cube." She winced. Bernie mispronounced it slightly, but he knew ... He knew!

 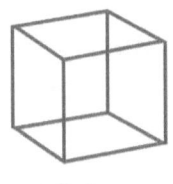 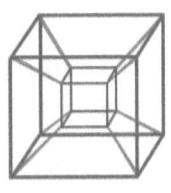

Square   Cube   Tesseract

Grandpa's diagram to explain the Tesseract as a 4-dimensional cube of cubes

"Bernie," she said softly as he was summoned to her desk that bright February day in 1943. "Don't talk about tesseracts or science to the other boys and girls here. They do not understand that. This will be our own little secret."

"Yes, Miss Oppenberg," he replied smugly. "I won't tell them. I learned about tesseracts from my Grandpa and the non-math illustrated books he showed me about solid geometry." Bernie amused himself by mentally running through the construction of basic structures of solid geometry while the other children 'tinker-toyed' away randomly. Only occasionally did they produce boxy constructs, striving for the promised reward of a large lollipop.

Meanwhile, Bernie used the Tinkertoy parts to busily construct hexahedrons, dodecahedrons, spiraled and truncated pyramids. He paused. "Miss Oppenberg, can I have my lollipop now? I finished my construction." In flustered embarrassment, she produced the lollipop and asked him, "Do you really like lollipops?" Bernie replied sarcastically, "Of course I like them. I am a kid, remember?"

She silently vowed herself to remember, and walked over quickly to the blackboard to post Bernie's earned gold star there. "Oh boy," he gleefully cried, clapping his hands. An inner smile reflected on her relieved face. Bernie was only a regular little bright boy after all ... even with his Tinkertoy tesseracts!

Years later, Bernie encountered Miss Oppenberg again by chance in a Lexington Avenue coffee shop after he enrolled as a freshman in CCNY to pursue a Liberal Arts degree. She had overcome the anti-German wartime prejudice of the City school system, which sometimes failed to differentiate between Nazis and their victims. By diligent practice, she had reduced her German accent to a barely noticeable level after she departed from her kindergarten class for the dignity of a college professorship.

That's how grown-up Bernie learned his kindergarten teacher's life story. They exchanged warm reminiscences over a cup of tea about her kindergarten teaching days. To Bernie's surprise, Miss Oppenberg told him that she was no stranger to four-dimensional concepts.

At Heidelberg, her father was a physics professor before the Nazis rose to power, and she heard much of his dinner talk to colleagues about the then new-fangled Relativity Theory, and the fourth dimension. She quietly told Bernie that Albert Einstein was once a dinner guest at her house! Her father, she told Bernie, assumed that such scientific talk was over her head. He assumed wrongly. Herr Professor Oppenberg had not considered science a suitable career for his daughter and refused to pay for such a college major. He offered her a compromise—to become a teacher instead. She had argued with him, but then reluctantly accepted his offer to pay for a teaching degree in a German college. She graduated before the Nazis came to power.

"What about Marie Curie? She is a scientist!" Miss Oppenberg challenged her father. He answered lamely, "That's the French. They are ridiculous anyway. No good German university would accept you for a major in science. Go for a degree in education." That ended the argument for the moment. But she still continued to ponder her future. Maybe in America? Women have more opportunities there. Miss Oppenberg was not a scientist herself, but an education major who took the only position offered to her as a refugee from Hitler when she emigrated to depression-torn America—the position of a Bronx kindergarten teacher in the United States of America.

12

Grandpa, My Hero

Since Grandpa was retired and past seventy years old when I was born, much of what I know of his life and career was told to me by my aunts and uncles. A leader of men in his working years, Grandpa ran his family as he had run his business—with a strong paternalistic hand. Yet he was indulgent to me as a favorite grandchild.

Grandpa's financial fortune vanished in the Depression, so only his great intellectual heritage remained to share with me. But what a heritage that was! Together, beginning when I was six years old, we left young children's books behind and delved into H.G. Wells, Tolstoy, Washington Irving and other exciting authors at a junior high-school level. I mispronounced many of their complex author's words, but I understood them.

Dear Grandpa! He was and always will be, my hero. But he was a product of his times, chauvinistic, favoring sons and grandsons over daughters and granddaughters. He believed that women were destined only for the kitchen and the baby nursery. But innocent of his male bias, I was too young when grandpa was still alive to wonder why his kisses were warm to me, but perfunctory to my baby sister Gloria.

Aunt Irma told me that after Grandpa left Ford in the spring of 1924, and up until the Great Market Crash of 1929, he led the life of a wealthy semi-retired management consultant in the New York City area. Four servants maintained Grandpa's townhouse residence on Lenox Avenue and 117th Street in tree-lined Harlem, then a mainly middle-class and wealthy white suburb of upper Manhattan. The household staff included a butler, a cook and a nanny who cared for Mom as a baby and her brothers and sisters.

There was an attached coach house that became a garage when Grandpa bought the mansion. It housed a luxurious Lincoln L7, chauffeur driven and maintained. Grandpa had sold his imported custom tobacco business to the American Tobacco Company after the First World War for a large block of their common and preferred stock. Then American Tobacco stock plunged in the Great Crash, together with his other investments, and he was reduced to near-financial ruin in his later years. To me, he was just Grandpa, the wisest man in the world. I had no idea as a child how wealthy he had been in his earlier business career.

Grandpa

Grandpa once dared, as a general manager at the Rouge River Complex, to confront Henry Ford, the autocrat of the automobile world, in Ford's private office, on the issue of anti-Semitism. However, Grandpa did not tell Ford that he was Jewish! Instead, he told Ford that anti-semitism was bad for business.

The 1920s were prime publishing years of the *Dearborn Independent* weekly newspaper, operating at a loss but subsidized by the Ford multi-millions. Henry Ford had bought this suburban Detroit newspaper in 1917 and changed its content from a suburban editorial style into a ranting 'rag' with screaming headlines of anti-semitic epithets and anti-Wall Street diatribes.

The paper was distributed in Ford auto dealerships and by Ford's own network of street newsboys all across America. Many urban newsstands and candy stores, fearing violence, refused to carry the *Dearborn Independent.*

As a Ford Motor executive, Grandpa had over a thousand men working under him at the Rouge River plant in Dearborn —the heart of the Ford empire. None of Ford's executives, or Henry Ford himself, ever suspected that Grandpa was not a Christian. Mr. Ford thought that Grandpa was Polish from his given name of Ralutzky. With no hook nose, and his cavalry officer bearing, Grandpa easily passed for a scion of Polish aristocracy, who appeared as if he would draw a saber on anyone who crossed him.

Grandpa was actually a devout Orthodox Jew. He wore a wide-brimmed dark brown or charcoal felt fedora during the day, and in the office. Facial hair was still common in American offices in the 1920s, so Grandpa's fierce facial mustache did not give away his Jewish identity. Tough guys in the movies of the '20s and '30s wore hats indoors, as did Harry Bennett, Ford's own personal thuggish enforcer, whose official job was head of the Service Department. 'Harry the Hatchet man' they called him (behind his back of course!). Harry wore a slouchy snap-brim fedora.

For two years, Grandpa lived the logistical nightmare of a double life at work—by day a secular Ford executive and by night a devout Orthodox Jew. He left his office early on Friday afternoons, but took home a briefcase full of papers to disguise his intended Sabbath observance.

Today, I can now only guess how Grandpa evaded Saturday golfing outings, business meetings and other Ford executive events. As for taking the Jewish holidays off, for instance, I always wondered how he managed that? I was never told how he did it, but I suppose it may have been a combination of sick leave, vacation time, and personal leave.

Grandpa never discussed with me his ways of passing as a Christian within the Ford management team, except in a brief reference or two to the widespread anti-semitism of the Roaring Twenties. New workers applying for employment with Ford in the post-World War One era were routinely strip-searched, and physical details such as circumcision were duly noted. Grandpa, as a senior executive, was spared this humiliating process.

The workers endured this indignity because Ford paid higher wages than any other factory. No one in the Ralutzky family ever bought a Ford car again after Grandpa resigned, long after old Henry departed from this world in 1947.

In later years, I tried to explain to my family that Ford's grandson and successor, Henry II, had done much to atone for the old man's prejudices, including the creation in 1957 of Israel's first car assembly plant in defiance of the Arab boycott. There was also a $3 million donation from Henry Ford II, to the University of Jerusalem, and $12 million more to fund Israeli scientific and educational projects.

My arguments about the Ford family making amends for old Henry's anti-semitism fell on deaf parental ears. They told me, "You are only a boy. How do you know what Ford did in the old days to insult our people?"

But Grandpa knew what happened at Ford Motors in the 1920s. He also showed me some old issues of the *Dearborn Independent*, blaming the world's financial problems mainly on the Jews, with an occasional sideswipe at Wall Street and the bankers —his other targets.

On the lighter side, Grandpa once showed me a tidbit from the 1914 Ford personnel manual to illustrate a point he was making to me about personal hygiene. "Employees should use plenty of soap and water in the home, and upon their children, bathing frequently. Nothing makes for right living and health as much as cleanliness." In other words, 'Cleanliness is next to Fordliness!'

One early May day in 1943, I asked Grandpa, "Why did you go to work for Henry Ford when you knew he was anti-Jewish?" Grandpa replied, "I thought that as a general manager, I could help change that policy. Mr. Ford was thinking of running for President in 1924 against Calvin Coolidge. He needed to soften his notorious 'it's all the Jews fault' image. The anti-Jewish stories may have played well in the Deep South, but not in the East or West Coast states that Ford would need to win Republican Presidential electoral votes.

Grandpa continued, "I prayed for Mr. Ford to get a real change of heart, and that someday he would no longer vilify Jews and denounce them in his newspaper. And perhaps then, as a new day dawned free of prejudice at his company, I could stop hiding my Jewish faith and become an influence to bring Jewish employees into Ford Motors, with their traditional strong work habits."

"Wow, Grandpa!" I exclaimed. "Why did Mr. Ford back down from fighting Coolidge for the White House?" Grandpa stroked his mustache thoughtfully. "Maybe he realized it took more skills to run America than it took to build cars. Perhaps Ford would miss his beloved auto and aircraft plants. Perhaps he realized that as President, he would lose national hero status in the perceptions of most American non-Jews. Perhaps Mrs. Ford quietly influenced him against running."

Whatever the reason, the 'Ford for President' movement fizzled out, and the *Dearborn Independent* shifted its editorial focus from attacking banks and Wall Street back to its earlier anti-semitism, blaming the Jews for all the world's woes. Grandpa was appalled by Mr. Ford's renewal of anti-Jewish hostility after his brief Presidential campaign ended. Dismissal of the few known Jewish employees of Ford (after his 1924 abortive run for the White House had ended) was happening at lower company personnel levels, where they had earlier been grudgingly tolerated by Mr. Ford.

Aunt Irma told me about the dramatic May morning in 1924 when Grandpa left his modern high-collar business suit and vest hanging in the hall closet and carefully donned his Orthodox Jewish apparel—yarmulke, caftan and shirt with tasseled fringes and no tie. He had always worn fringed tzitzes discreetly tucked into business shirts before going to work, but this day they were displayed openly.

Grandpa marched directly into the private offices of Henry Ford where as a senior executive, he had direct access to Mr. Ford himself. He stormed past open-mouthed staring secretaries and clerks too stunned to stop him. He slapped his written resignation directly on Old Henry's desk.

Grandpa then marched out and slammed the office door behind him while Henry Ford harrumphed and sputtered, trying to find words to respond. Grandpa drove home to his rented house in suburban Grosse Point in his Lincoln L-series Brunn coupe, a Christmas bonus from Mr. Ford. An insistent klaxon beep summoned the family to the front porch.

"Pack up!" Grandpa announced. "I've had it with Henry Ford and his anti-Jewish phobia. We came to Detroit disguised as Polish Christians, now we will go home to New York openly as proud Jews. I am selling the car and we will return by second-class rail coach on the New York Central."

Now, a generation later, the outward bitterness of Grandpa towards Ford had abated. After losing most of his wealth in the 1929 Crash, Grandpa returned to the tobacco business on a much smaller scale, making a living by hand-rolling Egyptian cigarettes in his modest work-a-day Bronx apartment. But every Friday night, the apartment was transformed and sparkled for the Sabbath.

The dining room was large enough to seat up to a dozen family members for Friday Sabbath dinner. A few sterling silverware pieces and grandpa's easy chair were all that remained of the former splendor from the old Lexington Avenue townhouse, before it was sold at auction to pay his debts. Now only a few cheap pieces of furniture barely filled his flat, purchased from a second-hand store.

In confidence, Grandpa once told me: "I sacrificed my Ford career for Jewish moral principles and never regretted it. Now I live in a war-torn world which I pray will someday be a better place to live in than the present world, after Hitler is defeated." He looked at me thoughtfully and mused,

"Will this dear bright grandson of mine one day have to choose between his Judaism and a business career? Gott soll abhiten! (God forbid!)"

13

The Twins are Born

Mom was expecting again in early 1943. I was five years old, and more observant of pregnancy happenings than when Gloria was born two years earlier. I had seen pregnant dogs and puppies shortly after birth, all wet and wiggly, but did not see the births. I could not get any adult relatives to explain it to me. Grandpa cut off any discussion of the subject by saying he would explain it later. He was uncomfortable with the topic.

Meanwhile, Dad asked me to understand that Mom would now be tiring more easily in the next several months, and asked me to be an especially good boy and not cause her any grief. I tried to be 'good', but it was hard for me to suddenly transform into a "little angel". I did pick up my stuff from the floor more often, and became more diligent in watching out for Gloria.

Aunt Irma willingly obtained adult books for me from the library, but drew the line at procuring any sexual or maternity material. This was a rarity --- all adult family members agreeing on a family policy --- no sex or pregnancy books for me! I retreated and resolved to learn what I could by direct observation and guesswork.

Lacking any knowledge of the uterus, I figured that babies grew inside the bellies of their mothers. I knew that milk was important, and wondered how babies were getting it while still unborn. I never saw Mom drink any milk herself, but she was always urging it on me and Gloria. There were several pregnant mothers in the neighborhood, so I began to do some discreet observation on the University Avenue park benches along the center strip of the street where they congregated with their baby carriages.

Aunt Irma related an old-wives tale to me. She said that Mom's double-bulging abdomen, riding high in her fifth month of pregnancy, was a signal that a boy would emerge as the firstborn of expected twins. That's because boys are supposedly more aggressive than girls and in a bigger hurry to enter the world, according to folklore.

It was early Wednesday morning, June 27, 1943 when Mom went into labor with the twins. Mom typically woke up at six a.m. to fix breakfast and get me off to school. But today was different. It was a few minutes after 4 a.m., when she awoke Dad from his slumbers.

"Danny, wake up, wake up."

"Wha ... whaat?" Dad grumped sleepily.

"It's time ... The babies are coming."

"Are you sure?"

"Yes ... yes, a mother-to-be is always sure. Five minute pains. Let's get going."

Dad then woke me up, and said that the twins were on their way into this world. While he called the taxi garage, fixed a quick cereal breakfast for us and then called Aunt Irma, I got dressed and readied for school myself.

Aunt Irma, who lived about a mile away near Burnside Avenue, drove over in a few minutes to pick up Gloria and see me off to school. Fortunately, Gloria did not ask me about how babies are born (not that I knew that then anyway!)

Dad scooped up Mom's overnight bag, prepared in advance for a five-day maternity stay, and drove Mom to Bronx Hospital. Grandpa and Grandma came to the hospital within an hour after they were called to welcome their new twin grandchildren into the world.

The doctor had predicted twins by an x-ray count of two heads in her womb, with gender unknown. Dad paced calmly up and down the maternity waiting room. He had promised to call me at school when Mom delivered the babies. I knew it was not the stork that would be delivering my new baby siblings, but our own family doctor.

Many of my classmates still believed the stork legend. But Grandpa had explained to me a few months earlier, the way in which new babies arrive in this world. He spared only the sexual details of impregnation but covered the topic of conception and pregnancy itself in a simplified manner. The hospital called my school at around 11 a.m., and the principal delivered the message to my classroom.

The teacher was all smiles, the kids congratulated me and rushed over to the cookies and lemonade fetched by a monitor for a brief impromptu party. It was a twin boy and girl! Mom later told me that Carol came into this world first, pudgy and dark-haired and round-faced. Her brother Mark arrived eight minutes later, thin and reddish-blonde—truly opposite twins. As Mark grew into babyhood and then childhood, his hair lost its reddish tones and became 'dirty blonde'. He was the only genetically blonde boy or girl in the family for many generations back of our Eastern European ancestry.

Mark was contrary in behavior from his twin sister. He cried and fussed while Carol gurgled and smiled at her new world beyond the womb. Their physical and mental paths diverged as they grew up, but they remained twinned in an ineffable bond that transcended whatever brief quarrels and differences they had in their earliest years.

On the second day of their lives, I gazed up at the windows of the seventh floor maternity ward, alongside Grandpa at the old Bronx Hospital on Franklin Avenue. We anxiously waited for Mom to appear at the closed window of her hospital room with the babies. I was too young to be allowed upstairs to visit the nursery or Mom's hospital room.

I saw twins in the street sometimes, in baby carriages. Triplets were much rarer. I never encountered triplets in my Bronx neighborhood.

Quads? What are they? The quad question, like all other big questions in my life, I referred to Grandpa for answers. I knew it was not unusual for dogs to have four or more puppies at a time, I saw the word 'quads', but did not understand it. I never saw quads in my life. Neither did anyone else I knew.

"Grandpa," I asked, "Are there any quads in New York City?"

He responded thoughtfully. "There could be a few, maybe. It's rare. One out of over seven hundred thousand births. Quadruplets seem to happen mainly in Sunday newspapers, not in everyday life. I never saw any quads in Russia when I was a boy, or in America either." Curiously, I asked. "Does any human mother ever give birth to more than four babies at a time?"

Grandpa smiled. "That's very, very rare! Five babies born together are called quintuplets, or quints for short. Three years before you were born, the Dionne quints were born in Canada—the Dionne quintuplets." He paused. "They were the first human quints in world history to survive and grow up into adults."

I perked up. "Grandpa, tell me more about twins."

"Bernie, do you recall the story I told you about Cleopatra, the Queen of Egypt?"

"Oh, yes. She was conquered by the Romans in battle and Julius Caesar became her boyfriend!"

"That's right. Her full name was Cleopatra Selene. That means she was 'of the Moon', and I will tell you something else about her that you did not know." He paused for emphasis. "She had a twin brother. His name was Alexander Helios, and Helios means 'of the Sun'." The royal twins were named that way because the Sun rules the heavens in daytime, and the Moon rules the heavens by night." Grandpa continued by explaining to me that after Cleopatra's reign as female Pharaoh, Egypt lost its power as a mighty kingdom and was reduced to becoming a Roman province.

I did not interact as closely with the twins in their baby years as I had done with Gloria in her infancy, and then continuing when she was a toddler. My school studies and developing interest in world affairs began to take precedence over playing with my brother and two sisters. However, I did continue and enjoy my ongoing 'big brother' role to them.

14

1943: Wartime Riot in Harlem

In the summer of 1943, the World War blazed on as its impact on America deepened. Uniformed soldiers and sailors on leave or military business appeared sometimes on the streets of the Bronx and the borough's local defenses became visible. Artillery was set up at the Jerome Park reservoir in the Bronx to protect against any potential German raids across the Atlantic to bomb the New York City water supply. Rationing had begun, and Bronx families in general accepted wartime sacrifice and shortages as their patriotic duty.

Black families were also patriotic, but were poorer than whites and had less to be sacrificed to begin with. Their economic resentment at higher paying jobs going to whites smoldered in the streets and ghettos. A general riot began in Harlem between Negroes and Whites, and against local Jewish store owners in particular on August 1st and 2nd.

A white police officer shot Private Robert Bandy, a black soldier, wounding him in the shoulder. He was protesting the arrest of a black woman, ironically named Marjorie Polite, in the Braddock Hotel at 126th Street and 8th Avenue for disorderly conduct. The hotel had a reputation for prostitution. It was classified by the Army as a 'raided premises', and a police officer was regularly stationed in the lobby to prevent crime. The police report claimed that Miss Polite became drunk at a hotel room party, and confronted the police belligerently as she tried to leave. The cops also claimed Bandy hit the officer and was shot as he tried to flee. There were other conflicting reports from witnesses of the incident.

University Avenue (on a foggy day)

Bandy told the press that he intervened and hit the officer for pushing Miss Polite. Since Polite's mother was also present, it was unlikely that there was any prostitution going on at that scene at that time. Bandy was taken to Sydenham Hospital and treated for his wound.

Exaggerated stories swiftly spread in the afternoon from Lenox Avenue east to Lexington Avenue, and from 116th Street north to 145th Street.

The rumors flying around in Harlem were that "The cops are beating up and busting a sister!" By the time the wild tales had spread across Harlem, the story had shifted and magnified into cops killing a Negro soldier trying to protect his elderly innocent mother from arrest. A crowd of about three thousand blacks formed by 9 p.m. at the police station, wielding knives, clubs and crowbars.

Other crowds also formed around the hospital and the hotel. At the same time, Mayor Fiorello LaGuardia met with police authorities and black leaders to inspect the riot area. The Mayor then ordered 6,000 more city police officers into Harlem plus 1,500 volunteers and 8,000 national guardsmen on standby from New York State. All vehicular traffic was redirected to detour around the Harlem perimeter.

Trolley car on fire

After returning from battered Harlem, the Mayor spoke on the radio and urged Harlemites to go home. NAACP leader Walter Francis White also addressed the black community, appealing for the return of peace to Harlem.

White declared, "The rumor is false that a Negro soldier was killed at the Braddock Hotel tonight. He is only slightly wounded and is in no danger. Go to your homes! Don't destroy in one night the reputation as good citizens you have taken a lifetime to build. Go home now!" Unfortunately, the crowds did not listen. Late in the evening, matters got ugly as violence erupted again. At 10:30 p.m. curfew was imposed, and Mayor LaGuardia issued orders to shoot only if necessary to protect life.

Gangs of between fifty and a hundred men formed from the crowds and began to roam the Harlem streets. Windows and street lights were smashed. The liquor stores were looted first. This fueled the rioters to move on further in search of store stuff to steal. A few futile shots from storekeepers were fired fearfully from behind the counters, but this failed to disperse the mob.

Roving the glass-shattered streets, the angry rioters impartially smashed Jewish and Christian-owned stores alike. The few black storekeepers hastily scrawled signs stating "I AM A BROTHER" and came out in front of their stores to greet the rioters. Some of the storekeepers handed out cigarettes and sodas, and all non-white stores were spared.

One 'color-blind' drunk heaved a rock at a black-owned music store window, and was dragged away and beaten by the crowd from which he sprang forth. A mob leader apologized and handed the storekeeper a fistful of stolen cash to pay for the broken glass.

Smashed windows

Looters leaped into the broken stores and handed goods to the hordes outside, who then scurried off with armfuls of looted merchandise. The ranks of departing plunderers were swiftly filled by new rioters with outstretched hands clawing at the windows, smashing them with bricks and sticks. In all, nearly one thousand five hundred stores were burglarized.

The mobs hesitated in front of the few Harlem banks, as stout doors and barred windows blocked them, backed by shotguns aimed streetward by grim-faced guards. Shrinking away from confronting the banks, the mobs then attacked easier targets nearby. Bank guns were not fired as the guards had instructions only to shoot to protect bank property.

On the next day, sirens sounded, and thousands of New York City police were positioned for riot duty. Under this show of force, the mobs thinned out by late afternoon. Miraculously, there were only five people killed, about five hundred injured, and another six hundred or so arrested. Prohibition (of liquor) briefly returned to Harlem that week, a decade after it had been abolished.

About five miles away from troubled Harlem, Bernie and his Grandpa chatted the next day while they sat together in a shaded part of Crotona Park, away from the hot overhead sun. Bernie focused on the riot news. He asked, "Why did the black people attack the Jewish stores?" Grandpa gathered his thoughts to answer.

"It's because Jewish merchants own many Harlem shops, and the black people believe that Jews overcharge them for food and other goods."

"Is that really true?"

"No, it isn't. Big stores do not go into Harlem because they need to pay too much for security to safely do business there. Some of them also don't like Negroes, and won't hire them for anything but low-level labor, but will take their money if they shop in the white stores."

He continued. "Some smaller Jewish owned stores do business in Harlem and take the risk. They charge more because they pay more for goods on a smaller buying scale from the food companies. Maybe a hundred quarts of milk a day, for instance, for a local grocery. A & P supermarkets may do several hundred quarts a day, so they can charge customers less. But A & P has no Harlem stores." Grandpa sighed. "That's the way it is." The phone rang insistently, and Grandpa excused himself to answer. It was a local merchants' committee asking him to attend a hastily-called emergency meeting of Bronx businessmen to cope with a potential spreading threat from the Harlem riots.

With no time left to send Bernie home, his Grandpa decided to take him along for the experience. Off they went in Grandpa's Pontiac Streamliner Coupe to the Lewis Morris Apartments on the Grand Concourse. This major boulevard was modeled on the famed Champs-Elysees of Paris, but longer and wider, separated into three four-mile long roadways of eleven lanes each separated by tree-lined dividers.

The 'Lewis-Morris' was the tallest residential building in the old Bronx, already fading in the fifties from its pre-war glory days as one of the premier apartment houses in the borough. Its fourteen-story yellowish façade, built in 1923, showed signs of wear and tear, but it was still a grand sight to behold from the street level above the arched overhead of the Concourse viaduct. The building still had a doorman and carpeted hallways during the 1940s. It was named after a signer of the Declaration of Independence, Lewis Morris, who owned a large part of what is today the South Bronx. None of the seven other store owners gathered there knew Bernie, but they all knew and respected his Grandpa.

Grandpa Ralutzky introduced Bernie as his six-year old grandson and said the boy would act as his secretary at the meeting. Eyebrows were raised at this, with one man arguing that I was too young to be counted in a minyan. Grandpa replied, "Yes, he is too young to be counted if this were a minyan, but we are not in a synagogue or prayer group. This is a business meeting, and he will not have a vote or speak." With that non-minyan comment, the group's objections subsided, Bernie took his seat and busily began taking notes. Bernie was feeling very important and grown-up, and resolved not ask his Grandpa how to spell any grown-up words spoken at the meeting.

The men decided to strengthen their own store security by pooling contributions into a fund to hire private guards to patrol in case of any violence outbreak against stores in the Bronx. There were no opposing opinions. With the city Police fully occupied with the Harlem rioting, there was no possibility of seeking more Police protection for Bronx merchants. The meeting then adjourned.

Afterwards, Grandpa praised Bernie's accurate notes, and then rewarded his grandson's diligence with an extravagantly dripping two-scoop thirty-five cent strawberry sundae at Ruschmeyer's Ice Cream Parlor on University Avenue.

Ruschmeyer's was styled with hotel bar room elegance underneath its dark plum purple exterior sign. Mahogany paneling inset with oversize black plush leatherette booths loomed over customers, most of whom were too young to be in an alcoholic barroom. Perched atop the high stools, young boys and girls ordered fountain service from the onyx bar countertop.

Ruschmeyer's Ice Cream Parlor on University Avenue was an innocent after- school hang-out for teenage Bronx boys to practice the social graces of paying for a girl. Many older students had their first date experience there *(or so they told me!)*. In those days, it made a boy feel like a real 'big shot' to treat a girl to an ice cream soda for a quarter.

The soda jerks behind the counter were not 'jerky' at all in the modern insulting usage of that word. In their clean, crisp white jackets and matching caps trimmed with thin blue striping, they were local young countermen serving customers. For thirty-five cents, a deluxe banana split with two scoops was served.

An ice cream soda was twenty cents. Aunt Claire taught Bernie in tipping etiquette, so he would grandly leave an extra nickel tip for the soda jerk as an adult would do. He reveled in being addressed as "thank you, sir," with all the dignity that a first-grade schoolboy could muster.

15

First and Second Grade: Knowing Too Much

Two short blocks away from the apartment where I lived, PS 82 squatted atop the crest of Macombs Road. Its red brick five story façade faced diagonally west towards University Avenue. On the first September school day morning in 1943, I entered the first grade there. The school building adjoined the Park Plaza Theater, which was sometimes used for school events and graduations, and a small optometry shop where I was fitted for my first pair of eyeglasses.

At the breakfast table that morning, Mom cautioned me to behave (behave as spelled C-O-N-F-O-R-M) on my first school day, and every day thereafter. Parents had been asked to come to school with their first graders for registration and briefing on the school year ahead.

In our walk-in apartment, we had our meals in a narrow foyer next to the kitchen. First eating turn at the small table was taken by Gloria and me, then the twins ate in their highchairs next to Mom and Dad. When Mom was cooking, she became fierce and distractible. No one dared approach her. Dad sometimes tried to help, but was usually rebuffed. "Out! Out! You get in my way," she would snap at him. "Yes, dear," he replied sweetly. But he soon tried again, never taking her rigid 'no' as a final answer.

After breakfast, Mom and I marched off to PS 82 for first grade registration. We walked through the oaken double doors that were cracked and peeling with age, and then headed for the school office. *Books, instead of toys, awaited me inside,* I thought excitedly. *Books … BOOKS!*

The clouded skies over PS 82 were quiet on school opening day. After being signed in, we went to the auditorium and received the welcome packet, with parental forms for Mom and student ID tags for me. Then the teachers took charge and escorted the kids to their classrooms. My new teacher, Miss Jones, shifted classroom priority from kindergarten play time, with a little reading and writing, into a first grade reading and writing mode. My kindergarten teacher, Miss Oppenberg had kept my advanced literacy a secret from Miss Jones. Like my Grandpa did, she cautioned me not to appear overly bright to other teachers or students.

At first, heeding Grandpa's particular warning not to show off, I dutifully followed Miss Jones' instructions by writing out, in block format on graph paper, the letters of the alphabet. I did this slowly, and with a good pretense of pencil-pushing struggle. Growing ever more resentful and bored, I began to doodle on the graph paper. Nothing fancy or meaningful—just swirling patterns and funny faces. The teacher frowned from her upfront desk as she noticed my doodling and rebuked me sharply. While other first-graders were just starting their struggle to learn the ABC's in school, I read newspapers and magazines at home.

At night, I read books by flashlight under the bedcovers at home, and listened to news from a hidden radio at low volume after the family was asleep. It was mostly the Moms who came with the kids to school registration that first day. Dads were working, or afraid to be seen there if they were not, because then everyone would think that they were unemployed. Several grandparents also came in to enroll their grandchildren.

PS 82, also known as Macombs Junior High School, was a very ordinary-appearing elementary school for kindergarten through third grade. The school building was shared with junior high school classes of 7th through 9th grades. The high-ceilinged halls were gloomy and faded in appearance. Classrooms had dowdy fixed desks with hinged lids to store books underneath. Rounded inkwells, recessed into the angled desktops, remained unfilled for the first grade. They would be filled for older classes. I noticed tell-tale graffiti left behind from the previous year—naughty words scratched into the desk that first graders would know verbally, but could not write.

Miss Jones seated me in the fourth row. I tried to act like an ordinary child of average intelligence. Grandpa feared the teacher would put me down as a 'wise guy' to be reined in and dumbed down to the common learning level of the class. There was no accommodation for bright kids, or slow kids either. So, for me, it was conform, conform—and try to hide my scholastic skills as best as possible.

For a few days, my pretense to be an average-intelligence kid worked. I dutifully penciled the assigned work of copying block letters 1 ½ inches high and squared them off onto graph paper. Then deviltry got the better of my good conforming intentions, and I began doing the letters in flowing handwritten penmanship. I practiced penmanship as shown in writing manuals borrowed at the public library on Grandpa's card.

Quietly sneaking up behind me, the teacher hissed, "Where did you learn to write like that?" "From my grandfather," I replied. "Well, don't do it again" she scolded. "Write like everyone else is doing, and learn the alphabet properly—the way I teach it!"

Chafing at this unfair rebuke, my Grandpa's warning melted away in my mind. I protested, "but I really DO know the alphabet! And I can write in script too. See!" Proudly, I demonstrated by swiftly titling my paper as 'My Calligraphy Lesson'.

To Miss Jones, that was the last straw! I was banished to the back of the room while the class snickered in glee. In a few moments, my punishment became reward, as I discovered a back shelf treasure trove—seventh grade books from the previous year's class in that room. I selected Washington Irving's *"Knickerbocker History of New York"*. Then, I decided to deliberately misbehave often to get sent to the back of the room to pursue my self-education there.

So, while the class struggled with block letter ABCs, I delved into the adventures of peg-legged Peter Stuyvesant, the last Dutch Governor General of New Amsterdam (which later became New York City). I learned that in the early 17th century, New Amsterdam (at the southern tip of Manhattan) was the capital of the Dutch colonial province of New Netherland including parts of southern New York, New Jersey, Connecticut and Delaware.

During the first school week, Mom and I took the University Avenue trolley car to Woolworth's 'Five and Ten' on Fordham Road for school supplies. At age five and a half, I was now tall enough to peek over the counter and see the school supplies. Mom diligently checked off her school shopping list, and filled up the shopping basket with the required items—crayons, pencils, graph paper, ruler—but meanwhile I had sneaked over to the high school students' supply counter—protractors, compasses, triangles and slide rules! Wow! That was what I wanted to work with ... real drafting instruments!

Dad and the Summer Trolley

Mom firmly said, "No ... that's an extra two dollars for the slide rule. I cannot afford it. Besides that, you are too young for drawing tools anyway. The compass has a sharp point, and you could hurt yourself on it." I sulked. It was no use arguing with her. I would ask Grandpa to get it for me, when his legs felt better.

Sometimes I became Grandpa's 'legs' when he sent me to the local library to take out adult books for him on his library card, and secretly for myself as well. Grandpa stayed on in his East Bronx apartment after my parents moved to the west Bronx. Now that he lived several miles away, I saw him only once or twice a week, traveling by a twenty-minute trolley car ride east on the Tremont Avenue line.

As trees began to blossom and leaf into their summer splendor for 1943, my walks with Grandpa and Beauty, his circus dog, became shorter, and we paused more frequently for him to catch his breath. Beauty trotted alongside us, patiently stopping at the corners to check traffic before crossing. She was always unleashed and would not detour for cat chasing or other doggy distractions. Grandpa's entire neighborhood marveled at Beauty's intelligence.

"Good dog," said Grandpa. "Take a bow for Bernie." Beauty stretched out her front paws and dipped her head. I sometimes imagined Beauty, as Grandpa told me in his stories, as she once was in her performing days as a star doggie act before the Nazi invasion caused traveling circuses to flee for their lives. Since many circus performers were gypsies or Jews, they feared persecution if they stayed in Europe.

Grandpa joked about Beauty's circus, life saying that they had a dog act because they could not afford to feed a bear. A refugee from Europe who owed Grandpa some money gave him Beauty in settlement of the debt.

Autumn school days arrived again the next year, 1944, as I entered the second grade. My crafty school-time pretense continued that I was only beginning to read and write. My rebellious spirit grew, and I sometimes let it slip out accidentally in class that I knew more than I was supposed to know at that age.

It happened that after a basic arithmetic drill my academic cover was blown—the pretense of being an average kid. Miss Lerner had run through addition and subtraction drills in the last few classes while I pretended to write in my notebook, meanwhile making magic squares out of the two-digit numbers.

These numbers totaled the same whether added horizontally or vertically. In case Miss Lerner came around to look, I had a cover sheet of 3+2, 1+4 entries, and so on. I became absorbed in horizontal and vertical 'magic' calculations then challenged myself to make diagonal magic squares!

The teacher sneaked over to my desk and snapped, "Let me see what you are studying so intently!" I responded softly, "Magic squares". Magic . . .what?" she asked.

"Magic squares in arithmetic," I replied.

She declared angrily, "You are supposed to be doing the drill!"

"Yes, Miss Lerner, but I know this basic stuff already." (At least, I had the good sense not to say 'baby stuff' to her!) Miss Lerner squinted critically at my paper. "Where did you copy this from?"

I replied defiantly. "I didn't copy it. I know it." She smirked at me. "We will see what you know. Come with me to Mrs. O'Donnell's office after class." After the bell, we marched into the grim smoked-glass cage of the principal's second floor office. Mrs. O'Donnell was a stereotype of an old maid schoolmarm, and a strict disciplinarian. Thin, gray-haired and hawk-nosed, she pierced teachers and students alike with her angry glare.

Mrs. O'Donnell was widowed, and I overheard gossiped rumors by teachers around the school that her husband, who died in World War I, initially had a draft exemption, but pulled some political strings and enlisted in the Army. It was whispered around the school that Mr. O'Donnell had preferred facing the Kaiser to facing his wife, and died in battle. Ironically, his death awarded her civil service exam points as a war widow preference for the principal's job.

Meantime, Mrs. O'Donnell's scholastic war against me had started. I had been sent to her office before, for various minor misbehaviors. Some of my previous offenses were 'shouting out' answers in class and disputing teacher's facts to the class. My defense was that 'I was right!'. That excuse didn't 'cut' it with Mrs. O'Donnell!

Still doubtful about my math abilities, she asked me to do the multiplication table in my head ... up to 12 times 12, which was as high as the class went. Little show off that I was, I kept going up to 20 times 20! Then she started asking me for three digit mental multiplication, and I did that too, but more slowly.

Mrs. O'Donnell's mouth dropped open, and she said in a more kindly voice, "Well, Bernie, I see you know your arithmetic! But let this be our little secret. That's between you and me and Miss Lerner. The other kids will resent you if you show you are too smart."

We made a deal. No demerits, no detention, and I promised to keep my scholastic skills secret from the class. I mostly kept that promise for the rest of my elementary school days, with only an occasional small slip.

I continued pursuing my own selected studies alone, away from school. In the public library I did self-assigned homework in addition to my regular school homework. I did the class homework nearly perfectly, then inserted a few deliberate errors, so that the teacher would not think that I was too smart.

16

The Twins: Early Years

Carol began to read at age three as I had done. She eagerly eyed my stowed-away *Golden Books*, which I had first saved for Gloria. While I was reading one early spring day, Carol tried to match words to pictures, so I began to teach her the alphabet in the same way that Grandpa had taught me.

By age three, Carol also showed early musical talent. She tinkled out nursery tunes on a toy piano after hearing them played once by Mom. Then, as her fingers grew longer, she began to play on Mom's upright piano in the living room. Soon, Carol outgrew Mom's teachings and began taking professional music lessons at home with Mr. Aaron Greenstein. He was paid three dollars by Mom for each weekly lesson. With her black curls flying, Carol bobbed her head rhythmically sideways to keep pace with Mr. Greenstein's metronome at the piano.

Tiptoeing into the living room softly, I sometimes watched Carol's absorbed practicing as her cascading chords rolled out across the keyboard. She was often not aware of my presence until the end of her session. Once, I exclaimed proudly, "Carol, you will play in a concert hall someday." She blushed. "Please don't talk like that, Bernie. You'll give me a swelled head."

Even the birds outside seemed to quiet down when Carol played the piano. After two years of lessons from Mr. Greenstein, Carol played like a born princess of the keyboard. Mom bought her a metronome as a kindergarten graduation present, and I warned Mark not to tinker with it. For once, he listened and never touched the metronome.

I also tried giving reading and writing lessons to Mark, but he quickly became bored and went off to work with his tools instead, while Carol and I read together. His literacy dawned slowly in the first grade, barely keeping pace with the other kids in his class. His early talent for manual dexterity enabled him to handle adult tools by the time he was six years old. I browsed many second-hand shops to get him real, but often rusted, handyman tools which we cleaned up and used together. Among other tasks, he fixed broken chairs, and hung shelves on the walls

At first, Mom and Dad were nervous about Mark handling sharp-edged tools, but soon they accepted his mechanical skills. Mom required that either Dad or I had to be in the same room with him during 'tool time,' however. Some of the things we built together were a dollhouse for Carol and a puppet show stage.

Carol also liked to play 'school teacher' She sat her dolls in neat rows at six-inch school desks and 'taught' classes in reading, writing, good hygiene and manners. Mark scrounged up some small cardboard boxes to cover over her dollhouse classroom.

My siblings grew and blossomed in the full sunshine of their childhood innocence during the war-torn years of the 1940s. The clouds and shadows of family tragedy that were to deepen and change the lives of the Seiden family came later on. Much later.

In elementary school. Carol became an honors student in the

second grade. She earned 'honors' awards every year afterwards into high school. Mark, on the other hand, barely scraped by in class, struggling to eke out at least a C minus grade with his sister's dogged assistance. Without Carol's patient coaching, he would not have passed some classes at all!

As an honor student, she was embarrassed by Mark's poor grades. She was always in a different class from Mark, since it was school policy then to place twins or triplets into different classes to prevent classroom competition between them.

In the five years that had passed since I went to those same classes as my siblings, Bronx school attitudes towards bright students began to change for the better. In my early elementary grades, the teachers often discouraged advanced students from venturing beyond the standard curriculum in order to maintain an average class norm. In the late 1940s, some local elementary schools finally began to encourage bright students with enriched programs and extra credit for tutoring slower students.

Carol was quietly modest about her intellectual and musical talents, and was very caring towards less-scholarly Mark. She often spent an hour or two after completing her own extensive homework to help Mark with his homework struggles.

Meanwhile, Mark developed tool skills and he intuitively repaired mechanical and electric appliances. Skinny and tall for his age, his yellowish brown hair was in a perpetually tousled state. Furrowing his brow in concentration, his stubby, but strong and often dirty fingers rescued old radios and other appliances from the garbage bin. He learned by his mistakes—smashing several old radios before getting one to work again. After repairs, he sold them for a dollar or two.

Sometimes Mark was 'too clever' for words, rigging things up as intended practical jokes which only he thought were funny. Once, I remember he rigged music to come out of the radiator instead of steam heat. He hid a small radio behind the radiator, blocked the steam valve and substituted a radio On/Off switch.

Sneaking out of the living room, lest a giggle betray him, he exited through the ground-level window of my room onto the street behind the hedges that framed the outside of my window. The window stayed open, so he could follow the reaction of our parents. It was not 'hide and go seek', it was 'peer and hear'.

As I look back today, I realize that much of the mischief that Mark made as a young boy was done out of jealousy towards Carol to win attention for himself. I remember the time when he attached a secret microphone to our living room radio, and interrupted the music show with a pseudo-news bulletin of Russian paratroopers landing in New Jersey.

Only Mom and Dad and I heard this broadcast. They seemed to believe it. I immediately suspected otherwise, It sounded to me like a muffled Mark taking a page out of the Orson Welles "War of the Worlds" play. But I said nothing for the moment and let the gag play out for a little while.

(Quote from "War of the Worlds" Radio Show, 1938)

"Ladies and gentlemen, we interrupt this program to bring you a special bulletin. A large strange-shaped fireball has landed in New Jersey. It looks like a spaceship. It's opening on the side and strange pointy guns are peeking out... BZZZT---- it's a ray gun! Rays are shooting out and zapping everyone in sight. People are running for their lives...." - Quote from the original "War of the Worlds" radio show in 1938.

Mom and Dad listened in open mouthed wonderment, not knowing whether the broadcast was real or not. Mom turned white as a sheet and started shaking. In a quavering voice, she said, "Maybe it's the Nazis coming with secret weapons." Dad just stared and frowned confusedly, not wanting to contradict Mom in front of me.

A smart kid can disguise his or her voice, but then still sound like a kid! And I knew that radio networks would not use a kid to warn the world of an alien invasion! So, I checked the radio and turned it around to look at the back cover.

There it was!—an extra wire (not the plug line or an antenna cable). I followed its snaking trail along the wall baseboard, angling up behind the curtain and out the living room window. Disconnecting it, I proclaimed, "Aha! Got you!" Raising my voice, I called out, "Mom! Dad! It's Mark, not the Martians! This is a microphone cord!"

Dangling the cord at my parents, I explained, "This is just another of Mark's pranks. Maybe he was inspired by my telling him a week earlier the old scary story of Orson Welles 'War of the Worlds' broadcast of October 30, 1938. It panicked thousands of people."

"Oh, yeah", Dad said. "Now I remember the big scare about that Orson Welles show. I didn't hear it on the radio myself, but some people I know packed up and fled north towards the Catskills." He smiled. "That's as good a place as any in which to face the end of the world. How do you know the radio date? You were only a baby when it happened?"

I replied, "Grandpa once told me about 'War of the Worlds', and I heard a rebroadcast of it a few months ago. The radio show described an imaginary invasion of our world by Martians. But it was done in real-time news bulletin style by interrupting a music show. A lot of people panicked and thought it really was an alien invasion."

Mom firmly declared, "I wasn't fooled by this Martian nonsense back then, and not today, either!" Dad added soothingly, "Yes, Rosie, we know you are too smart to believe that stuff." Then he secretly winked at me. I heard scrambling in the shrubbery outside and 'little brother' vanished from sight outside the rear window. I knew his hideout, but did not betray him. This was parent business to deal with Mark, not 'brother business'.

The next day, I saw he had trouble sitting down, so I knew he had been spanked for the Martian mischief. I could not resist teasing him a little about that. "I'll bet your behind is now as red as the planet Mars." He pouted and stalked out.

Around the time that they started to read—Mark slowly at age 6 and Carol, earlier and more advanced— their imaginations captured their play imagery and they began to act out some of the roles from Golden Books. I became their Director and helped to set the scene for them. Pirates and princesses, doctors and nurses, pilots and passengers, Little Red Riding Hood and the Big Bad Fox. *(you read that right! It was my sequel to the Big Bad Wolf adventure and portrayed Little Red Riding Hood going off in the woods again, this time ensnared by a Fox!)*

17

A Quiet Retreat to the Library

*I*n the first grade, my learning frustration continued to mount. I was bored with the elementary level of reading, writing and arithmetic being done in the class. Grandpa gave me what support he could in my studies, and allowed me to use his library card to borrow adult books supposedly for him because he could not come to the library himself. I wrote out 'his' book list in an adult handwriting style which passed scrutiny at the desk with hardly more than a glance.

As my reading intensity and comprehension level increased, I became more sensitive to the ongoing chaos in my family's apartment. It distracted me, even with my room door shut, against the constant bickering between Mom and Gloria. More and more, I turned to the High Bridge Public Library at West 168th Street and Woodycrest Avenue to find peace and quiet for my readings and studies.

The library was a squat, stone, two-story high-ceilinged structure with dark mahogany shelves and gloomy vaulted windows. Dusty chain-suspended bowl-encased light bulbs shone over long oaken tables and chairs. Verbal communication was in tones barely above whispers, and the few boisterous children were swiftly silenced by frowning librarians. The hushed tones focused my attention on the rows and shelves that delineated each section of the library. The fiction area, particularly the science fiction, led me into worlds and civilizations that I never could have imagined, and may not happen in this world for many centuries to come, if they happen at all. The interplanetary worlds of Isaac Asimov and Robert Heinlein were among the favorite literary destinations of my boyish imagination.

Only once was I ever challenged for taking adult books to the check-out desk. That was when I tried to check out a copy of *Gray's Anatomy*. The medical language was far too complicated for me, but I wanted to study the pictures of the human anatomy. The librarian very curtly told me that "my grandfather would have to come and check that one out himself!"

The other books in my stack that day were checked out without comment. I usually took out five books and read through them within thirty days—rejecting several volumes that were too disappointing or boring or too difficult to finish.

I was aware of the pending midterm and final exam dates for the upper grades in my school, since I observed that those students became more subdued in their shortened play times, were less likely to harass younger school students, and they began to 'crack' their books more often.

On a freezing wintry day in January, 1944, I answered Mom's objections that it was too cold to go out to the library by bundling up in my warmest coat, and putting on my mittens and scarf. I promised Mom to 'walk fast' the six blocks to the library. Off I went to Highbridge with reddened face and enthused heart. Inside the library doors, while thawing out, I saw a familiar neighborhood girl, Florence—my sixth grade babysitter!

Highbridge Library

There she sat in her flaxen hair and pigtails, preparing for midterms. I especially liked her because she was not as bossy as previous babysitters had been with me and my siblings. She was a buxom twelve-year-old neighborhood brunette whom Mom hired once or twice a month at fifty cents an hour, so that she and Dad could go out to a movie.

Her brow frowned in concentration as I approached her table. "Hi, Florence", I said cheerily. "What are you studying?" I answered my own question by noticing the oversize *Hammond Atlas* spread out before her. She seemed surprised by my interest in her work.

"I am studying Greenland. It's in the far North."

"I know that", I said. "It's a Danish colony."

"How did you know that? You are only a little kid!"

Smugly, I retorted, "I know a lot of things that older kids and grown-ups know. I read adult books and understand them. What would you like to know about Greenland?"

Florence asked, "When did it become part of Denmark?"

I thought about it briefly, then looked up the topic in the *Encyclopedia Britannica* on the reference shelf. Next only to my grandpa, the *Britannica* was to me the wisest source of information in the world. I explained to her that Greenland had been ruled by Norway in the Middle Ages. Napoleon's defeat in 1814 freed Norway from French rule, and brought western Greenland under Danish rule. Norway occupied part of eastern Greenland and the two nations agreed to bring their territorial dispute to the International Court at the Hague. In 1933, the Court recognized Denmark's sovereignty over Greenland, settling a decades-long dispute with Norway.

Florence's eyes opened wide as I told her about how the International Court settled arguments between nations that were submitted to them by the disputing countries, and that they also advised the United Nations. I told her that even though the Court had no enforcement powers, its influence was often felt in the world of diplomacy.

I always took the precaution of checking out one or two *Golden Books* from the Library for myself besides the stack of books supposedly for Grandpa. That way, if I sat in the library to read or study, the illustrated children's books provided a cover for my real adult-level reading. (I could always say to a curious adult that I was "just looking at the pictures" in the adult books. Fortunately, nobody noticed that my adult books often did not have pictures!

Florence smiled and said to me, "I'd like to make a deal with you."

"Yeah, I'm listening."

"When I come to baby-sit, I will let you stay up later if you help me with my homework."

"Okay, you've got a deal."

We finished our studies at one of the big library tables, and I checked out my borrowed books and went home.

18

Bernie's Dad Tries to Buy a Taxicab

*B*ernie began his school years in the midst of the Second World War. The '30s had passed into history and the big Depression of 1929 and its lesser sibling, the Second Depression of 1937, had come and gone. In the Forties, wartime jobs lifted the economy from its 1933 lows. However, unemployment remained high and racial segregation limited job opportunities for black people. Some fortunate non-white laborers migrated to the factories of Detroit and other Northern cities to work there.

However, *John Strasburgh*, a city historian, estimated in his book, *Victory City*, that only 142 black workers out of approximately 29,000 workers held defense jobs in New York City in this time period. This may have been a contributing factor to the Harlem Riots of 1943. As the nation entered a war-time boom, idled factories reopened and began second and third shifts for the war effort.

Shortly after Pearl Harbor, GM and Ford swiftly converted their assembly lines from autos to armaments. Henry Ford, who had been sympathetic to Nazi Germany, did an about-face in attitude towards the Axis and now acted as a patriotic American. He converted his Lincoln Continental assembly line to tank production within a record-breaking six weeks!

American women joined the workforce in factories and offices—eighteen million of them in all, inspiring the iconic muscular 'Rosie the Riveter' posters that are still admired today. They took off their aprons, donned coveralls and replaced young men who were drafted into military service. Grandpa and many other family men felt or hoped that working women would quietly give up their paychecks and return to the kitchen and child care after the war.

Ration coupon books, with their paired official double eagle seals framing the imprint of the United States Food Administration, became a feature of daily life at local retail stores. Many consumer goods prices were frozen by the US Office of Price Administration (OPA).

In the early war years, Bernie's parents did not own a car because gas rations for private citizens were limited to four gallons a week. Running 8 to 10 miles per gallon in the car engines of those times, four gallons would not get you very far. Natural rubber for tires was also scarce. The Japanese had cut off most of America's regular tire supply previously shipped from occupied Indonesia.

But taxicabs were granted gas permits and Bernie's dad, as a cab driver, could sometimes sneak in a quick little local trip for the family in his cab. He often drove military officers and government personnel from LaGuardia Airport into Manhattan and the other boroughs.

Dad's New York City taxicab

Tips were good from those who were traveling on government expense accounts. Officers took taxi rides for five dollars plus change, and often would tip Dad with keeping the change from a ten dollar bill. It was government money for travel expenses, not out of their own pockets. So they could afford to be generous. For the first time in his life, during the War years, Dad was able to save some money for the future.

"Rosie, I want to buy a taxi medallion," announced Dad one Sunday in the early summer of 1943. Dad proposed to move up in the world from taxi driver to taxi owner. Any assertion from him to Mom on financial matters was unusual because he usually just followed along meekly with Mom's plans, whenever and whatever she made them.

For ten years, Dad had patiently plodded away behind the wheel, driving ten or twelve-hour shifts and earning about fifty or sixty dollars for a six-day week behind the wheel. That was a typical lower middle-class income for the 1940s. Semi-skilled male laborers made only a little more than that for a five-day forty hour week.

Every day, Mom counted out Dad's cash earnings on the kitchen table. Dad had to empty his pockets for her when he came home after work. But he hid a quarter each for Bernie and Gloria in his socks. Who says that young children cannot keep a secret! That one was kept. And Mom never found out!

An Irish friend of Dad's, Jack Sullivan, owned a taxi medallion and was ready to retire. Since 1937, New York City had frozen the number of taxi medallions at 11,787. The price began to rise afterwards, since the only way to get a new medallion was to buy one from an existing owner. Some medallions were reserved for individual owner-drivers—nearly one-third of the total, and two-thirds went into taxicab fleets for leasing to drivers.

Bernie had been shooed into his room at bedtime, after Gloria was tucked in and asleep. Mom and Dad began to discuss the taxicab situation in the kitchen in low voices. But Bernie listened through the door, as usual. It was a sultry late June evening and he could not sleep anyway. His parents argued late into the night about the taxicab.

"Jack wants to sell me his medallion for two thousand dollars. That's a good price. I know some guys are getting twenty five hundred for their medallions plus selling the cab itself. He wants to give me a break on this deal. Twenty years of driving on the streets of New York are enough for him. He's going home to Ireland after he sells the cab."

Mom sneered. "How much does he want for that old wreck?"

"An extra thousand dollars."

"Oy vey! Then there is the cost of fixing it or buying another cab. And the expenses ..." She sighed, "Dovid, you know you have no head for business."

"Rosie, Jack told me he pays a bookkeeper $20 a week who tracks the income and expenses for him." In a raised voice, Mom exclaimed, "Twenty dollars ... TWENTY DOLLARS!!?? What about gas and oil? That's more money on top of that!"

"Rosie ... please listen to me for once," Dad pleaded. "Even with all that you say, I would still be making over a hundred dollars a week, twice what I am making now. And I could lease out the cab to a night driver and make even more."

Sarcastically, Mom responded:

"Yeah ... and get a phone call at two in the morning that your cab is parked halfway up a tree in Harlem."

"Rosie! Rosie! I know who the good drivers are in my garage. I will not hire any single guys, drinkers, gamblers, or ticket-getters. I will pay them a higher commission then they are making now."

Mom was adamant. "No, no. I won't let you buy a cab! You are a working man, not a boss or a business owner." The argument went on for awhile, as Bernie continued to listen, ear to the door, straining to catch every word. But, as usual, Dad eventually gave in. In the following days, Bernie watched him for signs of disappointment, but Dad had placidly accepted his fate. No medallion. No taxicab business. Only continuing to work for Mr. Ackerman, taxicab fleet owner, stock market investor and entrepreneur.

Near the end of the war years, Bernie sometimes joined his Dad, riding around in the cab for a few after-school hours. He began reading New York City guide books and soon became familiar with the major tourist attractions of Manhattan and the Bronx. Sometimes Dad picked up famous passengers, but it never happened while Bernie was riding with him.

Once, Dad picked up Bob Hope at LaGuardia Airport, going to Columbia Presbyterian Hospital on 168th Street and Broadway in upper Manhattan. Dad said the ride was very quiet, and Mr. Hope wore dark glasses and did not crack any jokes. Obviously, he was trying to avoid being recognized. The next day, the *Daily News* revealed that Bob Hope had checked into the hospital for treatment of an eye condition. At first, Bernie was peeved that Dad did not seek an autograph from this famous Hollywood star, but Dad patiently explained his belief that it would have been rude to ask for an autograph.

19

The Family Gathers at Grandpa's

*I*n the 1940s, my extended family often converged at Grandpa's home on Friday nights for Shabbat dinner. Grandma stayed mostly in the kitchen, a background figure toiling away, preparing meals for the family gathering. At the table, Grandpa regained some of the past aura of dignity from his pre-Depression years as a successful businessman and Ford executive.

Little of Grandpa's former luxury from the Roaring Twenties remained in his Crotona Park apartment when I visited there. The Dresden china and Waterford crystal for our Shabbat dinner, Grandpa's gold watch, cufflinks and some of Grandma's jewelry remained. The 1929 Crash took away the upper Manhattan townhouse and the four servants of the Ralutzky family.

Grandpa, in the early years of the twentieth century, had built up a successful business of importing high-quality aromatic Egyptian tobacco for smokers willing to pay the premium price. Then, around 1908, Grandpa sold his small firm to the giant

American Tobacco Company (ATC) for stock and cash, and stayed on with ATC as a manager.

In those days, tobacco was a respectable business, and one measure of a man's success in life was the quality and cost of the leaf that he smoked. Gold cigarette cases, and hand-carved meerschaum pipes were status signals of the wealthy and those who wished to appear wealthy. About once a week, Grandpa smoked a plain store-bought meerschaum, not hand-carved. He smoked one pipe while reading the morning paper, and another after dinnertime. But not on Holy Days or the Sabbath. I remember a conversation we had on June 6, 1944 about D-Day when the aroma of his afternoon smoking was still lingering in the air. Grandpa never smoked during my visit, after school.

"Good afternoon, Grandpa," I cheerily greeted him at the door. Over his shoulder, I saw the dark meerschaum in his pewter bowl, still wafting curlicue smoke wisps into the living room air.

"Allies Land in Normandy" screamed the New York Times headlines on his coffee table. Grandpa had been absorbed in the story of the Allied invasion of Europe, and forgot that I was coming over. "There's big news today, Bernie," he said somberly. "General Eisenhower is leading an invasion of France by American, British, Canadian and French forces. They came ashore in three waves in Normandy, and the fighting is heavy." He paused briefly. "Let us pray for their success."

"I know the older classes in my school can discuss the war news, but nothing is said to the first grade about the War," I complained.

Grandpa sighed. "Bernie, when will you understand? Your school believes that war news is too adult for children your age."

"Then why don't they have a special class for kids like me that want to know what's going on in the world?", I asked. "Perhaps someday they will, Meantime you can always come over and discuss these matters with me." He smiled benignly.

I was starved for adult-level conversation. Mom and Dad had never gone to high-school, and could not comprehend much of what I already knew about the world and its events. My teachers were mainly concerned with keeping order and did not encourage me or other bright kids intellectually.

The other relatives on my mother's side of the family were often fighting with each other and with Mom, and so I could rarely get to visit them. Petty disputes all about who said what to whom and when in the family often lingered on for years to create ill will among them long after the original dispute was forgotten. Sometimes it was yesterday's insults and snubs, sometimes it was from before my generation was born, but we were not supposed to ask questions about family quarrels. Or worse, my siblings and I could not even try to 'make up' with anyone else in the family with whom our parents were at odds.

Far away in northern France, it was a cold, post-stormy June day in Normandy. The invasion had already been delayed twice, and Eisenhower gave the go-ahead signal at dawn on June 6th. Feeling the importance of D-Day, I hugged Grandpa, my small arms clutching around his waist. At age six, I still needed a little-child's closeness with him, even when we were discussing adult-level topics.

Grandpa was somewhat stiff and formal in his everyday life, but he privately unbent with me. He chatted away with Gloria on a nursery school level, but with no 'baby talk'.

Gloria was different from me in disposition. She was a freckle-faced little redhead in pigtails with a fiery and stubborn temperament. Bright and sharp, Gloria was direct and responsive to learning. She loved Grandpa, and looked up to him, literally, with her pug-nose tilting up towards his whitish gray mustache.

Mom cooked nourishing meals, keeping Dad and her children well-fed on a limited budget. She knew many ways to make leftovers, without their tasting the same way twice. Her cooking often used combinations of noodles, vegetables, chicken or meat with lots of gravy. I helped wash and dry the dishes in an old-fashioned chipped porcelain two-part kitchen sink and tub. When she got a little older, Gloria shared kitchen clean-up chores with me. I washed and she dried after the meal. Our kitchen was small and we had to do a little 'do-si-do' dish-washing dance to avoid crashing into each other.

As the oldest child, I had my own room. Gloria slept in the living room. The next year after Mom gave birth to the twins in 1943, Gloria had to share her partitioned living room/bedroom with the babies.

The musical talent in my family was concentrated in Mom, who played popular music by ear on the upright piano in the living room; and Carol, who was gifted and progressed rapidly with private music lessons at home. Mom had only taken a year of lessons, but she had a natural feel for piano chords and sang to accompany herself, and played the mandolin.

Uncle Rudy, Mom's brother, was a professional musician, playing the accordion and piano. He had accompanied silent movies and vaudeville houses in the 1910s and '20s—never in the big time, only playing on local circuit theaters. He also performed at burlesque houses and saloons where the atmosphere was unsavory, but the tips were good. He never admitted any of these non-movie employments to the family, but my cousins told me about it.

After retiring, Uncle Rudy sold and repaired pianos at his Bronx home workshop. He was aloof, graying and wore thin spectacles perched on his sharp nose. Rudy did not really ever relate to me as an uncle. The few times I saw him in later years were uncomfortable encounters for both of us. Rudy and Mom were 'on the outs' for many years because he once sold her a 'bargain ' piano for $200 with a hidden crack in the baseboard. Mom complained bitterly, believing that Rudy had done this deliberately to take advantage of her. Forty years later, he was still snubbing us.

Uncle Rudy refused to fix the piano, and Mom did not want to sue him. But then why was he angry at me? I could not understand this, and tried years later as an adult to develop a relationship with him, to no avail. He wanted nothing to do with the family, condemning all for my mother's accusing him of cheating her on the piano purchase.

Another uncle sometimes present in my life was Eddie. He lived far from the Bronx in central Brooklyn, and came to visit us occasionally. His wife, Aunt Mae, was a big whiny-voiced complainer who did not get along well with Mom. Maybe because Mae's woes were a one-way sounding board—she did not have any patience to hear Mom's problems. But everyone got along well with Uncle Eddie.

He was a small narrow-faced man in his mid-fifties, kindly but sickly and aging before his time. A regular 'Mr. Fixit', he owned a hardware store on Flatbush Avenue in Brooklyn.

But my interests were elsewhere. I had stars in my eyes. Literally. Not the Hollywood kind. Real stars, the astronomical kind. My stargazing started at my sixth birthday party, hosted by Grandpa at his apartment. Grandpa had a special surprise present for me which needed a 'preview', he said, with a knowing wink in my direction.

Grandpa brought a long thin box out of his closet, which I excitedly unwrapped. It was a pair of stargazing wide-field binoculars. Wow!

The previous week, at the library, I had chanced upon a

copy of Camille Flammarion's nineteenth century work, *Astronomy for Amateurs,* which was not on Grandpa's list for me. I requested it anyway and received it from the librarian without question. The language was a little archaic, but Grandpa and his dictionary helped me out with the stylized poetic words of the old book.

I sat entranced at the imagery, squinting at the yellowing pages. *"O night, diapered with fires innumerable! Hast thou not written in flaming letters on these Constellations the syllables of the great enigma of Eternity?"*

"Grandpa, how can night be diapered?" I asked quizzically. "Night is not a baby!" Pausing, I added, "Constellations have twinkling stars, not flaming letters!" "Bernie, you are not a baby, so I will give you an adult answer. This language is called poetic imagery. You know what poetry is. This is fancier poetry than I think you have seen so far. It is the way that poets used to write when I was a little boy."

I laughed. "It is so fancy that few can understand it, I think."

"Yes, but it is beautiful. A modern poet might say 'blanketed' instead of 'diapered'. But it means covered, in either wording."

Grandpa then discussed stars and planets, explaining that twinkling was an atmospheric effect, and that in the vacuum of space, stars and planets do not twinkle. The sun was setting and I had to get home, but my newfound interest in astronomy had been kindled by the flaming words of Monsieur Camille Flammarion (1842-1925), the mystic poet and late President of the *Societé Astronomiqué de France* After that night, I asked Dad to take me to the Hayden Planetarium in Manhattan. I knew he would be much happier taking me to Yankee Stadium instead, but I persisted.

"Dad," I said, "I want to learn more about the stars and planets."

"Bernie, I can't help you with that. Why don't you go with Grandpa?"

"Because I asked him already, and he cannot walk around that much."

Dad was embarrassed that his lack of education prevented him from mentoring me on science subjects. His formal education ended in the eighth grade. I had been 'educating' him on our street walks since the 1944 election, when an ailing Roosevelt won his fourth term over Tom Dewey.

America did not elect Presidents with mustaches after the tenure of William Howard Taft (1909-13) in the White House. A few years later, Taft and Teddy Roosevelt had a falling out over issues, but their mustaches were not a topic between them.

Dad and I typically discussed sports, current events and politics in our dog-walking sessions along Macombs Road towards University Avenue. On the left side was Nelson Avenue and the hilltop block of Macombs Road with Dorn's Drugstore, the Hobby Shop and the Esso gas station at the intersection with University Avenue.

On the right, we passed PS 82, in its five-story square red brick building. Its chain-link yard fence abutted the south brick wall of the Park Plaza Theater building with a six-inch gap, which made an ideal drop-in hoop for basketball played with a tennis ball. No round 'hoop', just a 12-foot high gapped backboard. No slam-dunks, high-leaping shots, or out-of-bounds fall forwards were possible here even for the tallest kids. One either ducked or crashed into the wooden lower fence. I was a tall kid, but height was no advantage in this kind of pickup game.

On impulse, Dad and I sometimes stopped off to do a few set-shots using the spaldeen in my jacket pocket. He was one of the few Dads in the neighborhood who played ball with his son, and I loved him even more for doing it.

"Litte Fat Comedian" Lou Costello, Five-foot-five basketball player. Free throw champion of New

Lou Costello, Comedian, Actor (the way people remember him)

Dad was pudgy and short, just like comedian Lou Costello who was a basketball foul thrower champion in New Jersey in his younger days. That was before basketball rules changed to favor tall players. Clownish Costello had also boxed professionally under the name of 'Lou King' before teaming up with Bud Abbott as a comedy duo. Dad beat me in basketball that day, ten points to three. I won these one-on-one games with Dad sometimes, but in later years, he denied ever throwing a game to me.

Like Lou Costello, Dad was a jokester. As we talked and walked, Dad commented that FDR's opponent Tom Dewey had a little 'groom-on-top-of-the-wedding cake' look about him with his slick little mustache.

I played the Bud Abbott part to Dad as a straight man and seriously lectured him on Roosevelt's plans for the postwar recovery, while he made Lou Costello jokes. Then he grew serious and listened as I updated him on political affairs and other current events.

The balmy days of spring and early summer in 1944 flowed by in a leisurely way. Six floors above the sidewalk, when the skies were clear, I mounted our apartment house stairs to the asphalt roof, armed with binoculars, star atlas and red-lensed flashlight to adjust my eyes to the dark. I busied myself in observing the craters of the moon and star clusters of the Milky Way and Andromeda galaxies. It was to be another year before I was permitted to travel downtown by myself into Manhattan to the Planetarium. My elementary school term ended in late June, and summer playtime childhood joys descended upon the neighborhood.

I felt good then to be a young boy, cherishing my little sister Gloria and nurturing the twins, Carol and Mark, on their early years in this world. That good feeling was soon to end in tragedy that summer as Grandpa's health continued to decline.

Then, the unthinkable happened. . .

20

Grandpa Goes To Heaven

Suddenly, in September 1944, the unthinkable happened. Grandpa acquired a dog! Her name was Beauty, and she was a retired circus dog—a Spitz-Pomeranian mix, and well-behaved. When I went to see him one late afternoon in October 1944, there was Beauty in his lap. In surprise, I exclaimed: "Grandpa . . . YOU with a dog? Why? How did this happen?" Grandpa explained, "Bernie, I am an old man living alone now, and this dog was given to me to settle a business debt from a circus owner who brought her here from Europe to perform. She responds to commands in five languages—English, Russian, Yiddish, Polish or German. But she is old now and no one else will adopt her."

"So, if I cannot shelter Beauty as a pet, I can still shelter her as a war veteran. She will earn her 'keep' here." Beauty chimed in with a bark and a wagging tail, as if to agree.

'Beauty' was the first dog in my life or in Grandpa's life. Dad and I agreed to take Beauty home with us each weekend to give Grandpa a rest. A few weeks later, one afternoon after school, I knocked on Grandpa's door and Beauty opened the door by turning the knob. Grandpa had put a special rubber cover over the brass doorknob so Beauty could grip it in her mouth. The pitter-patter of starting raindrops told us that this day would be a 'rain walk'.

Grandpa ordered "fetch umbrella" and Beauty brought it to him in her mouth from the umbrella stand in the foyer. She was learning new tricks! "Good doggie," said Grandpa "Take a bow for Bernie." Beauty stretched out and dipped her head.

I imagined Beauty, as Grandpa told me in his stories, as she must have been when performing before the Nazi invasions caused traveling circuses with the gypsy folk to flee for their lives.

With a little peaked clown hat tied around her doggy chin, taking that same stretch-pawed bow I now saw here. I pictured Beauty, bowing before the applause of hundreds in a circus tent somewhere in rural Russia. Grandpa joked that the gypsy circus had a dog act because they could not afford to feed a bear.

This perky-eared shaggy little dog quickly snuggled its way into our family's hearts. During the week, Grandpa sent Beauty to the store every morning to get his daily newspaper. Beauty watched her street crossings carefully on the way, and had a little neck pouch into which Grandpa inserted a nickel and, by pre-arrangement with the store, Beauty would receive two cents change.

Each morning, rain or shine, Beauty trotted off to the store. Putting her paws up on the counter, Beauty barked for attention. The clerk would then place the wrapped newspaper into her mouth, take the nickel and put the change into the pouch. Beauty trotted home to Grandpa with paper and change intact.

One spring day, Beauty did her usual errand, but there was a different result. A new clerk in the store knew a dog would come in to pick up the Daily News, but he had not been briefed about the change due. He gave Beauty the newspaper, but pocketed the two cents!

Beauty made a big fuss, barking and carrying on. The manager came out and the embarrassed clerk put the two pennies back into the neck pouch. Grandpa told me about it later, and we had a good laugh together over Beauty's canine arithmetic. I used to wonder what would happen if the clerk had put one penny in, or three pennies, or gave the wrong newspaper to Beauty? I never found out!

Mom stopped by Grandpa's apartment twice a week, Tuesdays and Fridays, to clean and cook for him. She made several meals in advance, so all he had to do was heat them up, which he managed after Mom taught him some 'stove basics'. Grandpa never quite learned to cook, although under Mom's urging, he tried.

"Beauty the First" Grandpa's Circus Dog (with her coin pouch and tag)

Grandpa was an old-fashioned husband and father who never cooked a meal or did any housework. Now that Grandma had passed on, Mom told him it was not unmanly to make a meal for himself, but old habits died hard. He was used to being served by women in his house. Sometimes, one of my aunts came over to help Grandpa, but they all lived further away than my parents, and could not get there regularly.

On the first Tuesday in August, 1945, Mom went to Grandpa's and knocked on the door of his apartment, as usual. There was no response. Mom called the building superintendent to open the door and they found him crumpled up in the bathroom.

The police came, ambulance wailing behind them, but it was too late. The medic said that Grandpa had probably died of a heart attack the previous day. It was more than two hours later that Mom came home in a cab with Beauty. She was crying as she came in. Dad held her around the shoulders, in a rare moment of her acceptance of his comforting efforts. Beauty trotted along quietly next to Dad, her tail drooping low. Most often, Mom pushed Dad away when he tried to hug her. But not today. She sighed and gathered her voice, as I went into the foyer to greet them.

"Bernie," she said, still choking a little. "Grandpa is dead." My heart sank. I began to cry too, and hugged Beauty. Even Dad cried a little—he was very fond of his father-in-law. My own world, the world of the Bronx, spun around my ears.

I thought, *Grandpa dead? Who can I talk to now? Who will explain and discuss things, and not talk to me like a little kid?* I felt lost. I reached out to Dad and we hugged. And hugged and hugged.

Then Dad went in to see Gloria, putting on his rarely seen 'serious face'. Gloria, precociously perceptive of adult moods and emotions, knew instantly it was some 'big stuff' going on when Daddy called her by name instead of "sweetie pie".

"Gloria, I have something to tell you."

"What is it, Daddy? Is it why Mommy was crying when you both came home in the cab with Beauty and she was pretending not to cry?"

"Well, yes, it's about Grandpa. He has died and gone to Heaven."

She looked up at him quizzically. "Is that further away than Brooklyn?

"Yes, much further away," he sighed.

"Will he come back and bring me presents?"

Dad stroked her hair and struggled for words. "No, God gives us life when we come down from Heaven as babies, and takes us home to Heaven when our life is done. Some die early, some die late and live to be old, but sooner or later, we all die when our bodies stop working."

He paused. "Your present from Grandpa is love for you, which you will always have and remember." I listened and smiled from behind the door. Dad handled it well, I thought. Now Beauty will come and live with us.

The next day, the mid-day heat wave had broken. White clouds scudded along the pale blue sky, pushed by a mild northern breeze as Grandpa was laid to rest in Montefiore Cemetery, near my uncles and aunts who died before him. The temperature had dropped into the low seventies. I stood and recited the Kaddish prayer. Grandpa would have been proud of me.

The men gathered upfront at the gravesite, and the women kept to the rear. All were Jewish except for one man. Someone gave him a yarmulke. He stood and bowed his head in uncomfortable silence.

I sneaked forward from the gathered women, where my cousins, all older than me, stayed with their mothers. I quietly tried to join the men. There was muttering from some of the orthodox mourners who were not from the family. But my uncles and my father said "Yes, let him recite the Kaddish!" All looked at the Rabbi, who stroked his beard and declared: "Sha!" shaking his finger at the men.

Fortunately for me, the Rabbi was Conservative, not Orthodox. Sternly, he declared, "If the boy wants to read the Kaddish, let him say it!" A few mourners joined in the 'Amen'. The others did not interfere or object.

The Mourner's Kaddish began in Aramaic, which was the everyday language of ancient Israel—the language that Jesus of Nazareth spoke. Not a lamentation, this prayer is an acceptance of Divine Judgment and Righteousness. The Kaddish praises God, and yearns for establishment of His kingdom on earth, but does not mention Death.

"Yit'gadal v'yit'kadash sh'mei raba. Amen. b'al'ma di v'ra khir'utei. Amen

v'yam'likh mal'khutei b'chayeikhon uv'yomeikhon uv'chayei d'khol beit yis'ra'eil ba'agala uviz'man kariv v'im'ru. Amen. Y'hei sh'mei raba m'varakh l'alam ul'al'mei al'maya Yit'barakh v'yish'tabach v'yit'pa'ar v'yit'romam v'yit'nasei v'yit'hadar v'yit'aleh v'yit'halal sh'mei d'kud'sha B'rikh hu. L'eila min kol bir'khata v'shirata toosh'b'chatah v'nechematah, da'ameeran b'al'mah, v'eemru. Amen. Y'hei sh'lama raba min sh'maya v'chayim aleinu v'al kol yis'ra'eil v'im'ru. Amen Oseh shalom bim'romav hu ya'aseh shalom aleinu v'al kol Yis'ra'eil v'im'ru. Amen. *

* ENGLISH TRANSLATION: Let the glory of G-d be extolled, let His great name be hallowed, in the world whose creation He willed. May His kingdom soon prevail, in our own day, our own lives, and the life of all Israel, and let us say: Amen. Let His great name be blessed forever and ever. Let the name of the Holy One, blessed is He, be glorified, exalted and honored, though He is beyond all the praises, songs, and adorations that we can utter, and let us say: Amen.

For us and for all Israel, may the blessing of peace and the promise of life come true, and let us say, Amen. May He who causes peace to reign in the high heavens, let peace descend on us, on all Israel, and all the world, and let us say, Amen

---

When the week of mourning observance passed after Grandpa's funeral, I enrolled to summer day camp at the Washington Heights Y. This was the old 'Y' Jewish day camp on Fort Washington Avenue, in Washington Heights overlooking the Manhattan approach to the George Washington Bridge. Years later, it was torn down and replaced by a Port Authority bus terminal. All the camp kids had signed a condolence card for me. I was very touched by this.

Still mourning for Grandpa, I threw myself into the day camp scene to subdue the hurt in my heart. I reconciled myself to the fact that Grandpa had gone to Heaven, and I had to carry on my life without him.

Much to my bereaved surprise, I made two new camp friends that year. There was Marvin and there was George. Both were about a year older than me. Both had sisters. Both hated girls! That was no coincidence. I did not hate girls—I just could not figure them out. That is a major problem for many young boys. It was an even bigger problem if they did not have sisters to relate to. The three of us hung out together that summer, but Marvin and George lived far off in Westchester, so I never saw them again after camp ended that year.

The youthful sports and camp experiences partly filled the empty void in my heart that first summer without Grandpa, and summers for years afterwards. I missed Grandpa so much! *Without an adult intellect with whom to discuss world problems with, I felt resentment towards God for taking Grandpa away from me.* I lost interest in after-school Hebrew classes, only keeping open a little spark of personal interest in History.

For the next few years, until age twelve, I was spiritually adrift, gradually forgetting my Hebrew lessons and becoming estranged from religion, except for its history. But after my years of pre-teen and teenage rebellion, I rediscovered my Jewish faith as a young adult.

21

The Great Blizzard of 1947

On Christmas Day, Thursday, December 25, 1947, the New York City weather was relatively mild, with a high of 33 degrees during the day and a low of 22 degrees in the evening hours. There was a trace of snowfall (1/25th of an inch) and the winds were calm. The US Weather Bureau forecast was for "New York City and vicinity, cloudy with occasional snow ending during the afternoon."

The next day, a major snowstorm hit the east coast by surprise. The forecast called only for 'occasional flurries.' Huge snowflakes fell thickly and quietly, without any wind, blanketing New York City streets and highways from  curb to curb. The snowfall started at around 3:30 a.m. Friday morning, Dec. 26th. It continued steadily all day into the evening, at over three inches an hour, a total accumulation of more than twenty six inches—an all-time record.

There had been only a dozen white Christmases recorded in the Bronx since local weather record-keeping began in 1869. Weather patterns in the northeastern United States tend to follow prevailing winds and flow from west to east, clocked and broadcast by weather stations along the ground path across the nation. This unusual counter-clockwise post-Christmas storm swept in without warning from the Atlantic Ocean, where no permanent weather reporting stations existed in 1947.

The 1947 blizzard moved through New York and New Jersey towards Pennsylvania and Ohio, diminishing to a light dusting by the time it reached the Midwest. It was the heaviest snowfall in New York City since the Blizzard of 1888.

New York City traffic ground to a halt by mid-morning, with cars, trucks and buses stranded in the middle of the streets. Elevated trains stopped running for several hours, then resumed on a limited schedule as tracks were cleared. Parked vehicles were buried beneath ten-foot snow drifts. Pedestrians were unable to reach the streets.

New York City schools were shut for the Christmas holiday week, and many local businesses also remained closed for the week. Some intrepid adults ventured outdoors on skis or snowshoes. In my neighborhood, snowball throwing began informally on the second day, then escalated into a snowball 'war' of 175th Streeter kids versus Macombs Roaders, with about a dozen boys on each side. It was agreed that the captain for each team would be the stickball team captain from the past summer's street rivalry. A few girls tried to join in the snowball war, but were quickly shooed away by the captains. Smaller boys were also sidelined. It was also agreed that older, teenage boys would give either side an unfair advantage, so they were also banned.

The team captains conferred to set ground rules and prepare for the forthcoming snowball combat. Physical fighting or pushing was not allowed, nor any weapons other than snowballs.

The two rival sides, Macombs Roaders and the 175th Streeters, had played some close, hotly-contested stickball games that past summer and autumn, and the continuation of their rivalry in a snowball war was a natural consequence of their ongoing competition.

New York rarely had twenty-plus inch snowfalls. These blizzards became a great opportunity for local snow battle fun. Hardly any vehicles were moving anyway, so there was no objection to blocking off 175th Street at each end of the block with empty garbage cans retrieved from neighborhood basements. One boy was stationed at each end of the block as lookout to warn of oncoming traffic. Bernie was one of them. Parked cars became additional barriers. Both sides were careful not to disturb the cars to avoid angry backlash from vehicle owners.

Each side built a traffic-facing fort on the sidewalk in the middle of the block. Cardboard boxes filled with snow formed the walls. Small flags made from colored socks were placed in each fort to be defended. If a sock flag was captured, the war would be over and the captors declared victory according to the team captains' rules. Macombers had a blue tag pinned to their hats and the Streeters had yellow tags. These tags were scrounged from left-over Christmas decorations.

The snow 'soldiers' wore winter hats. Capturing an opponent's hat meant that soldier was 'dead', retired to the spectator sidelines and out of the snowball war. All preparations for the war were completed within two hours, the forts were built and both teams retreated to their own side of the street. Macombs Roaders positioned themselves on the left side and 175th Streeters on the right. One of the older teenage boys, John Liguori, who was not a combatant, agreed to act as referee, and both sides chipped in a dollar each to pay for his efforts.

He was deemed especially qualified by the neighborhood boys because he had a loud voice and owned a whistle that he used to call his dog. Also, John lived on nearby Nelson Avenue, and therefore was presumably neutral between Macombs Roaders and 175th Streeters.

The boys clustered into a football-style huddle at each fort, then three boys were dispatched as guards to the right and left sides of the forts to protect the flanks. The piercing referee whistle sounded and the battle was on. Each boy prepared up to six snowballs at a time, then reloaded their stash.

Several Macombs Roaders charged forth in a wave of concentrated firing on the left flank. They were driven back by a wave of 175th Street snowballers returning their fire.

One Macombs Roader lost his hat in the scramble and two 175th Streeters moved out under heavy covering volleys to retrieve it and claim a defeated 'soldier.' A 175th Street counter-attack, with six 'Streeter' boys snowballing the other side, crossed the street and pounded the enemy fort on the left side at point-blank range. Three more Streeters left their fort and attacked from the right side. Three Macombs hats were taken and their team asked for a truce.

Sensing an imminent defeat, the Macombers surrendered in good spirits and the snowball war was over. It had lasted about an hour, with no casualties other than a little facial bruising. The hats were all returned, the street was unblocked with garbage cans removed, and everyone shook hands and went into a nearby luncheonette for some hot chocolate and donuts. It was the only store still open in the entire neighborhood. The snow remained on the ground for the rest of the week. There were some individual snowball fights, but no more snowball wars were fought in the neighborhood that winter.

Bernie built a three-foot high snowman for Gloria, decorated with a rolled cardboard top hat and large buttons. His little sister proudly told her playmates that she had the best big brother in the whole world.

Bernie had another ongoing Bronx snow adventure during the post-Christmas Blizzard of 1947. About a mile north of Macombs Road, facing University Avenue, was the 'Hall of Fame' campus of New York University, which later became the home of the Bronx Community College in 1959.

Behind the sweeping facade of the famous curved colonnade of bronze busts, there is a small, but steep hill that slopes down to Sedgwick Avenue. It ended in a ten-foot long flat plate at the bottom, rimmed by a cast iron fence about eight feet high.

There was no need to look around for a way to sneak in—Bernie had a college connection there! Four neighborhood boys persuaded their Dads to drive us to the campus entrance with our sleds. One of the Dads was a professor at the college and had a campus ID with which to enter the Hall of Fame gate with his son and a few young guests. A 'flash of green' may have also expedited our campus arrival, but the boys were still innocent of ways of friendly bribery in he adult world. The lone security guard at the gate was lax since it was Christmas break for the college, and the campus was nearly empty except for the sledders. Both Macombs Road and University Avenue had been plowed and were barely passable to entering cars. The college had cleared its own campus roads, and the sledders were able to drive up the crest of the Sedgwick hill in back of the Hall of Fame.

The snow glistened whitely, unpolluted by city street trash. It was piled over four feet high in some spots, and had hardened to the point of being a walkable but crunchy surface. The boys' booted footsteps sank about two inches down, but no one slipped or fell. The hill definitely looked sledable. So we unhitched our four 48-inch American Flyers from the open car trunk tie-downs and lined them up at the edge of the hilltop. The dads separated the sleds by twenty paces to lessen the chances of crashing into each other. They each chipped in one dollar to create a five dollar prize for the winner—the first one to reach the bottom and not crash into the fence.

There were no checkered race flags or cheering crowds there, but the boys felt the thrill of the race as if it were the Winter Olympics. One of the dads called out, "Man your sleds!" And 'man' them we did…

"Ready, set, GO!" The boys pushed off from a prone sledding position, and Bernie took a slight early lead from the starting momentum of his size ten feet—big for a boy his age. He began braking about three quarters of the way down by dragging his left foot off the rear of the sled. In less than a minute, he was at the bottom, finishing in second place after pivoting safely to the left and dragging his foot deeper into the snow to make a safe stop about three feet short of the fence. The first-place sledder came in about two lengths ahead of Bernie but skidded sideways on his turn and bumped lightly into the fence as he rolled off his sled to avoid a head-on crash. Luckily, he was only scraped slightly. That disqualified his 'first-place' finish and Bernie was declared the winner.

Generously, Bernie declared that his prize would be invested in treating everyone, dads and kids, to hot chocolate and donuts. After another hour of sledding along less-perilous gentle slopes, we returned to the cars and went off to University Avenue for our treat. There was about a dollar left over, so there was an ice cream bonus for us all.

Within a week, the snow began to melt, buses and trolleys resumed their routes, and automobile traffic returned to local streets. Snow sledding and games returned to the streets, dodging traffic and cops, with only an infrequent trip to enjoy the untouched snows of Van Cortland Park as a special event.

22

Dad in Danger

Never does a boy forget the day he becomes a man! For Jewish boys, it is traditionally set on the day of Bar Mitzvah at age thirteen. For others, it is the day they go off to college and live away from home, or the day of marriage or enlistment in the military. For me, it was the day I rescued my Dad from great danger. At age ten. That was the day I became a man.

It all started in the basement garbage room of my apartment house. To get the national magazines I needed to keep up with what was happening in the world, I made a deal with Mr. Flanagan, our building superintendent. He gruffly allowed me to rummage among discarded magazines for back issues. *Life Magazine*, *Popular Science* and *Popular Mechanics* were my particular favorites.

I was very careful to restore magazines to the papers pile, and retie the bundles when I was finished collecting what I wanted. In early 1947, all this changed when Jack Flanagan, the super's younger brother, came over from Ireland to live with the super and his family. I noticed the increase in whiskey bottles from the trash almost immediately after his brother arrived, but said nothing.

The super's brother had a nasty streak in him that got worse when he was drinking. I said hello to him when I first saw him, and he growled an obscenity back at me, his breath reeking with liquor. I hastily retreated. He had decided, on his own, that when his brother was not around, he was in charge of the building.

A few days later, he confronted me in the garbage room after school.

"What the hell are you doing in here?"

"Your brother said I can take magazines if I leave the trash piles neatly in order," I protested.

Cursing, he boxed my left ear and my head rang with waves of pain. I yelled and ran upstairs crying. It was 4:30 in the afternoon and Dad had just come home from his day shift. I told him what happened in the trash room, protesting that I had not disturbed the magazine or newspaper piles in any way. With my ear still smarting, Mom and Dad went back downstairs with me. There was a grim, determined look on Dad's usually placid face which I had never seen before. Pounding on the super's apartment door, we confronted the Flanagans..

When they answered the door, there was a lot of yelling, and curses were exchanged heatedly. Mrs. Flanagan brandished a vacuum cleaner pipe at us. The super's brother and Dad threw punches at each other, clinched and rolled over into the living room, crashing past a coffee table on the way. Jack Flanagan was about fifteen years younger than Dad, taller, more muscular and heavier. He was a typical Irish 'tough' who had worked on the Galway docks. Not the kind of guy one would want to start a fight with, especially my peace-loving Dad.

It all happened very fast. Jack was suddenly on top of Dad,

and pressing his heavy ring into Dad's eye! Dad screamed with pain. I momentarily forgot that I was only a ten-year-old boy about to take on a fully grown man in combat! My adrenaline kicked in and I dived past the super's wife into the living room. Jumping on Jack Flanagan's back, I dug my nails into his neck.

I went crazy, clawing and biting at Jack like a wild animal. He tried to shake me off, but I held on grimly like a bulldog, biting his left ear and drawing blood. Distracted, he swung around sideways, trying to get at me. Dad kicked him off, then swung at him and Jack crashed into a lamp, momentarily stunned.

I kicked Jack in the face, then slammed him with the lamp. He fell down again and stayed down. I knocked Mrs. Flanagan aside on the way out, while Mom grabbed the vacuum pipe and bopped her with it at the door.

We retreated to our apartment. Jack came after us, then stopped at the door. I yelled at him, "You come near me or my Dad again and I will smash your face in. I have a knife and I will use it! You want a war? I'll get my friends and their Dads after you and we'll run you off back where you came from!"

Jack hesitated, then turned and walked away. He may have realized that if he started a miniature 'Irish versus Jews' war in the Bronx, his brother would kick him out of the house as the troublemaker that he was. Inside our apartment, Mom busied herself trying to stop the bleeding from Dad's eye. He moaned, "I can't see, I can't see."

"Mom, I'm calling the cops," I cried. "They will come with an ambulance."

"No, no, don't do that! The cops are Irish, and the Flanagans will say we started it and broke into their apartment, and the cops will believe them. Call Dr. Weinberg across the street. Please, please. No cops, Bernie. No cops."

"Okay Mom, no cops." I scooted across the street to fetch Dr. Weinberg.

The doctor's ground floor six-room medical office was on the southcorner of 175th Street and Macombs Road. He was widely known in the neighborhood for his compassionate bedside manner, radiating an aura of trust and confidence. (Twice a week I ran errands for him after school for pocket money. We would talk about science and politics when his medical office was not busy.)

Dr. Weinberg snatched up his black bag, closed his office and came across the street to our apartment. He stitched up Dad's face, put a gauze patch on his bleeding eye, and called an ambulance from Bronx Lebanon Hospital. He rode with us to the hospital. The ambulance siren wailed and Mom and I clung to Dad's hand. He remained conscious and was far calmer than we were. The emergency room team worked frantically to treat Dad's eye, and an ophthalmologist arrived within a few minutes to examine him. The news from the eye doctor was good. Dad's left eye was blood-filled, but with no permanent damage. Thankfully, we took him home with a gauze patch and aftercare instructions.

Dad was very popular with the other drivers in the AAR taxicab garage, and they called or came over regularly during his convalescence: the Irish drivers brought stews, corned beef and cabbage, and some good Guinness Stout. The Black drivers brought soul food, and almost everyone in the garage contributed. There was some talk around the garage among the Irish drivers of beating up Flanagan, but Dad asked them not to engage in more violence, and his wishes were respected.

Dr. Weinberg checked Dad almost every day for the next two weeks. Then the eye patch came off and he went back to work.

A few days later, Dr. Weinberg's office suddenly closed

without notice. A taped voice message announced that the doctor would be on extended vacation. Years later, I learned that Dr. Weinberg's supposed 'vacation' had really been a suspension of his New York State medical license for a year. He had discreetly and compassionately referred a young unmarried woman 'in trouble' to a trusted colleague in New Jersey for an abortion. Unfortunately, she developed complications and died on the operating table from an unexpected massive hemorrhage.

Abortions were illegal then in New York State, so he had risked his medical practice by sending a patient there. Dr. Weinberg had done this before, without repercussions afterwards, but his medical luck on making risky abortion referrals out-of-state ran out this time.

My parents did not hold this abortion incident against him when he resumed his medical practice. Neither did I. Dr. Weinberg continued his practice quietly at his old Macombs Road office, beloved by his patients, for another twenty years before retiring. He was still there, ten years later, for my own newly started family. When I became a young newlywed father, he delivered my wife's first child.

23

Baseball and the Circus

Among Dad's favorite excursions with me were Sunday baseball doubleheaders in the summer at Yankee Stadium, and the annual Madison Square Garden arrival of the Ringling Bros. and Barnum & Bailey circus in the springtime. Dad was also into the sport of fishing. He sometimes went out fishing for the day with some other taxi drivers, but I asked not to be included in that kind of trip. Dad was at first a little miffed by my rejection, but I explained my negative feelings about fishing to him and he accepted them.

I still have these 'fishy' feelings in my adult life today. My gut feels that putting a hook into a living creature is barbaric, aside from the debatable question of whether or not it feels pain. I have no problem in eating fish, but only if it is already cleaned and prepared away from my view with the head removed. That way, it does not 'look dead' on a plate when served.

To this day in a supermarket, I avoid the ice-filled counter bins in order not to see the fish staring up with their mouths open. When I was with Mom on University Avenue and she shopped in a fish market, I stayed outside until she was done. She would come out with the fish gutted, filleted and discreetly wrapped in wax paper within a paper bag.

Dad and I were big Yankee fans. When we went to Yankee Stadium, a dollar got us two seats in the bleachers. Dad and I took along plenty of sunscreen lotion and we wore straw hats for protection from the overhead sun beating down on the bleacher boards. The twins were too young to go on these outings, and Gloria preferred doing 'girl things' rather than baseball. But she did go to the Ringling Brothers circus with Dad and me when it was in town.

Our appetites at the ballgame were satisfied with frankfurters that cost a quarter each, dripping with mustard and sauerkraut. Dad and I each got two hot dogs that were washed down with a soda for me and a beer for him. Since Mom would not let him have a beer at home, this was a special self-treat for Dad.

The rich Alabama tenor tones of Mel Allen, known as the 'Voice of the Yankees', were a broadcasting booth fixture in the '40s, '50s and '60s. In his fruity-rich voice, Mel announced the game and play-by-play action together with his Oklahoma sidekick, Curt Gowdy. Yankee home runs, announced by Mel as 'Ballantine blasts' (honoring the game sponsor, Ballantine Beer) or 'White Owl Wallops' (for co-sponsor White Owl cigars) were proclaimed with a 'going-going-gone!' followed by his famous half-shrieking catchphrase, "How about that!" That quote later became immortal when it was enshrined on his memorial plaque in the deepest centerfield spot of Yankee Stadium.

There was some boozing in the stadium in those days, but it seldom got out of hand, and fights among the fans were rare—not like today's ballpark rowdies. A few Red Sox or Tigers fans were jeered by the home team Yankees, and some garbage was thrown sometimes, but that did not corrupt me or my ballpark behavior. Yelling and cheering were OK, but Dad would not get rowdy or allow me to be rowdy.

I was sophisticated enough as a kid not to be shocked by seeing some adult drunkenness or other misbehavior. Years later, when I was a teenager, Dad and I were still going to Yankee Stadium games together. Most games I cannot recall individually, but the outfielders were memorable in action almost any day.

The great Yankee outfield trio of the early '50s was always a pleasure to behold from the bleachers. Joe DiMaggio and Hank Bauer were graceful outfielders and good power hitters. They greatly overshadowed Irv Noren, the often overlooked left fielder. Noren was one of the few professional baseball players who had also played pro basketball. Noren had spent two seasons (1946-47) with the Chicago American Gears of the early NBA, and his fluid grace in the Yankee outfield was the legacy of his basketball playing background.

I recall once seeing him make an 'impossible catch' in the outfield that brought the stadium to its feet with roars of approval.

The great catch happened on a cool Sunday summer day in the '50s at Yankee Stadium. Seagulls circled above as clouds gathered for a later rainstorm. Dad and I were seated in the far left corner of the bleachers, a few rows back from the front rail. In the game, the Yankees were leading the Tigers by one run in the seventh inning of the first game of a doubleheader. The Tigers were at bat with one out and a runner on third base.

Crack went the bat and a low line drive sped down the third-base line. Everyone in the bleachers sprang to their feet shouting. It looked like a double for sure, maybe a triple! Noren raced to his left, angling in from a deep outfield position. Then I saw the impossible happen!

In the last split second of the sinking ball's flight, Noren made a desperate ten-foot dive and caught the ball near the foul line! Still flying waist-high in midair, he snapped off a perfect one-bounce strike to nail the runner at home plate, then rolled over just short of the fence, rising unhurt as the fans cheered wildly.

The Tiger runner was halfway home and suddenly had to reverse himself back to third base to tag up and run for home plate. He was called 'out' on a close play. Irv Noren, in a swiftly passing moment of glory, became a momentary superstar outfielder, soon to fade back into everyday common player status.

I never took school athletics as a serious personal focus in my elementary school days. I was not a good athlete—just an average schoolyard player. Softball was a major PS 82 sport activity, in gym class and in after-school pick up games. I never made a great catch like Irv Noren did—not even close! Often, I was only the 'last choice' pick for a street team. At school, Mr. Stafford, the gym teacher, made sure everyone got a chance to play on the schoolyard softball teams.

After school, I was on my own and often got excluded from ball games as a supposedly poor player. I was not a jock, but I could hold my own on the ball field. Sometimes, if there were not enough kids to start a game, we did batting and fielding practice until more players came to join us.

There was an element of playground prejudice in the pickup team choosing process. Some of that bias was an anti-intellectual myth—smart kids were supposed to be poor sports players physically. I liked the game, and preferred to play the outfield to meet the challenge of trying to 'get the jump' on fly balls, anticipating where they would come down and trying to be at the right spot in time to catch them. I never quite mastered the trick of judging the distance a fly ball would travel from the sound of the crack of the bat. But I had a strong throwing arm and batters would not often try to take extra bases on me.

When batting, I often struck out since my reflexes were usually slow to track the ball from the pitcher's hand to home plate. Imitating one of my Yankee heroes, Gil McDougald, in his unorthodox batting position, I adopted a new near-flat-level batting stance that got me more base hits, but subjected my style to occasional teasing by the other boys.

Each February, a few weeks before the major league baseball season opened, the circus came to town. New York City was treated to the early morning spectacle of eight elephants debarking from the mile-long Ringling Bros. circus train and marching, with trunks and tails linked, through the Lincoln Tunnel to Madison Square Garden on Eighth Avenue between 49th and 50th Streets.

Every year, Dad, Gloria and I rode downtown on the Lexington Avenue subway line to load up on cotton candy and other treats in the sideshow area, and enjoy the Circus. There were several hundred animals to be seen up close in their cages, including lions, tigers, bears, horses, camels and zebras.

And there were the unusual people—a polite word for 'freaks.' As advertised, these included the bearded lady, the tattooed man, the strong man, the heaviest, tallest and shortest men and women in the 'world' (or at least in New York City!) I remember that the tallest man was over eight feet in height. The midgets were less than three feet tall. Arriving early, my family headed for the basement where dozens of animals were displayed from the menagerie. One ticket admitted the holder to both the menagerie and the circus combined. The smells of popcorn and sawdust were in the air and calliope circus music pervaded the atmosphere.

Gloria busied herself with the cotton candy—eating it and getting it all over her face. Dad very patiently cleaned her with a damp paper towel and told her to eat more carefully because Mom would get mad if she saw Gloria's face and hands smeared up. The lions and tigers restlessly paced inside their gaudy red and gilt animal cage wagons as their roars shook the arena air.

Kids from out-of-town shrieked with awe and delight at the spectacle of the animals restlessly prowling around their cages. As New York City kids, with one of the largest zoos in the world nearby for us to visit, Gloria and I were less impressed, but still fascinated since we could get closer to them in the menagerie than at the Bronx Zoo.

In 1956, rising expenses caused Ringling to take down its 'big top' tent on its annual visit to New York City for the last time and they switched to performing in stadiums and arenas only. I never experienced the Ringling canvas 'big top' since I always saw the circus in Madison Square Garden in Manhattan.

24

Mom Gets Jealous

Aunt Irma told stories of family history on both Mom and Dad's sides. My mother apparently believed that she was always right and the world was always wrong. Mom ran her own household with a harsh hand. To her, Dad was like the oldest of her four other children. She scolded him often—both privately and in front of the children. I was embarrassed for him, and did not understand then why Dad tolerated Mom belittling him. That comprehension came years later. It was for the sake of the Jewish concept of *'Shalom Bayis'* (peace in the home) that he endured her heckling.

Aunt Claire was a vision to behold when she drove up to Macombs Road to take me on an outing every other Sunday afternoon. She appeared as the very image of the Fifth Avenue princess that she was. Neighbor's windows popped open, and they were all agog at the unusual spectacle of a woman driving her own car.

Aunt Claire parked by our building and emerged from her fancy car with a sweep of glamour. All that was missing in her grand arrival scene was a mike thrust into her face, shouted questions and the pop of flashbulbs. Some local kids even asked me if she was a movie star. I said "No," but bragged that my aunt was a 'boss lady' at Saks Fifth Avenue. On a bright day, her shiny new maroon Buick gleamed in the sun. No **man** had paid for her customized Roadmaster V-8!

In later years, I came to understand the adult-level concept of 'patronizing' behavior which explained Mom's thinly-veiled hostility to Aunt Claire. My allowance was fifty cents per week, but Claire, in front of Mom, grandly bestowed a whole dollar on me each time she came to visit.

I still remember her final visit:

"Oh, hello Rose, how are you?" Claire chimed sweetly, as Mom greeted her at the door in her apron, with hands still dripping soap suds from the kitchen sink. Mom muttered a "Hello" back at her, and then I came out with a warmer greeting and kiss, all dressed up to go for a ride around town with her, and chat about the business world and my potential future in it. "But, Auntie, I love science the most of any school subject!" I once told her. She replied, "I believe that Wall Street will be the place for you to work in someday, not Saks Fifth Avenue or the science world. Then you will be able to afford to buy a shiny new Buick like mine. Scientists drive old Chevys; Wall Streeters drive new Buicks or Cadillacs."

"Auntie, isn't Cadillac the fanciest car?" I asked curiously. "Why don't you drive that?" She blushed. "I can afford a Caddy; it's just that I like Buicks better. More stylish!"

Aunt Claire's lasting legacy to me was her personality as a successful woman in the male-dominated business world, and that women could be more than just housewives or mothers in this world. (She also instilled in me a fondness for Buicks—the only automobile in the world of Scottish lineage. The Buick

Company was founded by David Dunbar Buick, a scion of the Scottish Clan Dunbar.)

Aunt Claire and I often went to the Concourse Plaza Hotel for lunch. That was the fanciest Bronx restaurant I ever encountered as a kid. Wow! Linen tablecloths, real silver service with waiters in tuxedos to greet us. My favorite dish was the Glazed Long Island Duck luncheon for three dollars—a princely lunch price in those days! Aunt Claire grandly left a dollar tip on the table.

I did not understand then why Mom was cool to Aunt Claire. Eventually, her ongoing hostility pushed Aunt Claire away from further contact with us. Dad meekly submitted to the banishment of his sister, but I was very upset about it. When I called Aunt Claire on the phone at the candy store, she told me it would make trouble in the family if she ever visited us again. She sadly warned me against trying to stay in touch with her. Our nephew-aunt closeness was shattered by Mom's hostility to her. Mom issued an ultimatum to Dad, Claire goes out of our life, or else!" He meekly complied. I never found out what the 'or else' meant.

I wrote to her, but the letters were returned marked "No forwarding address." Apparently she had moved away and vanished from my sight. I never found her again. This was an emotional blow to my young life.

When we left the Crotona Avenue apartment to live on Macombs Road in the West Bronx, we expanded from a one-bedroom park-facing walk-up apartment into a two-bedroom ground floor walk-in flat facing other drab concrete and brick building facades in monotone masonry and shabby shingled fronts.

For the first time, I had my own room. My own room! It was an exhilarating feeling to have this privilege for the first time, even though it was partitioned into two half-rooms for me and Gloria. Our windows jutted out barely above street level. Only the feet of passers-by were visible. Pipes ran across our slightly-cracked ceilings, connecting to the basement boiler room.

The apartment was clean, but dark, furnished from second-hand stores and the Salvation Army. A piano graced the living room, played by Mom and then later by Carol when she came of school age.

Macombs Road was a hilly street winding its way upwards from the 170th Street elevated train station on Jerome Avenue to University and Tremont Avenues. It was a gentle slope, and I often rode my bike downhill for eight blocks coasting along on brakes without pumping the pedal once. Diagonally across the street from our apartment house was Tony's barber shop next door to Eli and Meyer's candy store.

Meyer was a grizzled and frazzled middle-aged shopkeeper with a slightly nervous and neurotic manner. If you hesitated for more than a moment or two at the counter, he would shrill at you, "Wadda ya want?" I was annoyed at this, because I was a good little customer there, buying at least one dime comic book each week. Nevertheless, I swallowed his difficult mannerisms and stayed polite.

Eli, Meyer's brother and partner in the candy store, was a comical, but blunt-spoken old man who saved a copy of my favorite comics to sell to me every week. He spluttered a lot when he talked, mouthing his words with a thick Yiddish accent. But I did not mock him with imitations behind his back like some other neighborhood kids did. *He was somebody's grandfather too, I thought. He deserves some respect for that.*

I traded and collected *Classic Comics* bought with my saved-up dimes. I never quite accumulated the entire Classics set after trying for several years. Unlike many other young *Classic Comics* fans, I had also read the hard cover authors behind the comic Classics—like Mark Twain, Arthur Conan Doyle and Herman Melville, among other famous authors.

I enjoyed the comic book versions of their works greatly, devouring the heroic stylized drawings that were so different from the crudely portrayed Mickey Mouse and Donald Duck slapstick Disney animations of the 1930s and early '40s. In fact, the term 'Mickey Mouse' became an insult in common adult usage to mean something 'small-time' or 'trivial'. There was nothing 'small-time' about Disney cartoons, merchandising or movie productions then or now as I remember them.

As a little boy, at the movies I was bored by the 'crash-bam bingety-bang' style of most 'loony cartoonies', and often walked out on them after seeing the main feature film. The movies I enjoyed most were Cary Grant films, Marx Brothers comedies, musicals and science fiction.

Our neighborhood movie theater was the Park Plaza, rounding on the curved corner of University and Tremont Avenues, immediately north of PS 82. School events, graduations, and an annual Halloween Party were staged there during the school year.

I dressed my siblings each year for the Halloween contest, and Mom used her old millinery skills to create their costume hats. Twice, once for Gloria and once for Carol, they won the grand Halloween prize—free movie tickets and popcorn for a whole month.

The movie of greatest impact on my early childhood was Walt Disney's *Fantasia*, the animated masterpiece of the early 1940s. Many adults were puzzled by its sophistication, and younger kids who saw it were disappointed. They expected typical Mickey Mouse-style slapstick, and instead were treated to animated artistry that elevated Disney screen magic into a serious adult-level art form, accompanied by classical music conducted by Leopold Stokowski and the Philadelphia Orchestra.

Park Plaza Theater (P.S. 82 in background)

I sat spellbound as the movie unfolded, my popcorn untouched. The musicologist Deems Taylor was an imposing sight on screen in black tux and matching black gloves, as he introduced each *Fantasia* scene with the music of the Philadelphia Orchestra while Maestro Stokowski loomed onscreen in silhouette. As Mr. Taylor introduced them, the orchestra softly tuned up in the background.

And then came the unforgettable image, after the *"Sorcerer's Apprentice"* scene, of a silhouetted Mickey Mouse, in his dramatic screen debut as the Apprentice, taking a curtain call by shaking hands with tall, dignified Maestro Stokowski. In the animation for *Fantasia*, the ridiculous had transformed into the sublime. I delighted in seeing the fat hippos dancing their ballet 'on point' with ostriches and crocodiles in Ponchielli's "*Dance of the Hours*". My eyes grew big as they feasted on the dark grandeur of the satanic "*Night on Bald Mountain*" which then segued into a misted sunrise chant.

The scene closed with an early morning torchlight procession of pilgrims, as a background choir chanted "*Ave Maria*". The Great Monster folded his hooked bat wings and shrank back into his mountaintop lair, with one last snarl at the sunrise.

I was especially entranced by the Beethoven Sixth Symphony, the "Pastoral," with its prancing centaurs, Greek Gods and winged horses. The "*Pastoral Symphony*" became a lifelong favorite, which awakened in me a hunger to hear other classical composers.

Vividly, the prehistoric era came to life with Stravinsky's "*Rite of Spring*" as dinosaurs and pterodactyls rose and fell, with an epic battle waged between the huge tyrannosaur and the smaller plucky stegosaurus with the viciously lashing spiked tail.

I didn't have money to buy phonograph records, but received a portable radio from Grandpa as a birthday present, and discovered WQXR as my favorite classical radio station.

The Tremont Avenue trolley line, with its yellow streetcars outlined by dull red trimming, was my favorite ride across the Bronx. It rolled smoothly and sedately along its tracks, outpaced by passing cars as its overhead trolley pole tip sizzled and sparked onto the overhead cable line. The New York City subway and bus fare remained at five cents for two generations. It was a point of pride for City Hall to keep the subways and buses at a nickel for 44 years. Finally, trying to balance New York City's first billion dollar budget, Mayor William O'Dwyer 'bit the bullet' as the train fare doubled to a dime, and bus fare rose to seven cents on June 30, 1948 at one minute past midnight.

The *Daily News* noted the next day: "Sorry. Folks. Now New York City is a ten-cent kind of town." Modern postwar times had arrived. Even the new airport, New York International (Idlewild to old-timers, now John F. Kennedy Airport today), was finally opening for business on the very same day the transit fare first went up.

The airlines were still haggling with the Port Authority over leases and landing fees, and nothing but an occasional private plane was landing at Kennedy airport yet. In its first week of operation, the world's largest airport collected exactly $44.

Subway fares went up again from ten cents to fifteen cents in 1953, and remained at that level until 1966. Mom was happy that we had moved to a larger apartment in a good West Bronx neighborhood with lots of shopping nearby on University Avenue. This broad boulevard had a central leafy strip of bushes and many park benches. There was a kosher butcher, where she bought a chicken on Thursday mornings for our Sabbath meal at Grandpa's. There was a fish store, a Bronx Savings Bank branch, kosher-style Olinsky's Market and five blocks of other stores stretching south along University Avenue.

I loved shopping at Olinsky's with Mom, helping her with the bags and sampling the pickle barrel when nobody was looking. (PS: I never did get caught!)

But my main boyish interest was in Ruschmeyer's, an old-fashioned ice cream parlor in mid-block on the southbound side of University Avenue. Its dark maroon awning faced PS 82 across the street on Macombs Road. The interior was resplendent in dark mahogany paneling with oversized black plush leatherette booths with an onyx bar counter.

When I went to the neighborhood movies, it was usually a double feature or one movie and five cartoons. Many Bronx boys loved John Wayne-type 'shoot-em-up' cowboys versus Indians Westerns. Of course, most of them rooted for the cowboys, but I quietly rooted for the Indians to win. After all, they were defending their land from us! My favorite Indian hero was Osceola, War Chief of the Seminoles, because he defeated the US Cavalry in pitched military battles against the Indians and their colored freedmen allies. But I really preferred adult-level movies to Hollywood cowboys and Indians.

25

Let's Pretend and Let's Play

My lifelong love of geography began in my elementary school years. I was waiting with Dad in Dr. Weinstein's office to get a flu shot. Dad usually read *Dick Tracy* comics or the *Daily News* at the doctor's office. He was okay with that. I glanced briefly at the creased magazines on the waiting room rack, but seldom read them. The few, like *Look, Life* or *Colliers,* that seemed interesting were often shredded and worn. I would glimpse the cover headline and the start of a potentially good article, but the continuation pages were often torn out. Often, I brought a pocket-size paperback book along to read.

When I received travel permission to go downtown into Manhattan at age nine, I often visited the main map room of the Central Public Library on 42nd Street. It was love at first sight to encounter the detailed medieval Mercator and Ortelius maps, with their embellished scrollwork, reproduced from the original parchment paper and stored flat in long flat architect drawers. The picturesque sidebars of these old maps evoked images of medieval walled towns and galleons setting forth under full sail at sea. (Mercator invented the word 'atlas'). In the *Encyclopedia Britannica*, I learned that he was the first cartographer to project the curved Earth surface onto a flat page.

My imagination soared as I finger-traced the great rivers and mountain ranges of the world that were depicted in full color. Even their conjectured configurations of unexplored territories were emblazoned with curlicued fire-breathing dragons and sea monsters. My special favorites were the pre-Columbus Atlantic maps with ships sailing over the edge of the world into the abyss.

"Here there be dragons. Garde well thy ship and thy soul..."

After exhausting the library supply of earthly maps, I immersed myself in the *Norton Star Atlas of the Heavens, 1950 edition*. It was purchased at the planetarium, with my own saved money. I wanted to know where everything was in the world and in the sky, hungering for maps and more maps to read and read, draw and draw. As with my other advanced readings, this early interest in cartography sometimes led to problems with my teachers. When basic geography was being taught in the third grade, I became restless and bored. Often, teachers thought I was daydreaming, but instead I was doodling imaginary maps onto a blank notebook page.

However, when called upon in class, I usually gave correct answers. Praise came from teachers rarely, if ever. Glowering looks of resentment came sometimes instead. From their furrowed frowns, I could almost picture their thoughts ... *"that little wise guy Bernie, I'll catch him next time for not paying attention in class!"* (But they never did!).

I remember an elementary class lesson on American panhandles—(*geography, not begging*)—which were elongated peninsulas jutting out from some State maps. One somnolent summer day in early June, the teacher tried one last time to trap me. She pulled the United States map down from the ceiling on its rollers, then wrote some state names on the blackboard. My eyes glazed over—I had read these a dozen times or more. Then she chalked in 'Alaska' and turned to me in another attempted '*aha*' moment.

"Bernie, what is different about the Alaska panhandle?" I rose and declared, "The state capital, Juneau, is in the panhandle and is the only state capital unreachable by highway." I sat down triumphantly as the class giggled uncertainly. Some of them could not even spell 'Alaska'.

After school, my role changed from school student to home teacher of my siblings as students. I gave mini-geography lessons once a week along with general homework help. Their interest was piqued by natural curiosity about the rest of the world outside the Bronx. With pictures and cutouts from *National Geographic* and other magazines, I brought planet Earth to life for them.

In their pre-kindergarten years, they showed a normal sense of wonder and fantasy for their ages. They loved fairy tales and playing 'let's pretend' inspired, no doubt, by my paraphrased stories to them of Mark Twain's works and Malory's King Arthur legends. Sometimes, I joined my siblings 'let's pretend' games as Director, inventing roles for them to perform as we engaged in improvisational theater. These games continued for several years until they reached the age of disbelief in fairies, goblins and pirates. Meanwhile, I discovered science fiction as a more adult form of fairy tale to share with them, and our rekindled imaginations soared to renewed heights.

Several times a week, our 'let's pretend' sessions convened on the rug in a living room circle after school. Gloria, as the next oldest, perched on my right side, then Carol sat next to her, and Mark was on the left side. Their little faces were aglow in rapt attention as I constructed a play scene for the next day's performance. Mom made herself scarce when we began our play scenes, temporarily relieved from having to keep an eye on us.

I assigned roles to my siblings to be acted out, then scrounged around for potential scenery materials. Cloth scraps and scarves were fashioned into skirts, turbans and robes, then refashioned after the performance for another scene the next day or week. Play swords and guns emerged from the toy chest as we armed ourselves for imaginary action against our enemies.

During rehearsals, my brother and sisters sometimes asked me, as Director, questions about their parts and I responded, sometimes with a little history lesson as background. If I was a pirate captain that day, then one sibling became the pirate 'crew', and the others became the crew of the ship or fort we were attacking. Cardboard cartons, tapered to form a ship's bow, were our ships, and bed sheets our sails, furling out with cord on taped broomsticks.

We fitted out cardboard tubes as cannons, readying our scenery and props for the game. If it were a larger project, then we would build today for a fantasy game tomorrow.

I enforced Mom's 'let's pretend' permission rules with Gloria, Carol and Mark.

The rules were:

1) keep down the noise,

2) no bed sheets, pillows or linens. (Mom had veto power on stage supplies), and

3) clean up after the performance.

Mom stayed out of our way and busied herself with household tasks or went outside, after cautioning us not to 'make a mess', or her staging permission would be revoked.

Sometimes, we acted out a fairy tale from the Brothers Grimm or Hans Christian Andersen.

Gloria never liked being a captive princess. She preferred being a rescuer or a heroine instead. But she also liked to play such roles as Queen Elizabeth rallying the English against the Spanish Armada, or Elizabeth Blackwell as the first lady doctor in the United States.

Mark became fascinated with the craft of puppetry. I helped him construct a puppet theater, drawstring curtain and all, using discarded Christmas tree lights for stage lighting. He was our stage manager fixing the lights and assembling the stage components. Often, we were absorbed, playing for an hour or so until summoned for dinner. Later on, as our presentations improved, family and friends became our puppet-show audience. I made tickets and programs by typing in the text, then using scissors and paste to create tickets which cost ten cents each for kids and a quarter for grown-ups. Our puppets were made from discarded old socks.

When it was curtain time, a background lamp remained lit, while the main room lights were lowered. I would announce the play, and the acting roles, and then it was ... on with the show!

I felt fulfilled as a big brother by managing the puppet shows, and teaching my siblings in their early formative years, as Grandpa had taught me.

Just as my siblings were outgrowing their fantasy and puppetry phase of childhood, a new acting outlet, beyond our family circle, entered my life. In the local Sedgwick Community Center on University Avenue and 174th Street, there was an improvisational theater group—open to all ages. Members dubbed it 'The Improv'. Although I became one of the youngest members of the theater group, I felt comfortable relating to the older children and adults joined together.

'Thelma the Thespian', as I nicknamed her, was the only girl near my age in the group. She had actually taken acting lessons, and often smiled at me. At that age, I was not attracted to her, or any other young girls in my neighborhood. A few years later, when my adolescent hormones kicked in, that attitude changed for a more mature appreciation of the female sex.

The Sedgwick theater group was not 'child's play'—it was adult improvisational role-play. The group leader would set a short scene for us to perform while sitting in a circle. To me, this was easier than trying to remember lines from a script. Once or twice during the improv session, the floor was opened to scenes suggested by members.

Fred was our group leader. He was a slender young hazel-eyed guy in his early twenties. His shoulder-length chestnut-brown hair was neatly swept back from his pleasant, but slightly rakish face. He conducted the improv and drama groups at the Sedgwick Center once a week while pursuing theater arts studies at CCNY.

One sunny Thursday in the early spring, Fred gave us an 'improv' scene of particular poignancy. It was a wartime homecoming scene wherein the young soldier comes home unharmed, but his family greets him with sad news. His brother, a year too young to join the Army, had died a few days earlier in a civilian street accident.

With that scene set for the group, we continued without script or dialogue, just by reacting on the spur of the moment to whatever was said by the others. There was a stir in the group when that scene was announced. One young girl turned white as a sheet, a man winced as if stabbed with a needle, and another boy shook his head negatively.

They did not want to talk about it. They had actually lost one or more family members in the World War. This scene had hit home to them—literally, but not to me. Fred nodded. "Okay, no more war homecoming scenes, then. Anyone here have another idea?"

Freckle-faced Thelma spoke up. "How about a spin-off on *Romeo and Juliet*? I could be Juliet's kid sister, with a crush on Romeo!"

Fred responded warmly, "That's a great idea! Who wants to be Romeo?" Empty silence in the room and squirming. I sighed. As one of the few young boys in the group who had two kid sisters that I actually liked, I felt obliged to volunteer. I responded, "I volunteer to play Romeo."

Fred briefed us on our roles. "Juliet was fourteen and Romeo was sixteen, according to Shakespeare's play. Her kid sister, who is imaginary—let's make her …" Thelma piped up. "I am eleven. That's the right age for a kid sister."

Fred responded. "Okay. Eleven it is." "Someone in the back asked me, "Do you have any experience in kissing girls?" That was answered with a group giggle. Fred wisely ruled, "let's do another scene instead. No romance this time."

I raised my hand and proposed a different skit in which the court undertaker complains to the King that the new jester is too successful. The merriment he brings to the court caused funerals to slump sharply. We ran the scene forward from there and had a merry old time with it. I do not remember the details of the scene as we played it, but, inspired by a growing opera interest from the radio, I named the lead role with a Rossini flourish—Dismalo, the Undertaker.

Dismalo bewailed the loss of funeral business from the antics of the new court jester. Patterned loosely after Figaro, the Barber of Seville, my heroic villain plotted and schemed in an operatic-styled Improv idea to bury the jester in a special soundproof coffin just in case he objected to being buried alive.

As an opera-loving boy regularly listening to classical music, I knew about settings for operatic tragedies and comedies. These inspired some of my own Improv scenes at the Sedgwick Community Center. I also brought scenes home to use for my sibling 'let's pretend' plays.

Later, I also joined an indoor floor hockey league with several boys near my own age from school. We played in each other's living rooms. The flat side of six-inch rulers became our hockey sticks, and pennies became pucks. Boundaries were set up by stretched strings, and goals were small cardboard containers cut out on one side. The goalie was a quarter coin and it did not move, but could be repositioned by a player. We played three twenty-minute periods on our living room floors, using a kitchen timer.

For outdoor games, neighborhood boys informally organized soapbox derbies on a nearby steep hill—down 176th Street from Grand Avenue to Davidson Avenue, then a sharp left-angle turn down a lesser slope on Davidson Avenue for about a hundred yards, and finally a flat stretch to coast to a stop past a finish line. Parents helped by getting the local police precinct to close off the block to automobile and truck traffic for two hours during the race.

I warned Mark that if I ever caught him racing down Davidson Avenue by himself without supervision, I would ground him, lock up the soapbox racer and withdraw my help for him on any future projects. This time, he listened to me and stayed safe.

The soap box derby was run once in the spring and again in the summer. In the winter, the hill became a sled racing course with lookouts posted to watch for traffic, and garbage cans were set out as street obstacles to protect sledders. Kids under ten were not allowed to race by their parents or whoever was watching them. I rode down the hill a few times myself without racing anyone else.

Some of Mark's friends were also building soapbox racers for use on local hills and in parks and playgrounds. These were milk or orange crates nailed onto the end of a two-by-four plank. Roller skates or baby carriage wheels were attached, and wooden handlebars were improvised and added on for steering. I helped Mark with the construction and we decorated it by painting and trimming it with bottle caps and flags.

Starting in the spring, when outdoor winter activities ended, vendors in trucks and horse-drawn wagons appeared on Bronx streets. The knife-sharpening truck, announced by cowbell, was a regular street solicitor. Other street vendors came calling, building up to a crescendo of purveyors of Good Humor ice cream, various fresh vegetables and watermelons from a pushcart or truck—among other goods. Also coming to our local blocks were mobile amusement rides, turning our neighborhood streets into an instant carnival. These included the Whip, the Half-Moon, mini-Ferris Wheel and sometimes even a pony ride. In the summer, hydrants were opened with spray caps and younger children frolicked in the spray. These were happy and exciting times in my old Bronx neighborhood.

26

Exploring the Bronx

In my early teen years, I began to explore the Grand Concourse more extensively, roaming its north-south length as far as I could walk, usually between 161st Street and Fordham Road. It is a broad boulevard about a mile east of Macombs Road—a larger, but less elegant Bronx boulevard than its model, the famed Champs-Elysees of Paris. It is divided by center strips into a north-south main road flanked by two side roads. East/west vehicle traffic crosses the Grand Concourse by street underpasses at major intersections.

The newly-built IND subway line opened along the Concourse in 1933, with train stations recessed into its arches. The subway travels along Sixth and Eighth Avenues in Manhattan, then swings over to the Grand Concourse in the Bronx before finally curving west to its northern terminus at 205th Street near Mosholu Parkway. It sparked a tremendous growth in the Bronx with the migration of those upwardly-striving workers who were fortunate enough to be spared from the mass unemployment of the 1930s. They rapidly inhabited nearly three hundred Art Deco and Art Moderne five and six-story apartment houses constructed along the Concourse.

Concourse Plaza Hotel

The Grand Concourse was the most upscale boulevard in the Bronx. My family could not afford to live there on a cab driver's earnings, so my earliest Concourse experiences were the luncheons that Aunt Claire and I enjoyed in the linen-draped banquet halls of the Concourse Plaza Hotel. The Concourse Plaza opened in 1922, a few months after Yankee Stadium opened a few blocks downhill on 161st Street. It was the first business-class hotel ever built in the Bronx.

The Concourse Plaza hosted the New York Yankee teams and the stars they attracted to major league baseball for forty years, then it declined, together with the Grand Concourse itself, into mid-century shabbiness. As a young boy, I never dreamed that such a dreary future decay loomed ahead for the Bronx, followed by a partial revival that took many years to unfold.

My favorite Concourse building was the thirteen-story Lewis Morris Apartments, with its filigreed yellowish facade perched high above the 174th Street viaduct. It had a sweeping panoramic view of the entire Bronx.

North of the Concourse Plaza Hotel were block after block of Art Deco six-to-ten-story apartment houses, many with doormen and carpeted lobbies. Along the Concourse was the 168th Street 'YMHA'. Further north was Tremont Temple, a Reform Jewish synagogue north of Burnside Avenue. That is where I joined the singles group in my late teens and began to meet girls socially.

Past Burnside Avenue, the northbound Concourse became busier, dotted with some small enclaves of upscale stores. The Ascot Theater stood out from its boxy storefront apartment house neighbors near 183rd Street on the east side of the Concourse.

With its striped terracotta frontage, the Ascot Theater was the only Bronx movie house that featured foreign films (with subtitles). The Ascot's Hollywood offerings were among the more cultural films of the mid-20th century era. A typical example of this genre was Shakespeare's *A Midsummer Night's Dream* (released in 1935) with Mickey Rooney, Olivia de Havilland, James Cagney and Dick Powell.

Often, I was the only child in the entire theater. Once, at the box office, I caused the eyebrows of the ticket agent to rise as he remarked to me patronizingly, "There are no cartoons here, kid." I replied sharply, "I am no kid. I am paying an adult price of one dollar, and I expect to be treated as an adult patron!"

There was no matron or children's section in the theater. The ticket agent turned red, then dispensed the ticket. Simone Signoret (in French) or Marlene Dietrich films (in German) or Shakespeare in English did not appeal to most Bronx teens or pre-teens that I knew.

Continuing north on 183rd Street, was the old Concourse Center of Israel synagogue, where my parents were married in 1935. Sometimes, I walked as far as Fordham Road, a mile further up the Grand Concourse, a few blocks past the Loew's Paradise Theater. Skipping the bus meant an extra twenty cents in my pocket to spend. Just past the Concourse roadway dipping into its only north-south underpass on the Concourse was the splendid facade of the Loew's Paradise, the acclaimed faux-Venetian premier theatre of the Bronx.

The wide theater screen of the Paradise was especially suitable for early Cecil B. DeMille biblical epic films, which I remember seeing there. These included the first Cinemascope film, *The Robe*, and its sequel *Demetrius and the Gladiators*, *Ben Hur*, and *The Ten Commandments*. These were projected on a screen almost three times as wide as standard movie screens. The Paradise was one of the last theaters built in the Atmospheric architectural style, which recreated the illusion of an outdoor villa atrium under a nighttime sky. The theater's interior walls were lined with Moorish grottos back-lit by dim red and dark blue lamps. Smartly-uniformed ushers attended to audience seating on the orchestra, mezzanine and balcony levels.

Loews Paradise Theater

In the grand foyer of the Paradise, there was an elaborate Carrara fountain which contained a goldfish pool with shimmering koi splashing under its flowing waterfall. If I arrived early for the movie, I sat there and watched them swim languidly around the fountain, trailing diaphanous fins in their wake. Stars twinkled in the deep purple celestial sky of the theater dome, as wired moving clouds drifted over the audience It was beautiful—enchantingly beautiful.

Loews Paradise Theater interior

Once a month, on Sundays when Dad was off from work, my family went to Burnside Avenue and ordered lunch from Foo's Chinese Restaurant around the corner on Davidson Avenue. Aunt Irma lived halfway down that block, but never joined us for lunch at Foo's, even when she was on speaking terms with Mom. The first Sunday after my first payday as a delivery boy at the *Bronx Home News*, I planned to surprise my parents for the occasion. Only Gloria knew what I planned to do, because I wanted to treat her to a special dessert with my new earnings.

At Foo's, we sat down to lunch as Dad made a pretense of studying the menu. It was a futile exercise since Mom did all the ordering and it was always the same for everyone in the family—Chicken Chow Mein—the seventy five cent special.

For years, I had glanced longingly at the imagined exotic dishes on the menu, most of which were over a dollar, an impossible luxury for our family. That first payday, with a pay envelope in my pocket, I fixated on Beef Chop Suey as my secret surprise menu choice, conservatively priced at ninety five cents. Today was to be the fulfillment of my dreams. I would buy my own lunch!

On the way to Foo's, I held Gloria's hand and slowed my long steps to match her shorter ones. Dad wheeled the stroller with the twins, as Mom walked alongside. They were getting too big for the stroller, but Mom felt it was too far for them to walk on their own.

Foo's was modestly Oriental in style and moderate in price. The gray stone-framed front window was draped in red symbol-festooned cloth, with several jade dragons displayed up front. Our hostess, Madam Foo, or the 'dragon lady' as I secretly called her, greeted us as we came in. She was brilliantly sheathed in a high-collared jade-green dress shimmering down to her ankles in sequined glory. All that was missing to complete her dragon lady image was the long cigarette holder. I always wondered if she had a stiletto under that sheath. I never got close enough to find out!

Mom did not even glance at the menu. The waiter approached and she began her usual order with Gloria and the twins to share one plate.

"Four chicken chow mein lunches, with white rice."

"Just a minute, Mom," I interrupted. "I want Chop Suey!"

Shocked silence. Mom's eyebrows raised up an inch. "What did you say?"

Slowly I responded. "I want to eat Chop Suey, and I am paying for it. It's my money and I want Chop Suey. I don't care if it costs twenty cents more, I am spending it!"

I placed the money on the table, a dollar and a quarter. Dad smiled. Mom gave him a dirty look for not backing her up, then shrugged. "All right, then," she yielded with ill grace. Soon I would go on to explore other delicacies. (Yum, yum. I can make my own menu selection now. Just like a grown-up!*)*

After lunch, Mom and Dad went home and I took Gloria to Ruschmeyer's for a 'my first job' celebration dessert. We sat in a booth instead of at the counter. A shadow of disappointment momentarily crossed her face as she could not spin the leatherette booth seat like a counter stool. But the treat of having a strawberry ice cream soda with me soothed her from her lost stool-spinning opportunity. Two scoops of strawberry ice cream in the soda was her reward.

* * *

I had few friends during my early years. The combined effect of the death of my playmate Harry, the death of my grandmother a year later, and finally, the passing away of Grandpa and Uncle Eddie when I was seven tended to estrange me from other children of my own age. These personal deaths cast a shadow over my socialization.

Many of my wanderings around the Bronx in my early school years were solo trips. I preferred to be alone in local travels so that I could study the sights without distraction or hurrying along to keep up with others. At the Bronx Zoo, for instance, I read the labels on the cages and lingered at least several minutes near the enclosures of each animal group to observe their behavior with each other and with humans. The Zoo is where I learned lifelong lessons in respecting and loving animal life.

27

Manhattan Adventures

At age nine, I was ready to voyage into the canyons of Manhattan. Dad interceded for me when I requested permission from Mom to go downtown by myself. She was reluctant to allow this adventure.

Dad declared, "Aww, Rose, Bernie is big enough to go downtown by himself now. He knows his way around Manhattan better than I do in my taxicab." With a few dollars saved up from my allowance, and a dollar from Aunt Claire, I rode downtown about once a month on the Jerome Avenue elevated line to 42nd Street and Lexington Avenue. Each time, I savored the stroll across the lofty concourse of the Grand Central Station, gateway to midtown Manhattan. Up the broad stairs I loped, stretching my legs after the hour-long subway ride, the first of many Manhattan subway rides to come.

My first stop, after leaving Grand Central Station, was usually the Horn & Hardart Automat on 42nd Street for a cup of hot chocolate and a donut. That cost a grand total of fifteen cents. For another quarter, I could get a tuna fish, macaroni & cheese or bologna sandwich. The window compartment turntables would rotate into position, then pop open with each purchase, and then close when the plate is taken from the shelf by the customer. Empty shelves were quickly restocked with the same dish.

There were Automats located throughout midtown Manhattan. Many were high rectangular restaurant rooms, the earliest of the fast food emporiums. They were filled with glossy lacquered tables—their famous food compartment windows embanked along curved or straight walls, and open cafeteria buffet-style steam counters for direct serving of hot dishes.

Horn & Hardart

'Nickel-thrower' ladies with rubber-tipped fingers gave change at floor booths that they punched out from a coin machine. When the change lines grew longer, the 'nickel-throwers' walked around to dispense coins more quickly from their hand-held coin dispensers.

Encamped at some Automat tables were homeless men and women, usually sitting alone, quietly, or muttering to themselves. They stank of tobacco and whiskey and were avoided by the customers. Often, they would sit for hours over a cup of coffee. Presumably, the managers were too busy to chase them, except in the unusual instances when any of them would make a disturbance.

Neil Simon, a famous Broadway playwright, described feelings similar to my own childish feelings of delight at the

Automat, when he said: "To have your own stack of nickels placed in your hands; to be able to choose your own food, richly on display like museum pieces; to make quick and final decisions at the age of eight; this was a lesson in financial dealings that not even two years at the Wharton Business School could buy today."

Horn & Hardart Automats first opened in Philadelphia in 1902 and ten years later in New York City on Times Square. The Automat was not only praised in plays and prose, but also in song. The Hardart was an eccentric musical instrument with sounds spewed from plucked strings, popped balloons and piccolo whistles. Peter Schickele, known publicly by his pseudonym of *P.D.Q. Bach* for musical parodies, composed a *Concerto for Horn and Hardart* which musically quoted Mozart's 29th Symphony. The third movement, *"Minuetto con panna e zuccero"*, translates in the Italian music score as *"Minuette with cream and sugar"*. Schickele's Horn was a regular orchestral-tubed horn. The Hardart instrument was a piece of machinery. As with the Automat dispenser, the orchestral Hardart had small windows next to which the musician had to insert coins into a slot. This opened the panes that played the Concerto instead of dispensing food. A final classical touch was the etched inscription on the Hardart: *"Minor Labis Matris"* (translation: *"Less Work for Mother"* the Horn & Hardart advertising slogan.)

A particular favorite Automat dish of mine was the chicken pot pie, with its flaky crust, more vegetables and less sauce than today's retail pot pies. Other favorites were macaroni and cheese casseroles and Boston baked beans in an individual bean pot.

Horn & Hardart had a strict 'no food left overnight' policy for its restaurants and retail shops. Any of the nearly 400 menu items leftovers at the end of the day were trucked to "day-old shops" in low-income New York and Philadelphia neighborhoods to sell at reduced prices.

At the Automat, there were 'dolphin-head' spouts pouring coffee and hot chocolate into your cup on the counter-affixed tray. Coffee was dumped and brewed fresh every 20 minutes. After two generations at a nickel, the cost of a cup of coffee or a glass of milk at the Automat rose to a dime.

I sat at a distance apart from adults to avoid attracting unwelcome attention as a youngster alone. I quickly learned to move a chair at a selected table to another table so that there would only be one seat at my table.

After the Automat, I often browsed in Macy's Herald Square, then the largest department store in the world. I enjoyed the beautiful window displays, particularly the animated display figurines revolving on tinseled turntables in tune to holiday music. I traversed the grand aisle along the main floor, then went up the clacking wooden escalator to the sixth floor Toy and Sporting Goods departments. When I had saved up some money, I comparison-shopped at Macy's and then bought the same items cheaper at Gimbel's, two blocks south on Sixth Avenue and 32nd Street. The great retail store rivalry between Macy's and Gimbel's persisted for nearly a century.

Sandwiched between Macy's and Gimbel's was the upscale department store Saks 34th Street. Saks and Gimbel's were joined by a connecting upper three-story copper-clad enclosed bridge. Store prices and decor at monochromatic, flat-ceilinged Gimbel's were plainer than at Macy's. But Gimbel's had some famous customers too. For instance, Mrs. Louis Armstrong bought his famous showy pocket handkerchiefs there!

I also enjoyed browsing the Stamp department on Gimbel's mezzanine level, and the famous Bargain Basement where

Mickey Spillane had once worked in 1940 before embarking on his career as a crime author.

Gimbel's Bargain Basement, with its mirrored columns, was the first of its kind. It opened during the Depression years. Burrowing in their basement bin for shoes and suits was a favorite pastime for many shoppers. My feet were large, growing to a size 14 by the time I was a teen. Most New York stores then did not carry shoes larger than size 12. In the bins, with shoe pairs all tied together, were piles of all different sizes with a few 13s and 14s. Sometimes the pairs separated, and my challenge was to find the matching shoe, often near the bottom of the pile, then try it on for fit with no service help. Shoes cost five dollars a pair in the Gimbel's basement bins. They were sometimes a little scuffed, but a quick shine made them presentable again. Gimbel's advertising motto was "Nobody, but nobody, undersells Gimbel's." They lived up to that motto. During Gimbel's final months, the *NY Times* reminisced on March 27, 1987, about the store's founding days. "The moralistic reserve of the building's design corresponds to a sort of missionary zeal about the store, reflected in a speech by one of the Gimbel brothers when the cornerstone was laid in 1909." Mr. Gimbel declared, *"A great modern store helps to make the buying of goods absolutely safe to even the most inexperienced. It is a great university for the training of character and upright dealing."* Macy's and Gimbel's were the twin retail royalty of Herald Square. The Gimbel's stores closed in 1987. *(Rest in peace, dear Gimbel's!)*

Sometimes, instead of going to Herald Square, I strolled west on 42nd Street after exiting from Grand Central Station. Passing the iconic marble lions, named Patience and Fortitude, which guarded the steps of the Public Library, I headed towards Times Square. Cheap electronic and clothing shops lined both sides of 42nd Street past Sixth Avenue westwards past Times Square and Broadway to Eighth Avenue. I once bought a sports shirt locally there for two dollars, but it fell apart and ripped at the seams after a few weeks. After that, I never shopped on that block again, having learned my first adult shopping lesson. 'Caveat emptor' *('Let the buyer beware').*

New York Public Library
Main Branch
42nd Street & Fifth Ave.

Crossing Seventh Avenue, I passed Hubert's Dime Museum near the southeast corner of Times Square and entered to spend some coins. There was a mechanical kicking soccer game, pinball machines that flashed and dinged when you scored points, live circus acts and Professor Heckler's Flea Circus. I sometimes paused at Hubert's gypsy fortune telling machine to watch it run. The old gypsy lady would nod and wink, pass her hands over her crystal ball as the lights dimmed to the tune of an eerie 'diddle-de-dee.' Then the fortune card spat out of the slot as the light went out and the machine went silent until the next play. The card would read, "a tall mysterious stranger will reward you handsomely for your services" or some other trite prediction.

The flea circus at Hubert's Dime Museum had a colorful, glass-enclosed, small table-sized stage with miniature props such as carts and autos being pulled, or Ferris wheels turned, by tiny strong-legged fleas that could move many times their own weight. The fleas were attached to the props by thin gold harnesses, and their efforts to escape resulted in random crawling motions around the stage. A ringmaster was in charge.

I researched the topic of trained fleas in the library, and was disappointed to learn that the fleas were not really trained and did not run purposefully. These were 'running fleas' by natural instinct.

There was another flea type selected by the ringmaster—the 'jumpers'. Their harnesses were attached to small ping pong balls. As the flea tried to jump away from the ball, they would be moving the ball instead, as if playing soccer. Since fleas only lived a few months, the flea circus would have to replenish its 'herd' often.

Among the attractions I remember was the Israeli 'Jewish Giant', Eddie Carmel, who was over eight feet tall. Then there was also the Bearded Lady, who used the stage name of Lady Olga. Her bushy black beard was over a foot long, with a mustache to match. Otherwise she was quite feminine in appearance. Her husband and manager was Mr. O'Boyle, ex-clown and sideshow barker.

Also, along 42nd street in the 1940s and '50s, there were seven or eight glitzy movie theaters between Broadway and Eighth Avenue. They blazed forth in neon signage touting their shows, ranging from first run movies to seedy re-runs and porno films. In between the movie houses were tourist-luring camera, clothing, and appliance stores of dubious reputation and deep discount prices. There was also a fast food luncheonette offering 10 cent hot dogs and 15 cent hamburgers. So a quick snack there was within my budget.

There were "No Minors Allowed" signs very prominently displayed outside on the doors or covered-over windows, and the stores enforced it. Painted ladies were lounging around in the mid-block hotel doorway, where they could retreat inside quickly if a policeman approached. Their skirts were very short, and they smiled at all the men passing or nearby. A few of them even smiled at me— *(I didn't know why then!)*. Innocently, I smiled back.

All New York City Mayors, since the days Grandpa was young, had publicly vowed to clean up tawdry Times Square from its crude burlesque, cheap entertainment and gaudy neon signs that beckoned and bedazzled tourists and locals passing by. Sideshow hawkers and hot dogs for a dime lured one and all for the loose coins in their pockets.

28

Palisades Park Beckons the Bronx

*A*cross the wide Hudson River, beyond Manhattan, were the flowing mysteries of the Jersey shore. There was distant Palisades Park, thirty acres of rides and amusements on the plateau atop the shore-line cliffs. It was a short ferry ride away on the Hudson River from Harlem.

A new black family had recently moved into the basement of the apartment house across the street from us. The father, Mr. Meyerson, became superintendent of his building. There were two sons, Henry and Randolph, and a daughter Becky. Randolph was around Bernie's age, eleven at the time, when we first met at PS 11 in the sixth grade accelerated class.

Henry, the oldest Meyerson kid, was fourteen years old and Becky (Rebecca) was age five. Henry was hostile to Bernie when they met and to all white kids in general. Becky was a little on the wild side, and dared to say 'hello' to Bernie once before Henry pulled her away.

Randolph, nicknamed Randy or 'Randy the Dandy' was a bright student who was diligent in class. He was slender, well-spoken, above average height and handsome with light brown complexion. The 'Dandy' part of his nickname came from his dressing sharply in conservative colors of shirt, slacks and sweaters. Unlike other boys, he did not wear dungarees, and took some teasing for that.

His answers, when called upon in class, were usually correct and well-reasoned. Randy and Bernie soon gravitated towards each other in friendship, and often walked home together after school. They talked about current events, sports, parents, classical music and girls among other subjects.

At first, Randy and Bernie were unconcerned about how others might feel about their being friends across color lines. It was an unusual 'hanging out' relationship between a black kid and a white kid in the University Heights section of the Bronx at that time. They were not trying to make any kind of racial statement. It was a simple liking and sharing of interests.

There was some pressure on Randy from his older brother to not "mess around with a white boy." When Bernie visited Randy's apartment, his brother was barely civil to him. However, his mother and father were more cordial. Bernie pretended not to notice the brother's hostility.

Bernie wanted to invite Randy over for dinner. He approached Mom with determination shortly after Dad came home from work the next afternoon. He asked, "Mom, I want to invite Randy over for dinner. Would tomorrow night be okay?" Mom looked startled. "What! You mean Randy, the super's kid from across the street?"

"Yes. Randy. He's very nice, invited me over to his place yesterday, and I would like to get to know him better." Mom objected immediately, but for a reason I did not expect. She complained,

"What would the neighbors think if they saw me invite a black boy over to dinner here?"

To Bernie's surprise, since he rarely opposed anything that Mom said, Dad chimed in.

"Aw, Rosy! Randy is a nice boy and I think it's okay to invite him." Mom relented grudgingly.

"All right, but we must keep the blinds down so no one will see him here!"

Dad and Bernie reluctantly agreed to close the blinds, and the Seiden family apartment became integrated.

The next day Bernie confided to Randy about his dreams of visiting Palisades Park. Dad offered to take the boys there together. But that trip with Randy never happened because Palisades banned people of color from entering their huge saltwater wave pool. It was filled by pumping water from the Hudson River, some two hundred feet below the Palisades cliff. The water was measurably salty. The pool was 400 feet wide by 600 feet long in size, and its surface waters were stirred by rotating pontoons from behind the picturesque waterfall. This created one-foot waves to enhance the pool swimming experience with an 'ocean surf' feel.

In his early school days, Bernie was innocent of understanding the concept of homosexuality. He thought the buzzword 'gay' meant being of a partying spirit, and that 'queer' meant being cuckoo. Randy belonged to the Drama Club at school, and performed in 'black boy roles'.

Palisades Park

Randy thought himself to be fully accepted there and not discriminated against. *After all, this was the Bronx, not Mississippi!* Then, in a spirit of his imagined color-blind acceptance, Randy tried out unsuccessfully for the role of Romeo in the Shakespearian romance for the school play "Romeo and Juliet". Fortunately, he did not audition to be Juliet! *Ironically, he might have landed that part, done well and never lived it down afterwards!*

From Bernie's readings in history, he learned that the style of young English noblemen (called 'dandies') in the late 18th and 19th centuries was to 'put on airs', flouncing around in ruffles, laces, and tight pants; dousing themselves with perfume and lavender. These were mannerisms that in today's world would be deemed effeminate. However, most of these dandies were basically masculine, and they would quickly draw their swords to defend against any slur about their manhood.

Poor Randy! He had no sword to draw. His own brother, John Henry, was usually indifferent to protecting Randy. Several white boys in the school began to bully him early in the school term. It started with name-calling. "Faggit!" "Girlie-boy" They shouted at him derisively. Each day, it escalated and turned uglier. Randy was afraid of retaliation if he reported them. The school authorities would only protect him in the building or on the school property, but not off their premises after school.

One Friday afternoon in early October, Bernie was coming out of school to meet near the Macombs Road side entrance. Bernie's final class of the day ran ten minutes after Randy's class ended. Three white boy bullies followed him across the street, taunting him repeatedly. Then they grabbed him and dragged him across Macombs Road onto a vacant lot on nearby Nelson Avenue. Bernie ran after them, and followed the bullies to the lot. No one else on the street nearby noticed or bothered to try to intervene. To his horror he saw that they had spread-eagled him bent over a large boulder and had pulled down his pants! In their blood-lust intensity, they did not notice Bernie right away, nor did they expect that any white boy would come to Randy's rescue!

With his right hand, Bernie grabbed a stout tree limb off the ground and a fist-sized rock in his left. One boy quickly fell from a clout to his head, then staggered to his feet and ran off. The second one turned towards me and was socked in the jaw with my rock. The third hesitated, then let go of Randy and scurried away screaming.

I helped Randy to his feet, adjusted his clothes and reassured him.

"It's OK, Randy. I'm here now. C'mon. I'll take you home."

"Oh, Bernie, I'm okay now. But I don't want to report this. White teachers and principals will not stick up for a black boy. You know that, too."

"Yeah, but there are some black cops who would listen. Are you willing to file a complaint?? I will support you as a witness."

"No, no! Don't make trouble. You gave them a good lesson not to be bullies. They won't bother me again. I'll start a rumor that a black high school gang from Clinton will protect me."

Bernie smiled. *Randy was good at gossip —it would probably work...*

He spontaneously hugged Bernie who felt a momentary unease. *Boys do not hug boys—it's unnatural,* he thought. Bernie was too young to grasp the adult-level concept of male homosexual fear underlying that principle. *It's okay to hug a man or boy if it's your Dad of family,* he thought. Hesitantly, he shook hands with Randy in 'Grown-up Man' style. Then Bernie walked him home, only two blocks away, with right arm around Randy's shoulder. He was not his usual exuberant self. Mrs. Myerson met us at the door.

"Land sakes!", she exclaimed. "What happened to you, Randy?"

"Three white boys tried to beat me up. Bernie stopped them."

Bernie shrugged. "It's okay. I would have done the same for any friend that was assaulted from my school."

Mrs. Myerson thanked Bernie and offered a five dollar reward, which he politely declined.

The shadow of racial discrimination outside the deep South hung over Palisades Park and its pool. This feeling intensified in

1946 as returning black veterans, who had risked their lives and fought for America, sought equal access to 'the good life' in leisure time activities at amusement parks and in other aspects of post-war life. African-American protesters began picketing the Palisades Avenue gate demanding:

"Jim Crow" must go!

This New Jersey anti-bigotry slogan appeared nearly ten years before Martin Luther King's civil rights demonstrations and the boycotts that began over that issue in the Deep South.

Wikipedia describes the civil rights turmoil at Palisades Park as follows: *"The summer of 1947 would see the protests continue and become larger in scope. Melba Valle, a 22-year-old African-American woman from New York, attempted to gain admission to the pool using a ticket purchased by her friend who was white on the morning of July 13, 1947. The ticket in Valle's hands was not honored and she was denied admission to the pool. According to newspaper accounts Valle was "forcibly dragged and ejected" from the Park."*

This rampant discrimination led to Congress of Racial Equality (CORE) demonstrations at the Park gates. Less than a month after Ms.Valle's ejection from the Park, eleven members of CORE were arrested. Demonstrators vowed to return to protest at the Park gates every Sunday until blacks were admitted entrance to the pool.

A copy of the flyer being handed out at the Palisades Park gates by CORE members was circulating among some of the older students in Bronx schools.

Dad and Bernie were very outraged by this discrimination and vowed never to go to the Park until that policy changed. That took several more years to happen. The stark language of the flyer (on exhibit in the Fort Lee Museum) speaks for itself. **"DON'T GET COOL AT PALISADES POOL"**

> *"Palisades Pool, in violation of the New Jersey Civil Rights Law, bars Negroes and persons with dark skins. Such a person is told that a club exists and only members can use the pool. Yet white persons who are not "members" are regularly admitted and then handed a "membership" card inside. Irving Rosenthal, the Park's owner, refuses to cease racial discrimination, although it violates the New Jersey Law. Members of our interracial group who tried peacefully to gain admittance to the pool have been manhandled by the Park's private guards and by Fort Lee police. On July 27 of that year, a Negro was blackjacked from behind by a park cop while other park 'goons' were shoving him on a bus. On August 3, eleven members of the CORE group were arrested on trumped-up charges, and two were beaten by the police."*

More of a deterrent to visiting the Park than the occasional bruises and broken bones of the other rough rides was the perilous Cyclone Roller Coaster, located near the outer cliff edge of the Palisades pool.

Less popular than the Palisades pool was the rough-riding Cyclone Roller Coaster, located near the outer cliff edge of the Palisades. Only ten percent of first-time Cyclone riders dared to repeat the bruising experience, compared with forty percent repeat riders on other typical amusement park roller coasters of that era.

Over the course of the summer, the continuing family pressure from brother Henry to curtail Randy's friendship with Bernie became too much to withstand, and their friendship sadly withered away under a barrage of cancellation excuses each time we were to meet. After awhile Bernie got the message. But he always cherished the memory of that summer of friendship with Randy.

Atlantic City Trip Interrupted: Aunt Dolly Elopes

*B*ernie's family took yearly auto trips to visit Aunt Dolly in Atlantic City, New Jersey. This was a highlight of the family summer season. Aunt Dolly was a petite, tough-looking brash blonde with a face wrinkled by many years of sunning on the Atlantic City beach. She was colorful, volatile and exciting. Dolly hung out at City Hall with the Mayor and his buddies—the only lady player in their weekly backroom politicians' poker game. She played a daring game, sometimes bluffing her way into a winning pot by drawing to an inside straight or faking the others out with a pair of deuces.

This was the old Atlantic City before the casinos came. The grand seaside hotels, the Boardwalk with its amusement arcades, the Heinz 57 Varieties exhibit pier, the Million Dollar Pier and others stretched out into the ocean. Longest of all was the Steel Pier with its famous Diving Horse act, and submarine Diving Bell. One admission ticket for three dollars covered all the attractions for a day-long adventure. Fralinger's Salt Water Taffy, feeding Boardwalk strollers since 1886, gave the oceanfront air an extra flavor with the sweet scent of cotton candy spun before the eyes of tourists.

Barkers hawked their wares to lure passersby as the roller chairs pushed past straw-hatted men and their ladies strolling along the Boardwalk. In its heyday, the sleek black, cream and silver Art Deco trolley cars of the Margate-Ventnor line could outrun almost any diesel-powered local street bus. The trolleys sped along their twin-tracked north and south right-of-way west of Atlantic Avenue.

Just before the annual Miss America Pageant in September 1948, an unexpected phone call came from Aunt Dolly in Atlantic City to Bernie's mother.

"Hello, Rose, how are you?"

"Hello, Dolly. How are you and Izzy doing? Are your kids still objecting to your dating him?" Smugly, Dolly replied, "Izzy is doing fine, thanks, and sends his regards."

Dolly hesitated. She had been dating her elderly boyfriend for nearly a year. Her adult children objected strenuously to his courting Dolly, fearing that their potential inheritance would be jeopardized. So they pressured any potential suitors, and did their best to chase away her occasional boyfriends on one pretext or another.

"Rose, I've got news for you. Izzy and I eloped last night to Maryland and got married!"

"What!" Mom nearly dropped the phone. "C-c-congratulations," she stammered.

"We just came home and I wanted you to be the first to know."

"You are not a love-struck teen-ager. How could you do this without any notice to the family? Was there a rabbi officiating, at least?"

"No, it was done by a Justice of the Peace."

Mom groaned. "Oy vey, not a Jewish wedding! The family will be very upset. I am upset too, but I wish you good luck, anyway. You will need it. Are you going away for a honeymoon?"

"No, not for a few days till I settle with my children about my marriage."

Mom said firmly, "I am standing by you on this matter. I will come down to help you talk it over with the family. I'll be bringing Bernie and Gloria."

Bernie often overheard what was being discussed when adults did not know he was nearby. As a last resort, to stop Aunt Dolly's love life, his cousins had even threatened violence against her boyfriend. The gossip line that whispered around in the family was that (a few months before the elopement) Cousin Sam yelled at some man on the phone, "Stay away from my mother or I'll break your neck!" *Was it Izzy?*

Yes! Dolly's new beau was … Izzy the Tailor! That's what the family renamed him mockingly. They assumed he was poor, because of his slightly shabby looks and clothes. Izzy was nearly eighty, spry and wizened in face and neck. He smiled nicely, with all his teeth still in place, and told funny jokes in English and Yiddish.

Izzy had met Dolly away from the house, so their romance stayed secret from the family for the first few months of their relationship. Dolly was finally found out by Cousin Sam spotting her a few months later, holding hands with Izzy on the Boardwalk.

The only adults in the family who took Dolly's side were Aunt Irma and Bernie's Mom. The others said "Dolly, you are too old to get involved with a man, anyway." Then, sneeringly, "Besides, he is a poor prospect for marriage and will live off you." That was the last straw. She shouted at them, "Izzy is not poor. He is just not a fancy-looking type of guy!"

Both Bernie's cousins, Sam and Hilda, Aunt Dolly's children by George, her late husband, had low-rent apartments living with their spouses in Dolly's main apartment house. She was the real estate tycoon of the family, and owned three small apartment buildings and a string of boarding houses near the Boardwalk.

Dolly had started her small real estate empire with one rooming house, bought with a three year mortgage in the Depression years, financed by late Uncle George's insurance policy. As the war years progressed, she pyramided her properties, buying a second house, then a third, and a fourth, etc.

If any politicos needed a few hours or an overnighter with their girlfriends, Dolly saved her fanciest rooms for them. Bernie saw one of these rooms once, when the door was open. He asked innocently, "Mom, why can't we stay in the fancy room with red velvet drapes and naked lady pictures?" Mom turned beet red and stammered, "That's a special room, not for us." Of course Bernie was too young to know what Mom meant by 'special'!

Dolly was widowed five years before Bernie was born. In the waning days of Prohibition, George, her first husband, had one too many drinks one night in a Pacific Avenue gin mill and decided to go for a midnight swim.

His body washed ashore the next morning in the Inlet, still clutching his last pint of Bud. Even in death, the booze stayed with him. Dolly shed a few ritual tears at the funeral, and then was back at her office the next day to close a real estate deal. She told Mom: "George would have wanted it that way."

Dolly liked to play the 'merry widow', and had a series of older boyfriends before Izzy, who were charmed by her sixty-ish youthfulness. In those days, it was expected that older widows would stay in black attire, withdraw discreetly to their parlors, and take to needlework and babysitting for grandchildren. Not Aunt Dolly! Aunt Irma shared the story of Dolly's elopement years later with Bernie when he was old enough to begin to understand adult romance.

Years later, Bernie learned from Irma how fantastically daring it had been for the elderly couple to pull off Dolly's elopement right under the noses of her adult children! Izzy had sneaked around to the back of the house, by pre-arrangement, to stand under Dolly's bedroom on the second floor. At age eighty, he climbed up the fire escape to spirit his sweetheart away! *What a guy he must have been in his younger days to still have that much energetic vitality left in his senior years!*

Dolly waited by the window. A soft tap sounded; and there stood Izzy, perched on the ladder, silhouetted in the moonlight. Dolly handed him her suitcase through the opened window and followed him down to his parked car around the back of the house. They sped off, like eloping teenagers, to Maryland in the middle of the night, where a local justice of the peace awaited them in his pajamas. After the ceremony, a Maryland 'No Tell Motel' awaited them for that night.

Of course, when Dolly did not come down for breakfast the next morning, the family became frantic and called the police. They said to wait 24 hours before making a report. Working the phone and searching the local neighborhoods all day, the family did not locate her. Just before dinner, Mom, Dad, Bernie and Gloria arrived at Dolly's apartment. A few minutes later, the newlyweds drove up and emerged from Izzy's Packard at the front entrance of the house for the first time instead of down the block or around the corner.

The family did not know that Izzy owned a 1948 Packard Super 8—that was not a poor man's car! Peeking out of a front window, the cousins watched in stunned silence as Dolly and Izzy emerged from the Packard and came to the door.

1948 Packard Super 8

Dolly barged into the dining room and triumphantly flashed her two-carat diamond ring. "I am now Mrs. Isidore Shapiro!", she declared. Cousin Sam nearly choked, the others managed to mumble congratulations. Mom kissed her sister Dolly and new brother-in-law Izzy, and beamed at the new 'old couple'. Welcome to the family, Izzy", she said. It was one of Mom's finest moments.

Invoking seniority privilege as the oldest child present, Bernie offered boyish congratulations to his old aunt and new uncle. "Uncle Izzy," he asked, "Can Gloria and I have a ride in your new car?" Bernie had never seen a Packard up close before. It was two-tone silver gray. It seemed, in his eyes, to be a half-block long. Izzy said "Yes," Mom nodded her approval, and off Bernie and Gloria went for a spin along Atlantic Avenue with Aunt Dolly and Uncle Izzy.

When they returned from their ride, the shocked cousins were arguing animatedly among themselves, now reinforced by Mom and Dad's presence. Gloria and Bernie were told to play in the next room. They were afraid to be caught listening at the door; but at one point, Dolly yelled loudly enough for all within earshot to hear the argument briefly. "I am sick of all your butting into my affairs. I am not a little girl to be forbidden to socialize with boys." About a half hour later, all were called in for supper and the cousins were all smiling. Something had been settled!

The family was staring out the window at Uncle Izzy's spiffy new Packard. And he was telling them about his four dry cleaning and tailoring shops in Philadelphia. "So," Aunt Dolly announced, "Now let's plan for a kosher wedding." A few days later, Bernie's parents went home to the Bronx and the cousins began getting ready for the wedding.

The phone lines buzzed—department stores, bridal shops, printers, limousines, orchestra and, of course, a Rabbi! All local Rabbis were busy before the High Holidays, but some extra cash offered made one of them 'un-busy' and family plans went full speed ahead for a traditional Jewish wedding two weeks later.

Atlantic City catering halls were impossible to book on such short notice, but due to a late cancellation, the family 'lucked out' and booked the Claridge Hotel ballroom at the last minute. Meanwhile, Mom had packed suits for Bernie and Dad, and a beautiful dress for Gloria.

Then came Aunt Dolly's 'official' wedding day. Izzy's family arrived from Pennsylvania, and his middle-aged son Fred served as best man. Now Bernie had a whole new set of cousins, all much older than he. Some were even older than Dad!

But Gloria and Bernie, as Dolly's young niece and nephew, were untroubled by the misgivings of their older cousins. Their congratulations and kisses to Dolly and Izzy were heartfelt. Later, as Bernie cozied up to Izzy, he revealed that he was an enthusiastic stamp collector. The new family bonding was sealed, and Bernie had a new uncle.

On the wedding day, the skies were bright and sunny, and

the seagulls circling overhead screeched and squawked. It was Sunday afternoon at the Claridge on the Boardwalk, and the wedding guests strolled among the potted palms, often greeting or sometimes avoiding each other.

The old Claridge, still standing today, is known as the 'Skyscraper by the Sea'. It was the Queen of the Boardwalk. Built in 1930, its 24 floors made it the tallest building in Atlantic City before the casinos came. Some local politicians and the Mayor also came to the wedding. Bernie's hungry pre-adolescent focus was fixed on the buffet table, not the distinguished guests or the fancy dining room.

The Claridge Hotel, Atlantic City

This was the first wedding that young Bernie and Gloria were ever invited to attend. They reacted as if it were the grandest spectacle in the world. At the buffet table, chopped liver on oval silver platters was sculpted into hearts lined with miniature tomato slices and greens. There were herrings and pickled beets and salads galore.

Bernie and his cousin Mikey briefly tried to chat with each other. He was bright and interesting, and only two years older than Bernie. Then his mother, Aunt Alice, swooped down and dragged him away. Aunt Alice did not get along with Mom, therefore Mikey and Bernie were forbidden to play or talk together.

Aunt Alice was afraid that Bernie would 'contaminate' her Mikey somehow. It took many years for Bernie to begin to understand family politics, which separated generations of his family into bitter quarreling factions continuing for decades.

It was not an orthodox Jewish wedding, so men and women were not separated at the ceremony. Afterwards, the symbolic glass wrapped inside a napkin was broken. Then the band played traditional Jewish favorites, striking up a lively Klezmer rhythm.

Dolly and Izzy led the way onto the dance floor for their first dance as a couple. She looked maturely radiant in pale blue chiffon, and Izzy looked like sixty, instead of eighty, in his blue tux with satin lapels.

But Izzy soon got winded and Dolly danced on with her brothers and Dad in turn, wearing them all out one by one. After about twenty minutes, she danced on alone, as others left the dance floor. With a final graceful twirl, she curtsied off the dance floor as the family applauded. This was a beautiful ending to a beautiful wedding.

The next morning, Izzy and Dolly took off for a honeymoon in the Catskills, and Bernie's parents prepared to return to New York. But first, Dad, Bernie and Gloria went for a final walk on the Boardwalk, strolling north along its herringbone-patterned planks, savoring the colorful seashore sights and reveling in Atlantic City's carnival atmosphere.

Seagulls swooped down along the way to snag a scrap or two, often stealing from each other in deft flapping and beaking maneuvers. Gloria giggled, but she did not want to stop to watch them. Not even the cotton candy spun by hawkers at their food carts tempted her. She had one fixed objective in mind: "Daddy, Daddy! Bernie!" she shrieked suddenly, pointing ahead. "It's Mr. Peanut!" For that, they HAD to stop!

And there he stood all his shelled glory in front of the Planters Peanut store. Resplendent in top hat and tux, and sporting his trademark monocle and white spats, he twirled his cane and bowed to Gloria. Gloria curtsied back to him, with pigtails sliding across her shoulders. He waved us into the store as she gave him a parting hug. The overpowering sweet smell of fresh roasted peanuts assailed us at the door. In we went for some nut snacks. Gloria could not decide between the honey coated peanuts or almonds. Bernie generously treated her to the almonds while Dad bought her the peanuts.

On the western side of the Boardwalk was the Planter's Peanut Store, and the Steel Pier was on the eastern ocean side, stretching one third of a mile out into the churning Atlantic surf.

Generously, Gloria shared the nuts with Bernie. Exiting Planter's with their cheeks stuffed, their eyes feasted on the Steel Pier across the Boardwalk, with its General Motors exhibit, three movie theaters and the world-famous Diving Horse.

They continued on north towards the Inlet. Mom joined them later for lunch at Hackney's Restaurant, run by Harry Hackney the self-styled 'Lobster King'. He was also famed for his Lobster Waitresses, past prize winners in the Atlantic City Famous Beauty Pageant Parade on the Boardwalk. When serving, they were known as the 'two hundred waitresses with two hundred smiles'.'

After lunch, Dad and the family made ready to forsake the sands of Atlantic City for the six-hour drive in stop-and-go local highway driving through New Jersey coastal towns to return to the asphalt streets of the Bronx. (The much faster New Jersey Turnpike and Garden State Parkway route for New Yorkers going to Atlantic City was still almost a decade away from construction.)

30

Truman, Israel and Junior Smuggler Bernie

Truman overrode the traditional mindset of the State Department and supported the creation of the Jewish state of Israel. He recognized the new nation eleven minutes after it was announced by David Ben Gurion on May 14, 1948 at 4 p.m. (Jerusalem time) before sundown and the onset of the Jewish Sabbath.

President Truman was called 'Harry the Haberdasher' by some newspapers. On election eve, reporters sometimes slipped (before the polls closed) and addressed Governor Tom Dewey as "Mr. President". The 1948 election, according to national popularity polls, seemed likely to elect the first Republican to the White House in twenty years.

Truman's Whistlestop Presidential Campaign of 1948

Bernie read about Truman's published accomplishments as President Roosevelt's successor, and became convinced that the press, the public and the polls had greatly underestimated him. Boldly, Bernie spoke out in social studies class and predicted that Truman would be re-elected. The teacher smiled indulgently, but brushed aside Bernie's arguments.

Harry Truman was 'giving 'em Hell' from the rear platform on his 'whistle-stop' campaign train barreling across the country. Bernie noticed that the kids who laughed the loudest at his political forecasting were the same ones who were dumbstruck when it came their turn to discuss the current events of the day.

Bernie's Dad, with his limited knowledge of world events,

knew that Tom Dewey was the New York State governor and a former district attorney; but he depended on Bernie to explain current events and politics to him. Bernie's Mom did not read the news at all, but she believed radio newscasts declaring that Roosevelt had been a good President. She had no political opinion on Truman.

Presidential Election Day, 1948 arrived. School was out in the Bronx, since lunchrooms and gyms were requisitioned for election machines. In the early evening, Bernie's classmates were out playing under neighborhood playground lights, while he was planted in front of the radio to hear a state-by-state election scorecard from WCBS. As results slowly trickled in, Bernie scribbled data and projections on a notepad. The early returns showed Dewey ahead in the eastern states. Bernie lost his battle to stay awake until the final results were in. He fell asleep dreaming of his planned consolation letter to President Truman if the President lost the election. After some Midwestern states swung to Truman, he held a close popular and electoral lead going into the morning hours after the election polls had closed. The rest of this 1948 election battle is history. After a delayed count, California swung to Truman in the wee hours of the morning, and his re-election was assured by daybreak Wednesday.

Bernie woke up, dashed out for the morning papers and gazed excitedly at the headline "HST IN!".

There, beaming all over the front page, was Harry Truman, laughing and holding up the famous wrong headline, from the Chicago Tribune, "DEWEY WINS!" "We did it, we did it!," Bernie yelled. *He wondered if Mr. Truman would have time to read a congratulatory telegram from a ten year-old boy?*

TRUMAN WINS

Soon after the election, Bernie was recruited by a local Israeli Boy Scout group, operating secretly among some of his schoolmates, to become a junior smuggler for the new nation of Israel. In mid-May 1948, Great Britain surrendered their Palestine mandate which was granted by the old pre-war League of Nations in September, 1923. Immediately after their declaration of statehood, Israel was attacked on all sides by Egypt, Jordan, Syria and other Arab states. The Jewish nation was plunged into an immediate crisis of weapons shortage. International groups formed to smuggle arms to Israel to supplement aid from governments that Israeli was receiving.

Bernie's group was disguised as an Israeli scouting and work program at kibbutzes in the Negev. The Israeli scouts wore uniforms with Star of David patches, sang Israeli songs and were sponsored by American supporters of the *Haganah*, the Israeli military forces.

This was very heady and exciting stuff for a young Bronx Jewish boy. The scouts trained with broomstick guns, and marched in military formations while puzzled parents applauded. Unlike official American Boy Scouts and Cub Scouts, the Israeli scout group did not have den mothers or den fathers. The meetings were held behind closed doors and on field outings with simulated arms training, on toy rifles with bayonets. The boys took an oath and were sworn to secrecy with a grim threat of retribution if we revealed anything about our 'scouting group' to parents or anyone else outside the group.

A super-secret 'presents for children in Israel' project began within the scout groups. The cover story was that we were wrapping and sending toys for poor Israeli schoolchildren's birthdays and Hanukkah holidays. What we were actually doing was painting real guns with cheap 'plastic gray' paint to look like toy guns! Secret connections were established with major toy suppliers to provide branded toy stick-on labels. Enclosed handwritten birthday, get well, or holiday greeting cards were stuffed in with the 'gifts'. They were packed for export to Israel as toys, and routed via the Port of Newark, where a sympathetic Irish customs inspector rubber-stamped his approval on the outbound boxes. Our scouts were a junior auxiliary to *Machal,* a Hebrew acronym for foreign volunteers in the cause of Israel's fight for freedom. Of course, it is not really known, even today, whether the Irish supported the cause of Israel out of sympathy to the Jewish cause, or were just looking for a time and place to fight their own revenge against Great Britain for its centuries of colonizing and suppressing Ireland. It may have been for both reasons.

Some Irish pilots also joined the new Israeli Air Force—which had no military planes at first, only Piper Cubs and other light civilian aircraft. The aviators carried bombs on their laps and they were strapped in so as not fall out with the bombs when they were dropped.

Among the first military planes procured by the Israeli Air Force were 25 Czech-built Messerschmitts 109s, purchased before the Iron Curtain rang down in East Europe. The Soviet Union later forbade its East European satellites from any further arms sales to Israel. These Messerschmitt fighters had been the backbone of the German Air Force (the Luftwaffe!). Reichsmarshall Hermann Goering would have been mortified at the spectacle of his finest aircraft becoming the founding air arm of the new Jewish state! They were shipped to Israel in such haste that some landed with hastily painted-over swastikas still showing through the gray battle paint!

31

The Melting Pot

There was little or no friction between ethnic groups in Bernie's West Bronx neighborhood. The local population was closely divided between Irish, Italians and Jews, together with a handful of Colored and Hispanic people. The Irish and Italian kids were both Catholic and many of them went to St. Mary's, a nearby parochial school on University Avenue.

The local Italian boys were not usually anti-semitic, but some of the neighborhood Irish boys were hostile—calling Jews 'Christ killers'. Several thousand Jews had lived at peace in Ireland, as a small minority in the Irish state for over a thousand years. The great nineteenth century Irish Catholic emancipator, Daniel O'Connell, had said of Irish Jews: *"Ireland has claims to gratitude from your ancient race. It is the only country I know of that was unsullied by any act of persecution of the Jews".* During the 1945-48 post-world war period, as Israel fought for its freedom, several thousand Irish volunteers came to the Holy Land to join the Jewish fight for freedom and nationhood against the British mandate.

Bernie reached a small milestones along the path of his personal independence by starting his first job, at age eleven, delivering the *Bronx Home News* after school. He read it eagerly, particularly the memorable columns by Eleanor Roosevelt titled *My Day (published 1935-62)*. He earned twenty two dollars per week to deliver a hundred papers along an apartment house route near the Grand Concourse. Yes, it was 'Grand' not to need an allowance from his parents anymore!

His route grew modestly to the point where he made almost thirty dollars per week delivering nearly 150 papers. He felt as rich as Rockefeller, and opened his first savings account at the Bronx Savings Bank faithfully saving ten dollars a week.

Eleanor Roosevelt

The *Bronx Home News* covered news in a feisty way to compete with the larger New York papers. It arose to journalistic heights with the daily *My Day* columns of Eleanor Roosevelt. She was Bernie's second-most favorite lady hero, next to Aunt Claire. He admired her outspokenness in sometimes disagreeing with her husband, President Roosevelt. When FDR died in office, she remained active and influential in national life. She served as First Chief Delegate of the United States to the United Nations (1946-52), chairing its Human Rights Commission.

Bernie saved for many years afterwards a *Home News* article clipping that Mrs. Roosevelt wrote as the era of postwar anti-communist paranoia in America dawned. It began: *"Oct. 29, 1947: I never liked the idea of an Un-American Activities*

Committee (in Congress). I have always thought that a strong democracy should stand by its fundamental beliefs, and that a citizen of the United States should be considered innocent until proven guilty. If he is employed in a government position with access to secret and important papers, then for the sake of security he must undergo some special tests. However, I doubt whether the loyalty test adds much to our safety, since no Communist would hesitate to sign it and he would be in good standing until proven guilty. So it seems to me that we might as well do away with a test which is almost an insult to any loyal American citizen."

32

Our Dogs: "Beauty the Second" and "Lucky"

Some of my pre-Bar Mitzvah stress had been relieved by the arrival of a new pet dog into our family. In the years since 'Beauty the First' died after spending her final year of life with us, several dogs came into and quickly left our family life. They were adopted from the Bronx ASPCA shelter. They were mostly disappointments, and were either not housebroken or had other behavior problems. After short-lived struggles to domesticate them, our hopes were dashed and we returned them to the shelter.

Gloria and I kept pleading for a new dog each time our family un-adopted one of these shelter mutts. We both promised to help take care of them. Mom finally decided to try again—this time at an advertised pet shop.

On the beautiful, bright Sunday afternoon of June 25, 1950, Mom, Dad, Gloria, the twins and I all set out on a two-mile family walk to the pet shop on Webster Avenue. It was a long hike, but there were no complaints as we stopped to rest along the way. Gloria and I debated as we walked. She declared, with pigtails swinging for emphasis, "I want a little puppy to pick up and hold and cuddle." I sighed and responded, "A larger dog is better for us to handle, and is less likely to get hurt." The twins sided with Gloria, "Yes, a little puppy, a little puppy." Sensing that I was outvoted, I gave in and said, "Okay, Mom. I agree to a small puppy."

In the middle of this 'animated' walk-and-talk' to the pet store, we passed a street news stand on the Grand Concourse. The headlines screamed:

"WAR!" and "NORTH KOREA INVADES SOUTH!"

My sisters and brother were too young to understand. The puppy was the big news event of the day for them, not Korea. Mom and Dad did not want to say anything about Korea to us kids, but I realized the major implications of what was happening, and the threat of a possible war confrontation with Russia and China.

There were two little black Spitz Pomeranian puppies in the pet shop window, about six weeks old. They were the 'ten dollar advertised special' for the day, including leash and ID tag

We held both puppies separately. One pup was somewhat passive, the other one squirmed actively in our arms. That made the canine choice simple for us—we went for the lively one. My family, on a rare splurge of ten entire dollars, went home in a taxicab with our new pet.

We decided to name her 'Beauty the Second'. She was a perky little black medium-sized female of erratic behavior, not nearly as smart as 'Beauty the First'. Mom handled her with the patience that she often lacked with us kids. Except for a routine veterinary check and spaying in her first year, Beauty did not see a veterinarian again until five years later. I walked Beauty alone in the morning before school. Dad and I walked her each evening together.

This was our 'man to man' communing time in a more relaxed way than if Mom had been with us. Our common bond was a mutual need to escape from her numerous sensitivities and suspicions. She constantly thought we were plotting against her, and sometimes verbally accused us of that after our walks. Sometimes, I was able to coax Gloria into doing the dog walk to relieve me in the morning, but not often.

Beauty the Second

On these walks, Dad and I did not discuss Russia, or the atomic bomb or other world happenings. I tried to educate him a little about current events, but most of it went over his head, so we spoke of local affairs instead.

Dad read only newspaper sports pages and the comics, leaving the rest of the paper to me. He was only too glad to escape from Mom's henpecking, with the excuse of walking the dog. Beauty knew the daily walk time, and always came to us ready to go.

Beauty was a happy dog during the Korean-war years, but later on she became lethargic, excessively hungry and thirsty every day, and needed to be walked several times daily. She began to lose weight and became mopey. I noticed these changes and expressed my concerns to Mom about her lack of energy.

"Mom," I said, "we've got to take Beauty to a vet. Something is wrong. She needs to pee too often. And she is sleeping during the day like an old dog. She never did that before." Mom hesitated. She knew vets were expensive, but for once, she agreed with me. She called and made a late afternoon appointment, then waited for Dad to come home. He readied the canine carry box, and Beauty did not resist being placed into it on a comfortable blanket.

Beauty wagged her tail, sensing that she was about to be taken someplace in the car. When feeling well, she enjoyed car rides, which often ended with a romp in the park. When we arrived at the vet, she sensed that we were not going to the park that day, and began to whine. The other dogs were starting to carry on, so everyone in the waiting room was busy trying to calm them down. After about a half-hour of paperwork, we were shown into Doctor Westmann's office.

The doctor was a middle-aged stout man with a slightly frazzled expression. I suppose that treating several dozen dogs, cats and other animals each day, then as now, can be a nerve-wracking experience. He spoke calmly and pleasantly to Beauty, calling her by name. Sensing that she would likely not resist, he waved off the nurse and lifted her out of the carrier himself onto the examining table. I knew that pet animals are comforted by the nearby presence of their owners when being examined. The diagnosis, based on a blood test and later confirmed by a urine sample was grim ... canine diabetes. A special diet was prescribed, without dry dog foods. Doctor Westmann wrote out a prescription, then told Mom and Dad:

"Beauty is going to need an insulin shot every day for the rest of her life. Which of you is going to do it?"

Dad said, "I guess I will have to be the one."

The doctor sighed, "It won't be easy."

Sensing my cue, I chimed in, "I will help by holding Beauty."

Doctor Westmann demonstrated canine injection to us. It is simpler to do with dogs than with people. It involves bunching up loose canine skin to inject beneath it—no pain or hunting for a vein in the animal. Thus began the doggy insulin ordeal that continued for the next several years. The daily shot was usually done after dinner. I sneaked around behind Beauty, then threw a heavy coat over her and held her down while Dad did 'the honors'. The injection only took two minutes, and it did not really hurt her. Then we petted Beauty and all was well again.

A few months later, things got more complicated to manage Beauty's diabetes. I observed that she was bumping into things more and more often when we walked. *Her eyes!* I thought sadly. *Omigod! Beauty is going blind!* Beauty gazed at me soulfully as I gently cupped her face with my hands. I picked up a flashlight from the kitchen drawer. "Easy, girl, easy," I crooned to her. Then I suddenly shone the flashlight at her face, and she did not blink, gazing at me steadily with her now-filmy eyes. I declared, "Mom, Beauty has gone nearly blind. She does not see the flashlight shining." She waved her hand in front of Beauty's face. No response. I shone the flashlight again, at close range. There was a slight squinting, but no blink. Mom looked stricken. "I will call Dr. Westmann and make an appointment."

At the vet, Beauty sat quietly on the table as he examined her. He frowned and looked at her eyes through a magnifying mirror. "Beauty has inoperable cataracts. Unless you want to have an expensive operation, with only a small chance of success, plus extended aftercare, I recommend that she be put to sleep". Mom looked shocked. "No, no. We will take care of her."

Busy as Mom was with cooking and household chores, I knew that the "we" meant both me and Gloria. She also said "Yes", but I knew that after her initial enthusiasm wore off, I would have to pressure my sister to keep up with her share of doggie nursing.

On a late dog-walking stroll one bitter cold night a few days before Christmas 1950, Dad and I were maneuvering Beauty through a snow-covered street trying to stay within the plowed channels wherever we could. Beauty wore little booties which Mom had knitted for her to keep her paws warm. She still had some vision left, and could sense the whiteness of snow, besides relying on her nose for guidance. Pure snow does not have a smell, but city snow picks up odors from the street which a dog can sense.

A block away from our walk-in apartment, as we passed by a building entrance on West 175th Street, we heard a puppy cry. Huddled in the doorway was a little mixed breed black mutt, shivering and trying unsuccessfully to get warm. We instantly stopped to pick her up. There was no other person in sight. A black car was rapidly heading past me down the block, speeding away and skidding on the snow.

I had two heavy sweaters on underneath, so I bundled up the puppy with my coat. I told Dad, "I better run back to the house now with this poor little pooch. Please finish up Beauty's walk and come home as soon as you can." The puppy did not struggle, and nestled close to my chest.

I entered our apartment. "Mom," I announced. "I have a little surprise bundle for you." I carefully deposited the puppy on the couch. Mom, sympathetic as always to the plight of animals, ran to the bathroom to get a towel.

"Poor thing. Poor thing", Mom murmured. "Where did you find it?"

"In a doorway on 175th Street," I replied.

"Well, we will feed it and warm it up. It must belong to someone. Who would leave a puppy out on a night like this?"

"Mom, I saw fresh tire tracks, and draggy dog footprints in the snow. I think the puppy may have been thrown out of the car and then it scrambled into the doorway to take shelter."

"Bernie", she scoffed. "You've been reading too many detective stories."

I shrugged. "I will ask around the neighborhood if anyone knows this dog."

But my diligent lost dog inquiries resulted in no claims of ownership. So the puppy became ours. Of course, we named her "Lucky", because if Dad and I had not happened along, this cute little doggy would have frozen to death.

Lucky

A few months later, Lucky unexpectedly solved the blind walking problem of Beauty! By coincidence one wintry March afternoon, Beauty and Lucky both felt the urgent need to relieve themselves at the same time. Beauty hesitantly bumped her way to the door, where her leash was hanging on the doorknob.

I attached Lucky's leash and headed for the door. Lucky sensed that we had to wait for Beauty's leash to be snapped to her collar, and then Dad and I would walk them both.

Then it happened. In a rare flash of super-canine intelligence,

Lucky pulled down Beauty's leash from the doorknob and brought it over to me. A sudden idea flashed through my mind ... *Maybe Lucky could walk her! Maybe? Maybe??* I hooked the other leash into Lucky's collar and deliberately left it on the floor.

I opened the door partially and then looked at our two anxious dogs. "Come on Lucky, come on." Beckoning to the door, I said "Take Beauty, Take, Take." Lucky knew the 'take' command—she had learned a few tricks with it and also, 'sit', 'lay down' and some others. What happened next was a huge surprise to me and Dad.

As I opened the door, Lucky picked up Beauty's leash in her mouth, stepped outside as we followed, then trotted off pulling Beauty along. Beauty followed her to the curb. Apparently, Lucky knew where to take Beauty and when to stop for her to sniff and 'do her business'.

Lucky's walks became the talk of the neighborhood. Neighbors and passers-by stared at the spectacle of the smaller 'Lucky' walking the bigger 'Beauty'. Lucky had always been a very meek, mild mannered dog. She was afraid of other dogs and cats, and was often bullied by them.

I recall Lucky shrinking back behind my legs when a cat half her size approached and hissed at her. Now Lucky had changed her manner. When she walked Beauty, timid 'Lucky' changed from a canine Clark Kent into Superdog, growling and showing her teeth to ward off would-be animal bullies away from blind Beauty.

Beauty showed no gratitude towards Lucky and sometimes snapped at her protector. Lucky just edged away from her and took the abuse stoically. Beauty lived on for another two years, before finally succumbing to canine diabetes. Lucky remained as our sole pet for many years afterwards.

A 'walking and talking' bond between Dad and myself developed over the next several years as we walked Lucky in the neighborhood. Most pre-teen and teen-age boys I knew locally had tenuous (at best) or rebellious (at worst) relationships with their fathers. I did not rebel against Dad. I loved him deeply, and felt sorry that his peace-loving disposition made him always give in to Mom's domineering ways.

Dad was a strong believer in the principle of *'Shalom Bayit'*, the Jewish concept of peace in the home. Sometimes he believed too strongly and kept quiet so as not to send Mom into a rage. He would agree with her even when she was wrong. An example of this was her fixation about finding free legal car parking spaces, no matter how long it took to land one.

In those days, local parking meters were a nickel for a half-hour, but Mom would make Dad waste gas and time by driving around a half hour or more to find a free parking space. He did not get irritated and usually submitted to her demanding ways patiently. Dad taught me a great lesson that would guide my relationships with women in my adult life. This was to be a respectful and loving companion to the women who shared their hearts and lives with me.

Dad was also a great gentle teaser. I fondly recall the times that I saw him give Mom an affectionate hug or kiss, and call her 'babe', only to be pushed away because she was 'busy'. But he did not get discouraged, and would try, try again. He told me on one of our dog walks, in a rare moment of philosophical wisdom, that women were the most wonderful of God's creations in the universe. I believed that too.

"Dad," I responded to this insight, "how come, if women are so wonderful, that the Bible says that God made Eve out of Adam's rib, instead of the other way around?" He thought about that. "Well, Bernie, I guess that creating Man was the preliminary design, and Woman was the finished product." I tried to fantasize what the world would be like if there were no women. *Surely*, I thought, *it would be a harsher and crueller place.*

Uncomfortable with abstract philosophy, our conversation soon turned back to the prospects of the Yankees to take the pennant again that year. Now, as the oldest child with three younger siblings in the house, I began to take an interest in child psychology. I read Dr. Spock's book *Common Sense on Baby and Child Care*, first published in 1946. Tenaciously, I began to carry 'Dr. Spock' around the house as my 'Bible', often quoting it to my mother's great annoyance.

33

Bar Mitzvah Preparations

As my Bar Mitzvah date approached, my parents enrolled me in nearby University Heights Hebrew School. I attended Hebrew classes for two late afternoon sessions a week.

I was still angry at God for taking Grandpa away from me while I was still so young. Reluctantly, I just went through the motions of Hebrew study, except for Jewish history classes where I participated in lively discussions of biblical events. It was just before Rosh Hashanah (the Jewish New Year), when I first questioned traditional Jewish theology. My challenge came after Rabbi Glick's lecture on Jewish symbols.

The Rabbi was dogmatic in doctrine, and did not encourage student questions. In my class, I innocently asked, "If Jesus had been hanged instead of crucified, would the symbol of Christianity have become a noose instead of a cross?" The teacher frowned. "We do not discuss Jesus in this school. It is forbidden! How dare you ask such an impudent question? Ask about Judaism, not about what the Christians do!"

A shocked silence came over the class. Then a few murmurs

and whispers, and a giggle or two. Regaining his composure, the Rabbi dismissed the class and marched me straight to the Principal's office.

Mr. Eli Kastenbaum, the Principal, was a practicing lawyer of cynical demeanor and judgmental responses. Struggling for words after hearing of my 'sinful' question, he called me a 'heretic.' It was his policy to grant little leeway in questions from pupils to teachers (mainly to clarify), not anything to challenge Orthodox Jewish theological tenets.

After the teacher told his tale of my supposed heresy to the Principal, I was asked if I had anything to say for myself. Refusing to cringe before the Principal's authority, I responded, "The question was asked in good faith. Where does it say in any Holy Text that Jesus cannot be mentioned in Hebrew School?" Silence and an angry glare was my answer.

To the accusation of heresy, I retorted, "That's what they called Spinoza, too!"

For a moment, Mr. Kastenbaum smiled at my rebuttal, then regained his sternness and ordered me expelled from the Hebrew School. If only Grandpa had been there to defend me! I missed him so much! Mom and Dad reacted calmly to this expulsion. They seemed to be actually relieved about not having to continue to pay Hebrew School tuition costs anymore. It was a whopping twenty five dollars a month, plus books and incidental school supplies. They did not try to enroll me in another Hebrew School.

My parents only went to the synagogue on the High Holidays for *'Yiskor'*, the late afternoon memorial service and did not stay for the full service. They arranged private lessons for me by a local rabbi on Nelson Avenue. After searching the West Bronx area between Burnside Avenue and 170th Street, Mom finally found a little 'hole in the wall' synagogue and Hebrew School on

Nelson Avenue, a few blocks from our apartment. It was a small, ratty cave-like three-story building nestled among six-story apartment houses. A tattered placard in Yiddish advertised the Hebrew School to those who could read the sign. After my bar mitzvah, I lost all further interest in Judaism during my teen years. Years later, I returned to an appreciation of my faith by example and discussion in a Jewish singles group, not rote repetition from an old text.

The building facades along Nelson Ave. were somewhat shabby, but respectable. These apartment houses were mostly red and yellow brick, interspersed with concrete cornices and scrollwork ornamentation. Their lobby flooring was of stained tiles, which hinted of a higher class origin in their earlier years. The windows probably had not been washed since the Hoover Administration, and sagged in their frames.

Two afternoons a week, I walked down Nelson Avenue to the little Hebrew School. The early 20th century houses blurred together in my eyes, casting a grayish pall over the street. I was sent to retired Rabbi Mendel for bar mitzvah preparation. He taught students by rote at ten dollars a month.

I quickly noticed that Rabbi Mendel allowed few, if any, questions. It was all rote memorization and chanting, droning on and on. I shut out my Jewish thinking processes and recited and recited and recited. Rabbi Mendel spoke broken English with a thick Yiddish accent which I did not understand very well. He was quite aged and very orthodox.

The weeks and months wore on as my Bar Mitzvah approached. I finally mastered my Haftorah portion to be recited and its chanting (the 'trope' or cantillation) just in time for the ceremony. The Holy Torah Scroll had an insert sheet with English subtitles clipped on below the Hebrew and Aramaic script. My still-childish treble voice resounded clearly in the sanctuary. (Fortunately, my adolescent hormones did not kick-in until several months later, when I lost my boy soprano voice forever.)

Nelson Avenue began on the southwest corner of Macombs Road and ran six blocks east past Featherbed Lane to PS 104, the public elementary school I attended for grades three, four and five. I had wondered about the meaning of the street name of 'Featherbed Lane', and found it in an old Bronx History book in the local library. During the Revolutionary War, the British redcoats were encamped nearby and blocked the roads to Manhattan. The local farmers were sympathetic to the American rebellion, and smuggled supplies to General Washington's army at night.

There are different stories told about how Featherbed Lane got its name. One version is that local farmers laid down featherbedding to aid soldiers to sneak past dozing British sentries. This is a colorful, but unlikely story. How could farmers lay down several hundred featherbeds and remove them each morning before they would be noticed by British patrols?

Another legend claims that the road was so rough that stagecoach passengers sat on featherbeds to relieve their discomfort. A third story contradicts the second, suggesting that the muddiness of the road smoothed the ride, making it as smooth as a featherbed. Finally, an article on the New York City Park's website suggests that the name dates from the 1840s when the area was home to a large number of prostitutes.

Since Mr. Kastenbaum had retired from the University Heights Synagogue shortly after my expulsion, there were no obstacles to my bar mitzvah ceremony being performed at the Synagogue. The arrangements were made and family and friends were invited. The congregation in general, and my relatives in particular, greeted my traditional pre-Bar Mitzvah conducting of the services with satisfied smiles. However, they were puzzled, and some frowned, at my choice of unusual sermon. My topic was "Who stood with us against Rome?"

When ancient Israel revolted against the Roman Empire in the year 66 of the Common Era, appeals for arms and supplies for Israel were sent out by courier to all Roman provinces and other countries. Only one nation (Armenia, later to also be subjugated by Rome) tried to help the Jewish people in their rebellion against Rome. I reminded the congregation that Armenia, in modern times, had suffered a holocaust by the Turks second only to the Jewish Holocaust at the hands of the Nazis. The congregation stirred uncomfortably at this reminder, and the lesson I proposed was that this analogy should create a special bond between Armenia and Israel! Today, in the Holocaust Museum at Queensborough Community College, special exhibits pay tribute to other holocausts of the twentieth century, including the Rape of Nanking by Imperial Japan in 1937 and the Armenian Massacre by the Ottoman Turks in 1915.

Today many Jewish organizations recognize the Armenian and other holocausts as horrific historical events, but such recognition was a novel concept for a Jewish congregation to hear recited from their synagogue pulpits in the 1950s.

At last, my Bar Mitzvah ordeal ended. The closing blessings were chanted and the attendees adjourned to the Synagogue dining hall. There was a reception for the congregation.

Mom had worked very hard in the kitchen, with help from my aunts on her side of the family. Instead of having the family reception in a catering hall, it was held in our small apartment. They had been busy since three days before my Bar Mitzvah to help prepare the banquet. Aunt Irma worked on preparing the fancy table settings and decorations. Extra chairs and tables were rented or borrowed.

I held my breath, praying that family frictions would not spoil my Bar Mitzvah day. Uncle Dave assumed the role of '*mashgiach*' (kosher kitchen supervisor) and made sure that everything was kosher, with a few technical culinary points that he 'overlooked' for the sake of convenience. A rabbi would have been much stricter in kosher observance, I am sure. But we could not afford to hire a rabbi for that task and settled for Uncle Dave instead.

Uncle Rudy brought out his accordion and played old Russian and Yiddish songs. Just when things were getting kind of mellow and the relatives were talking to each other, out came the soup being served from the kitchen—the first crisis of my celebration party.

When Mom and her soup tureen approached the table, Aunt Irma made an outsized sour face, lips pursed and nose wrinkled at the sight of Mom's yellowish matzoh ball soup. Aunt Irma announced her belittling opinion of Mom's cooking for all to hear at the table: "Rose, this soup looks like '*pishachs*'!" (a Yiddish slang word for 'urine'). A shocked murmur and some nervous laughter from the guests greeted this loudly scandalous declaration. Mom pretended she did not hear Irma. She blushed, and avoided any rebuttal that would have again led to a fight between the sisters. Only an hour of pleading by me and a little tepid support from Dad had resulted in Irma being invited at all, prevailing against Mom's initial refusal.

My sister Carol, all of eight years old, was one of the few at the Bar Mitzvah reception who took Aunt Irma's crudity with adult aplomb. She whispered to Mom, "That was a joke. Aunt Irma did not mean it." Then, loudly, "I think it tastes good. Give me some more, please." Gloria, embarrassed, fled the room quickly and quietly. I excused myself to pretend to go to the bathroom. I thought that Aunt Irma's remark about the matzoh ball soup was funny, but bit my tongue and remained discreetly silent. A few minutes later, I tiptoed into Gloria's room. Why had she not returned to the table? She was quietly raging. I could not tell Gloria that I privately agreed with Aunt Irma's criticism of Mom's soup. Of course I could not support Irma's outburst at the party, and I told her that when I met with her a few days later.

I loved my aunt, her brashness and all. Later, Aunt Irma apologized to me, asking to keep the apology between us and not tell Mom. I agreed to that. I did not want to pour gasoline instead of water on the fire of family relationships.

"Aunt Irma is mean. That was a nasty thing to say at a family party," Gloria declared. "I don't ever want to speak to her again." I tried to reassure her. "She has a big mouth, but a good heart. It was not right that she said that to put down Mom like that."

I patted her cheek. "It's okay. It's my party and I forgive her." Gloria gave me a quick hug. "I am lucky to have a big brother like you—so forgiving. I could never do that."

So now, Mom and Aunt Irma were on the 'outs' again for the umpteenth time. Over the past forty years, they had been on the outs most of the time—the Bronx version of the Hatfield-McCoy feud, except that Mom and Irma did not shoot guns at each other, only verbal barbs.

34

Sixth Grade at PS 11: School for Smarts

In the 1940s and '50s, bright students in New York City public elementary schools were often dragged backwards academically to conform with class learning pace for average students. Neither was any special help offered by busy teachers to the slow students who often fell further and further behind until they gave up trying to learn.

My emotional war with the school system lasted from the second grade through the fifth grade, with only intermittent periods of scholastic peace between myself and the teachers. In desperation at the difficulties of being trapped in school classes below my capabilities, I wrote a letter to the District Superintendent of Schools, enclosing a copy of an essay, with footnotes that I wrote in the fifth grade, titled "Gettysburg vs. Vicksburg: Which battle was the true turning point of the Civil War?" I argued in favor of Vicksburg. The school history textbooks taught that Gettysburg was the turning point of the Civil War, in which the Confederate invasion of Pennsylvania was defeated and forced to retreat back to Virginia.

On the same July 4th, 1863 that Lee's remaining forces retreated southwards—ending the Battle of Gettysburg, Confederate Lieutenant General John C. Pemberton surrendered to Major General Ulysses S. Grant at Vicksburg. This victory came after several previous Union attempts to besiege the fortress river port failed. It resulted in cutting off the Confederacy from Western America and gave the Union naval forces control of the Mississippi River.

A few days after Labor Day in 1950, an official letter arrived from the school Superintendent's office. It was addressed to me. Mom saw it and was troubled by its embossed address etched on the envelope. "Bernie, are you in trouble again?" she asked anxiously, insisting I show the letter to her immediately. To avoid another argument, I agreed. She received a copy of the same letter the next day.

P.S. 11

I had applied for transfer from PS 104, which lacked advanced classes, to PS 11 which had SP (Special) classes for bright students. My overworked, but conscientious and concerned PS 104 guidance counselor, Mr. Fields, had recommended the transfer as being in my best interest for scholastic advancement. At first, both schools objected because my grades were good, but my conduct was below average. Then I was sent for an IQ test and scored high at 144.

Finally, after further back-and-forth discussion, Mr. Fields persuaded PS 11 that the reason for my poor behavior was that I was not challenged enough by the standard elementary school curriculum. The letter read:

"Dear Mr. Seiden:

We are pleased to inform you that your application to transfer to PS 11 has been approved, as of Tuesday, Sept. 12, 1950. Please report to the Principal's office at PS 11 for placement in an S.P. 6th Grade class. We wish you the best of success in your new school."

WOW! I went the next day excitedly to report to my new school. Now for the first time, I would be in a class with my peers—other bright kids who took advanced classes in math, sciences and social studies.

I soon noticed the difference in classroom environment at PS 11 from my former school. At PS 104, as in most other city elementary public schools of that era, the policy was 'norm and conform'. *I was not 'norm', I was Bernie! And I did not want to conform either!* It was delightful to discover in my new class that I was not the only sixth grader who had read Shakespeare other than for a homework assignment, enjoyed classical music, and debated History and Social Studies topics.

One boy in my new class was working on a water desalinization project using solar power to steam the water. Another boy was studying the symbolism of heraldry and I remember a girl building an incubator for bird eggs that had fallen out of their nest. Most of them hatched and thrived under her researched care plan, documented by a carefully maintained diary. The few baby birds that did not survive were buried with due ceremony and respect. Halfway into the term, the surviving birds were released into the wilds of the Bronx when they were old enough to fend for themselves.

In 1950, there were two significant national events in America of which I was acutely aware. One was the Korean War and the other was the ramping up of the McCarthy 'Red Scare' era with reckless accusations of communist affiliation or sympathy for people deemed unpatriotic in their mannerisms, viewpoints or activities. Those citizens and aliens, deemed suspicious, were often government employees, entertainers, educators, 'left wingers', union activists and relatives or friends of these activists.

On Sunday, June 25, 1950; egged on by Communist China and the Soviet Union, North Korean armies invaded South Korea. The capital of Seoul fell in three days. The outnumbered South Koreans were pushed back within two months to the Pusan perimeter at the southeast corner of Korea, losing two-thirds of their territory.

The same day of the invasion, the United Nations Security Council met in emergency session, in the absence of the Soviet Union. The Soviets were boycotting the Council to protest UN recognition of the Nationalist Chinese as the representative of mainland China instead of the Communist government that had chased the Nationalists from the mainland. The Security Council quickly voted to assist South Korea to repel the invasion. The

United States was in the forefront of this action and sent forces to support the South Koreans.

I excitedly followed battle communiqués and war maps posted in the *New York Times* each day. I attached a *National Geographic* map of Korea on my bedroom wall with multi color push pins and stick-ons showing changing troop positions. I used tracing paper and heavy erasable marking pencils to show battle lines of the opposing forces, which I updated daily.

Dad jokingly said to me, "Bernie, if General MacArthur ever loses track of any of his troops, all he has to do is call you up to find them." I just smiled, and continued my military mappings. To me, wars were like a chess game, with moves and countermoves. Except that instead of eight pieces and eight pawns on each side, there were thousands of pieces, such as infantry, artillery, tanks and planes, and the battlefield was real geographic terrain instead of a checkerboard with sixty four squares. Grandpa had warned me of the horrors of real war, but after his death the warnings receded into my emotional background and war again became 'play' to me.

Meanwhile, the new school year started, and I settled in to Miss Toner's SP 4 class. I studied classic war battles and maneuvers from military history books from the library, and began to develop some ideas of my own on the Korean War. I did not dare discuss these ideas with anyone. On the second day of class, we were assigned to write a composition to assess our writing skills. My topic was the Korean War, illustrated by annotated maps, titled "Turning of the Tide in Korea."

Because of my Korea composition, I received a visit from the FBI at school! Yes, me! At age twelve, I was under suspicion by the FBI for espionage by unauthorized possession of classified military information because of an innocent English class composition based on publicly available sources at the library.

This is how it happened:

I conceived of a classic amphibious invasion to 'turn the tide' in Korea after UN forces (including American troops) were driven back to the Pusan perimeter. After studying coastal tide tables, I projected that the best strategy for UN forces would be to stage a west coast landing behind enemy lines on the peninsula of Inchon, twenty miles west of Seoul. There were only three likely landing points along the western coast of South Korea, and I chose the one closest to Seoul. I envisioned an operation similar to, but smaller than D-Day in Normandy, and proposed an amphibious assault with three waves of troops backed by naval artillery and air support. Little did I realize that about 250 miles away from the Bronx in Washington DC, top-secret meetings at the Pentagon were coming to military conclusions similar to mine!

The teacher stared at my report, then hastily gave the class a reading assignment and hurried into the Principal's office with my paper. Apparently, because of McCarthyism, teachers had been warned to be on the lookout for radical students.

When I came to school the next morning, I was immediately summoned to the Principal's office, where he awaited me flanked by two very grim-looking FBI agents, with lapel badges and gun bulges under their jackets.

I gulped, took a deep breath and then composed myself, remembering from detective stories not to appear nervous when confronted by the FBI. Especially if you are a suspect! *(Who, me? I am only a boy!)* The older agent was thin, sneering and arrogant. He snarled at me, flourishing the Korea composition in my face.

"Where did you get the information for this paper you wrote?"

"In the New York Public Library, sir," I responded in a small voice.

"What library?"

"The Main Library in Manhattan, on 42nd Street. I go there often. My sources were the *New York Times*, *National Geographic*, *Look Magazine*, and military history books. There were some other books and magazines, too—all public material. I constructed a Korean coastal map based on all communiqués published in the *Times*. If you read enough of that, you can get a pretty good idea of where all the troops are and what they may be doing. The rest is guesswork."

The older agent commented, "Pretty good guesswork, I would say." His tone softened a little. "Where did you get the idea of a three-wave assault?"

I replied proudly. "From General Eisenhower, of course. The battle plan he used for the D-Day amphibious landings. Is that a good public source?"

Grudgingly, the older agent said, "Yes, it is. But I will have to check it out." *I could almost sense the handcuffs being put away. How disappointing it must have been for them not to be able to arrest me!* But they didn't give up yet. Further questions followed, and my answers were, "No! My father is not a communist and has no communist friends.... No! I do not have any communist friends either... No! I have not marched in any protest rallies or signed any Peace Petitions," and on and on . . .

Finally they were satisfied. They confiscated my paper and warned me and the Principal not to discuss this investigation. Recovering my presence of mind, I asked the Principal, "Do I still get my A plus?" He answered, "Of course you will. I will take care of that. Keep up the good work, and try to avoid political topics in the future."

That ended the military secrets matter and the FBI and I both kept our word. They had come in swiftly and marched straight in to the Principal's office just briefly flashing their badges, so there was no buzz about their 'visit' to the school to investigate a very, very junior alleged 'spy'. However, some rumors spread among the school staff that I had been questioned by the FBI.

A few days later, at dawn on Sept. 15th, 75 thousand troops under General Douglas MacArthur landed at Inchon in three waves, supported by heavy artillery and air superiority. The North Korean army was surprised at Inchon, with inadequate forces on hand to repel the Allied attack, just like the German Wehrmacht had been surprised and caught under full strength in Normandy six years earlier. However, the Wehrmacht was a far tougher, more experienced and more determined foe than the People's Army of North Korea was to the Allies. I maintained a secret, smug satisfaction in my successful prediction of the Battle of Inchon, never talking about it until the memoirs in these pages began to take shape some sixty-five years later.

Despite the 'Korean War' notoriety of my opening days at PS 11, I was actually enjoying public school for the first time. PS 11 was a great revelation to me of what an enlightened school with SP classes could be like. No more was I at war with the teachers, or with slow elementary school curriculum far below my academic abilities and knowledge.

My SP class raced through the required standard curriculum and then on into more advanced work. Students had the option of choosing their own term projects for detailed study. I chose Mythology as my social studies project because of my interest in History in general and ancient Greece in particular.

From my own early Jewish History studies, I knew that in 332 BCE, Alexander the Great conquered ancient Israel. Some Greeks that settled in Israel were attracted to Judaism because of its monotheistic belief in a universal God. This compared favorably with Greek Gods who were little more than magnified and sinful mortals.

There was nothing very godly about Zeus, their King of Gods, who came down from Olympus to seduce mortal women and sire a breed of half-god heroes. The most famous one was Hercules. My term paper studied the human emotions of Greek gods and goddesses—the rages, jealousies, spites, adulteries and other deceits, and the detrimental effect this conduct had on human morals in those pagan times.

Even though the boys and girls in S.P. Classes at PS 11 were very bright, they also had their rowdy side. We played softball and basketball, just as other kids our age did. The only difference is that we argued about the rules more than most youngsters would do, using the official sports rule book as our back-up authority. Sometimes we had fights on the playground, when intellectual argument failed to settle our differences.

My classmates in the sixth grade were beginning to become conscious of the opposite sex. Boys were less sloppy than they were in the earlier grades and combed their hair neatly. Some girls began to wear makeup, either with parental permission or without. Those girls without permission secretly donned makeup in the bathroom before classes began, and scrubbed it off before going home to revert to a 'little girl' look.

My male hormones were still in boyish hibernation, so I did not try to befriend any girls in the sixth grade. Gloria kindly offered to 'fix me up' with one of her older girlfriends, near my age, but I was not emotionally ready for this early dating phase. Instead, I focused on my schoolwork and found great satisfaction in improved report grades which continued into the next school year in the seventh grade—when I returned to Macombs Junior High School (PS 82).

35

Macombs Junior High

To enter the seventh grade, I returned to PS 82, the same old building where I attended kindergarten through the second grade. The elementary grades occupied the second and third floors, and Macombs Junior High was on the fourth and fifth floors. Scheduling and recreation outdoor periods were carefully arranged to avoid having the elementary and the Junior High children cross paths inside or outside the school building. It was a precaution to prevent bullying or other problems.

Entering Macombs, I was placed in an SP (accelerated class) with elective program choices. I sensed a psychological barrier between the lower grades and the junior high school grades. For instance, in the lower grades, all students took the same required general science program. However, starting in the seventh grade, a student could choose either chemistry, biology or physics.

PS 82 (Macombs JHS)

There were three teachers I particularly remember from Macombs. The first was Mr. Coday, who taught seventh grade English. He was very tall and thin, about six-foot-six. He had the dignified British mannerisms of an Oxford professor, with speaking accent to match. I never understood why he was teaching in an American junior high, when his level of erudition was more appropriate to teaching at a college level.

Mr. Coday sprinkled his lesson plan liberally with Latin quotes, which went over the heads of the students, as did his blackboard eraser one day—over their heads, literally!

This is how it happened:

It was on a dry October day, a month after the school term began. The day was made even dryer by the discourse of Mr. Coday on conjugating irregular English verbs. Even the diligent students were nodding off after the first few minutes.

Then there was a stir among the seats. Someone had sneakily tossed a chalked-up blackboard eraser at Mr. Coday's back, lightly bouncing off its target. He calmly turned around, picked up the eraser and said to the class: "Everyone raise your hands, please. Palms facing front." He paused significantly. "Both hands." The class sheepishly complied.

Aha! The guilty eraser thrower had chalk dust on his hands. Mr. Coday suddenly picked up the eraser and aimed it at chalky Joe Stevens in the fourth seat, third row while shouting "*Vindicate dulcet*" (revenge is sweet). It landed squarely on Joe's forehead—a perfect throw. He did not translate, but I got the 'drift' of his Latinism.

I guessed privately that Mr. Coday had used the Latin root for 'vindictive' and 'Dulce' meant 'sweet'. Everyone in the room gasped. Several students had seen Joe throw the eraser at Mr. Coday. They applauded Mr. Coday's swift and accurate response. "Gratias," he replied, and we returned to our English studies.

Then, a week later, it was announced that Mr. Coday had the flu, and would be out of school for at least a week, and our substitute teacher was to be Miss Radice. Some of the boys that had been with her in another class began to smirk knowingly. But they would not tell me or the others anything about her. The next morning, she slinked into the classroom, slowly and gracefully, sheathed in a red woolen dress, cut low at her bodice to reveal the upper half of her ample bosom. A gasp echoed from the boys who had not seen her before. The others just smiled or smirked. The girls giggled, and then hushed up. All the boys continued to be distracted until her week tenure was up and Mr. Coday returned.

Then Miss Radice introduced herself, quite oblivious to the stir she caused, and settled into her teaching task as the students rustled in their seats. I fixated on her bosom in wonderment, and all the boys continued to be distracted until Mr. Coday returned. None of the other lady teachers in school were nearly as curvaceous and well-endowed!

My next most memorable junior high teacher was Miss Sheridan. I was fortunate enough to be her pupil in Math for both the seventh and eighth grades. She took a personal interest in me beyond my math skills.

After class, on her own time, she taught me Chess, and also allowed me to use chess probability math as an optional project for extra credit. Prune-faced, with her black hair swept back into a tight bun, just barely graying, she looked like the stereotyped image of an old-maid school teacher. But she did not act that way. Indeed, her wit was sharp, and she illustrated her math lessons with everyday examples of applied math. To demonstrate the lighter side of math and physics, she showed us a playful photo of Einstein sticking out his tongue at his 72nd birthday party in 1951.

My most 'unfond' memory of a junior high teacher was Miss Gomez. The school mandatory language class choice was either French or Spanish. I reluctantly chose French because I believed it to be more elegant. Miss Gomez taught both languages, so I would have been stuck with her either way. It was an unenthusiastic choice, but was needed for scholastic credits. My real preference was not to learn any foreign language at all.

For the first time in school, I did poorly in a subject. Languages were just not my thing. Miss Gomez was sarcastic, slim and sharp-featured. She looked the part of the strict 'duenna' that she acted out with her students. I sometimes fantasized an image of her as an older version of Carmen from Bizet's opera. In that image, *I pictured Miss Gomez with a knife in her teeth, a flower in her hair, and venom in her voice.*

She was also the coach for the student Drama Club. I joined Drama at the beginning of the term, before I realized that Miss Gomez led the club and that I might have a problem with her. The play, to be performed before the whole school, with parents and teachers attending, was Anatole France's *The Man Who Married a Dumb Wife*. I was assigned to play the Assistant Surgeon. This role fortunately had few lines of dialogue for me to learn.

The play is a comical farce about a man, Judge Leonard, who married a voiceless woman, Catherine, whom he adored. The Judge's role was ably played by my classmate Harvey Stewart. He had an amazing memory for dialog, and learned the entire role of Judge Leonard in two weeks. The Judge's wife was not dumb in anything else, but her tongue was mute. In desperation to give her the gift of speech, he hired a Surgeon to operate on her vocal cords. The surgical team was serious in its suturing act, with carpentry tools as surgical instruments, but the audience was in stitches.

Here is the famous Judge Leonard monologue which sets the stage, literally, for the ill-starred operation.

"My wife is dumb. Quite dumb. I admit, I noticed it before we were married. I couldn't help noticing it, of course, but it didn't seem to make so much difference to me then as it does now. I considered her beauty, and her property".

At this point, Harvey ad-libbed a wisecrack. "Aah, her property! Her substantial property!" The audience roared with laughter. Melodramatically, rolling his eyes, he continued his lines.

"And I thought of nothing but the advantages of the match and the happiness I should have with her. But now these matters seem less important, and I do wish she could talk; that would be a real intellectual pleasure for me, and, what's more, a practical advantage for the household. What does a judge need most in his house? Why, a good-looking wife, to receive the suitors pleasantly, and, by subtle suggestions, gently bring them to the point of making proper presents, so that their cases may receive more careful attention.

People need to be encouraged (ahem!) to make proper presents! A woman, by clever speech and prudent action, can get a good ham from one, and a roll of cloth from another and make still another give poultry or wine. But this poor dumb thing Catherine gets nothing at all. While my fellow judges have their kitchens and cellars and stables and storerooms running over with good things, all thanks to their wives, I hardly get the wherewithal to keep the pot boiling.

You see, Master Adam Fumée, what I lose by having a dumb wife. I'm not worth half as much. . . . And the worst of it is, I'm losing my spirits, and almost my wits, with it all. When I hold my wife in my arms—a woman as beautiful as the finest carved statue, at least so I think—and quite as silent, that I'm sure of—it makes me feel queer and uncanny; I even ask myself if I'm holding a graven image or a mechanical toy, or a magic doll made by a sorcerer, not a real human child of our Father in Heaven. Sometimes, in the morning, I am tempted to jump out of bed to escape from bewitchment.

Worse yet! What with having a dumb wife, I'm going dumb myself. Sometimes I catch myself using signs, as she does. The other day, on the Bench, I even pronounced judgment in pantomime, and condemned a man to the galleys, just by dumb show and gesticulation!"

In the operating room scene, a tray of carpenter tools was wheeled in to the surgical nurse at my side of the surgical table. The audience chuckled. 'Doctor' Harvey busied himself with the preparations and barked out his instrument needs to be handed in relay from the nurse to the assistant surgeon (me) to the 'Doctor' (him).

"Hammer." I passed the hammer to him.

"Chisel." Pause. *"Screwdriver."* I effortlessly passed these tools to him. *"Hacksaw."*

Oops! I fumbled it out of my sweaty hands in the nurses' relay and the saw flew out of my hands straight into the front row lap of Miss Gomez! The audience roared with laughter, and Miss Gomez placed the hacksaw on the floor next to her, so everyone assumed it was part of the show. I knew my junior high acting career was over before it began. I felt doomed to also fail her French class, which I did.

As I sailed along through the seventh, eighth and ninth year junior high grades, my classes were advised to begin thinking about what career direction we wanted to pursue, in high school and beyond, into college and the adult world. Adolescent physical and hormonal changes made us more acutely self-conscious and increased the difficulty of communicating with our parents and teachers.

As an outsider with few friends in school, I felt relatively immune to teen social pressures and group conformity. Dungarees and denims were the 'in thing' to wear for boys' pants in the 1950s. They were often styled with tight crotches and skinny legs. I wore regular pants instead—not to spite my peers or be an oddball, but because they were more comfortable.

As the autumn shadows of 1952 lengthened into the winter snows, I began to consider my choice of available high schools for the next year. Miss Sheridan tried to persuade me to apply to the Bronx High School of Science. I made an appointment with her for us to review the application papers together.

As we began, she cleared her throat. "Bernie, I have the Bronx Science application package on my desk here." She handed me a copy. "Let's analyze the qualifications and see if you qualify under their guidelines."

Hesitatingly, I began checking off, on paper and aloud, the topics that would not likely be disputed. "Hmm. Good attendance record. That's okay. Serious about schoolwork and homework." I paused. "Yes, or I would not be here now asking for your help." I continued down the checklist. "Academically successful in lower grades. Yes, from the sixth grade onwards at least. Except for failing French in the seventh grade."

Miss Sheridan remarked, "That might hurt you on the academic score. Go on."

"(Ahem) Well behaved." I blushed, then said "Yes" (with my fingers crossed)

Then there was another roadblock item. "Parents actively involved in my education!" These were not mandatory items, but were significant evaluation factors staring at me accusingly in black and white on the admission forms. I pondered the injustice of this question with puckered lips. Dad was working six days a week as a cab driver and never got past the eighth grade in school. Mom made it into the ninth grade, but did not finish because she did not have the academic skills or motivation needed to keep up with high school classes.

I thought, *how could my parents possibly become actively involved in my education anyway?* "List extracurricular activities" was next on the enrollment form. *Well, there was the Chess Club.* I smiled and entered it on the form. *I could not tell them about being a junior smuggler for the Haganah, sending real guns as toy gifts to Israel!* I shrugged. "Let's consider the other high schools. It seems that I have too many strikes against me to get into Bronx Science or Stuyvesant anyway. That leaves Taft or Clinton as remaining high school choices. The other schools are too far away."

Macombs Junior High School teachers were also advising their classes to begin thinking about what career direction to pursue in high school and beyond into college and the adult world.

My final choice had been simple. Most boys and girls in my neighborhood were going to Taft High. My contrarian nature, and desire to shed social connections with local teens led me to choose DeWitt Clinton High School instead.

In the ninth grade, while other boys were looking at girls, I was looking at tripod mountings for my spyglass folding telescope. It had four settings for 15x, 30x, 45x and 60x power. I worked on an old camera tripod to convert it into a telescope mount.

Two protractors were affixed to the top of the tripod to measure celestial altitude and longitude angles. From the sixth floor rooftop of my apartment building, my view swept across the Bronx horizon, and I marveled at seeing close-ups of cars and trucks on the Whitestone Bridge to Queens—several miles to the east.

I began going to the Hayden Planetarium almost every month to see the sky shows. The domed brick building facing onto West 81st Street was joined to the north side of the American Museum of Natural History. Approaching the five square columns of the three-story Planetarium facade, it felt as if I was approaching the portal to the universe. I would pick up my monthly copy of *Sky and Telescope Magazine*, then browse the 'sky shop' and exhibits. My favorite display was the fifteen-ton mostly-iron Willamette meteor near the entrance. It was discovered in Oregon in 1902, and later donated to the old Hayden Planetarium in New York when it opened in 1935. The Willamette was the largest meteorite ever discovered in the United States, and was estimated to have fallen over a million years ago. Today it sits as a focal point for the new Planetarium on the same site. The first time I saw it, I ran my fingers over the rough cratered surface, marveling at its metallic sheen. It obviously did not feel like an ordinary rock. When I went upstairs to the Planetarium dome, I settled down into the tilt-back seats to gaze upwards. The Manhattan skyline in silhouette ringed the deep purple of the darkening room.

The center of attention inside the Planetarium dome was the Zeiss projector—two multifaceted spheres connected by spidery struts, one for the north and one for the south celestial sphere. It could display the skies over anyplace on Earth, the Moon or planets in the past, present or future. Mini-projectors attached to the star balls displayed planets, constellation outlines or other sky show phenomena through multiple lenses imbedded in the spheres onto the dome.

The Zeiss resembled a giant spider waiting to pounce as the lights dimmed and the sky shifted into night mode. The lecturer's voice boomed in the room, softening in appropriate passages to coordinate with the celestial or planetary surface scene and ethereal music. I began to dream of becoming an astronomer. Later, I learned that much of the observational work is done by telescope cameras running at night, and analyzed by computer during the day.

At first, it seemed like a romantic career to stay up all night viewing the stars from a lonely outpost observatory. Then as I began to take some interest in the opposite sex, it occurred to me that I might have better things to do with my night life than watching stars or star photos. (*Like watching girls, for instance!*)

36

Gloria Comes of Age

"Bernie, a boy kissed me today in the school hallway and I got very mad about it." Gloria announced this event early in the spring of 1952. My protective instinct kicked in at this news, but as her older brother, I resisted the impulse to also get angry.

"Did you want him to kiss you?"

"No, he is icky. The other kids saw him sneak this kiss and they laughed about it."

"So that's what made you mad—that the others saw him doing it?"

"Yeah," she squirmed, sensing that a brotherly lecture was coming on.

"Gloria, I think it's time we had a little talk about boys."

I cleared my throat, trying to sound older than my fourteen years. Mom would have just screamed at her, saying, "Don't you dare let any boys kiss you!" Dad would duck the issue or fumble it. So it was up to me.

Gloria was coming of age. She was no longer a baby, but a

young girl of eleven years with a mind of her own and a stubborn streak to match. Her clashes with Mom grew more heated, and my role as mediator between them was being called on more often. Gloria usually listened to me, because I told her pointedly that if she did not, then she would have to face Mom's periodic rages and suspicions alone without my help.

"Gloria," I began. "It's only natural for boys and girls to like each other and, if they are friendly together, then kissing is okay too." Gloria made a face.

"It's still icky," she remarked. I grinned.

"Just wait a few years and you will not think it so icky any more. You will even like it, if he is the right boy for you to want to be friends with." On a sudden impulse, I leaned over and kissed her on the cheek. "Was that icky?"

"No, but that's because you are my brother. And you are good to me, not like other neighborhood boys I see with their sisters making faces and mischief at them." We laughed, and she hugged me.

These were the beginnings of Gloria's hostility towards Mom that would grow over the years ahead. It was not just that Gloria was a willful and stubborn little girl, but that Mom was a willful and stubborn adult. So, often I was in the uncomfortable position of having to support Mom's parental authority by saying to Gloria, "Do what Mom says."

In effect, I became Gloria's 'third parent', a heavy responsibility for a fourteen-year-old brother towards a sister only three years younger than myself.

In the late 1940s and early '50s, network television was building an excited new audience of millions of radio fans across the country. On Sunday nights, Steve Allen squared off on NBC against Ed Sullivan on CBS. That was sly Steve's comedy versus Sullivan's broad variety show. Gloria and I took sides in favor of

'Steverino', but Mom and Dad watched Ed Sullivan. A second television was an impossible luxury, so Gloria and I would watch the Steve Allen Show at friends' houses, when we could.

Gloria became a fanatic Eydie Gorme fan, and President of Eydie's Junior Fan Club, decorating her room with Eydie and Steve posters, pictures and articles from show business magazines. Eydie Gorme was then a rising young Bronx-born singing star and Taft High graduate. She became a Steve Allen show regular, together with Steve Lawrence, the singer she later married. I was very proud of Gloria for building up this fan club in the Bronx by her own efforts. Although invited, I tactfully avoided the club meetings at members homes in order not to overshadow her.

Like dark-haired Eydie, my redheaded sister had a pixyish look about her, and slight bangs curled across her forehead. In later years, I came to wish that Gloria could have learned some other charming traits from Eydie and Steve's rare stable, happy and enduring show business marriage. But that was not meant to be.

Gloria became conscious of makeup and lipstick at around age ten. A few of the more daring girls in her class at school began to try to look like grown-up women. They copycatted each other and mostly got it right, with the help of a 'cool' mother or older sister. Gloria did not have either of these female supporters. One day, I wandered past the open door of our bathroom when Gloria made her first attempt at lipstick and makeup. It was badly smeared, and she looked clownish. Fortunately for her, Mom was not home at the time, or there would have been a scene.

"That looks disgusting," I said. "If you are going to use makeup, then do it right!"

"Yeah, how would you know?" she sneered.

"Look at yourself in the mirror! That's how I know!"

With that, I snatched her head and poked it at the mirror. She cursed and tried to pull away from me. I quickly wet a face cloth. Using a towel would have been detectable by Mom. I scrubbed Gloria's face as she spluttered and cursed me. After she looked presentable again, I promised her, "I will try to get Mom to allow you to use makeup, and I'll get a girl from my class to show you how to do it."

Gloria looked skeptical. "You don't have a girlfriend! How are you gonna do that?" I responded firmly, "I will get a girl to fix you up properly and pay her five bucks." That was the easy part. I had the money from my newspaper delivery route. Obtaining Mom's consent was the hard part that I resolved to work on.

An opportunity came to bring up the subject of pre-teen cosmetics that evening after supper. Mom was in a good mood for a change. She had just bought some bargains at the local Jewish supermarket, *Olinsky's*. They were in a price war with a recently-opened branch of *Moisha's Dairy*, and Mom told us that she was lucky enough to be near the front of the line when the store opened. I warned Gloria to make herself scarce in her room, so that I could advocate her cause peaceably.

"Mom," I began. "I need to talk to you about Gloria."

"What's she done now?"

"No, no. It's not THAT kind of talk!"

"Okay, I'm listening."

"Gloria is facing social pressure from girlfriends to use makeup. Her friends are not bad girls or being fast for their age. It's just imitating their older sisters and harmless if it is done in moderation, as a part of growing up. She will not overdo it. It's better that she should be supervised than to sneak behind your back and do it."

"Who's going to supervise her?" Mom remarked sarcastically.

"I will," I answered quietly.

Mom sneered, "You are her older brother, not her older sister!"

"That's okay. I can keep better track of what she is doing than you can."

Mom winced. She knew that was true. I continued, "I've arranged for an older teenage girl in my class to advise and help Gloria with her makeup. She is nice and has a good appearance. And I am paying her for it."

After the makeup-smearing incident, Gloria began to mature. Her puberty began at age eleven, and it sharpened her childish temper. Emotional clashes with Mom became more intense and frequent, and more personal. When Mom tried to bring up the subject of the 'birds and the bees', Gloria told me that she had laughed at Moms discomfiture. "Why should I listen to you about sex when I know more about it than you do?"

Gloria had her 'moment of fame' when she was invited, a few months later, to be interviewed on a disk jockey show radio interview about the new Eydie Gorme fan club she had started with some school friends. She asked me to escort her downtown to the radio studio. The disk jockey asked me if I also belonged to the fan club and I responded, "No, this is Gloria's project. I love Eydie and Steve's music too. But this is Gloria's club. She started it with her school friends, and she runs it. So I keep out of it."

The disk jockey asked her on the air, "Gloria, do you ever ask your brother for advice on running the fan club?" She smiled sweetly and said, "No!" There I was, a surrogate Dad at age fourteen to a pigtailed freckle-faced eleven-year old sister!

A few days later, I came home from the library in the early afternoon when I heard tremendous screaming and crashing sounds coming from the bedroom. I burst in upon a scene of strewn furniture and bedding. Gloria was on top of Mom, choking her on top of what was left of the bedding. Mom was struggling to get my sister off her. Gloria was spewing a steady stream of curses and threats at Mom. I quickly grabbed her by the hair and pulled her off. Mom was panting for breath and ran into the bathroom to throw up. Gloria cursed and spit at me. I slapped her hard and yelled at her, "Don't you dare try that again or I'll call the cops on you!"

She laughed derisively, "You hate Mom too, and you know it!"

I replied, "I dislike much of what she says and does, but I do not hate her!"

"I saw you push her and restrain her sometimes."

"Yeah, but I never hit her or choked her. I will let this incident pass on your promise to never get violent with her again. When you have a problem with her, come to me, and I will try to settle it."

In a changed tone, she begged me, "Don't tell Dad."

I taunted her. "What's the matter? Are you afraid he will get angry for once and beat the crap out of you? You deserve it!" I paused. "I will let you get out of it this time, but it will be the last time!"

She tossed her head and halfheartedly agreed to restrain her behavior with Mom in the future. They continued to clash sometimes, but it never again escalated to the level of physical violence.

37

Seagate in the Sand

The summer of 1952 was hot and sultry. At age fourteen, I was not deemed old enough to stay home alone in the Bronx while the family went away for the summer. Aunt Dolly breathed a sigh of relief—the Seiden family would not descend upon her Atlantic City boarding houses this year! Instead, Aunt Irma went to Atlantic City by herself, paying her own way, staying in a cheap hotel not within Aunt Dolly's little real estate empire.

Aunt Dolly and Aunt Irma had a lot in common. They were both avid horse players, and regulars at the local racing track circuit. Aunt Irma was pretty adept at handicapping the ponies, and she seemed to be making some gambling profits.

This year's Seiden family vacation was to journey to the sands of Seagate, the semicircular western tip of Coney Island in Brooklyn. In the 1920s, Coney Island Creek, separating Coney Island's north shore from the Brooklyn mainland, had been filled in by developers and the Island became a peninsula.

I was not against the idea of vacationing in Seagate itself. My objections were just a general teenage rebellion at having to spend a summer in a four room family bungalow with Mom ruling the roost. I made the best of it, resolving to stay outdoors to enjoy the beach and to avoid close quarters with the family. And I resolved to go into downtown Coney Island as often as possible. Sometimes I'd take Gloria along, with Mom's permission, hopefully.

Seagate is a gated peninsula community of over 800 cottages on less than one square mile at the west end of Coney Island, thrusting out into Lower New York Harbor. Many residents there are permanent owners, with some cottages rented out on a seasonal basis It was founded in 1892, six years before the five boroughs (Bronx, Manhattan, Queens, Brooklyn and Staten Island) joined together to form New York City.

The old Coney Island lighthouse, built in 1890 at the western tip of Sea Gate, flashes its automated light which is visible fourteen miles out at sea. This skeletal white 75-foot tower is seen by all ships entering New York Harbor, rounding the eastern point of Brooklyn before they pass the Statue of Liberty.

The day after we arrived, I walked over to the lighthouse, a few blocks from our bungalow, took a few photos, but did not return to that site. Instead, I began daily explorations of the beach. Under the blazing sun, I swam and searched the sands in vain for other boys near my age to hang out with.

After a few days in Seagate, I had a nasty accident. While running across the beach, the big toe of my right foot was pierced by a jagged clamshell protruding above the sand surface. It was a quiet Monday. There was no one around to offer assistance, and no lifeguards nearby. They were only on duty for the weekends. After limping back to the bungalow in searing pain, Dad drove me to Kings County Hospital, where my toe was disinfected and wrapped like a mini-mummy. I was told to stay off my feet for a week and to limit my walking for a month afterwards.

I had some books and magazines to read and a radio, and flies to swat, but no television set and no air conditioning. An icebox, with ice restocked weekly by the iceman, together with a kitchen cabinet, provided our food storage. There were no stores nearby, and Dad took Mom shopping once a week in Coney Island. He continued driving a cab from his Bronx garage and took a week off for vacation at the beginning of our stay at Seagate.

I was saved from convalescent boredom by a major national political event broadcast on the radio — the opening of the 1952 Republican National Convention in Chicago. It was the first one ever to be televised, and the first in which I followed political events as closely as if were the World Series. As the rest of my family went off to the beach during the day, I sat by the radio, spellbound by the growing national excitement of the Presidential Convention and the prospect of a tight race between General Eisenhower and Senator Robert Taft for the Republican nomination.

In the New Hampshire Presidential primary on March 11, 1952 (the first in the nation), Eisenhower had won handily on a write-in vote (50% to 30% for Senator Taft). Eisenhower did not campaign or take a position on national issues. He then resigned as supreme commander of the NATO alliance in April. This heightened the springtime speculation that he would become a candidate for the Presidency. Without campaigning, he had won presidential primaries in New Jersey, Pennsylvania, Massachusetts and Oregon in April and May. Finally, in June, Eisenhower yielded to the urging of the Republican leadership, and announced his active candidacy for President. A groundswell of popular support for him, as a war hero, had built up nationally with the voting public. Eisenhower's first campaign speech was broadcast from his home state of Kansas.

I remember from newspaper photos how he looked that drizzly day. His balding pate gleamed at the cameras as his advisors visibly winced in the background. Newspapers reported that, grudgingly, Eisenhower agreed to hire debonair Robert Montgomery, the actor, as his media advisor. Even more grudgingly, he agreed to use makeup to dull the baldness gleam and improve his public appearance.

There was a tight race on for delegates between Senator Taft, leader of the conservative faction; and General Eisenhower, a moderately liberal Republican. The Republican convention was literally a political blow-by-blow contest, with Taft delegates shoving and getting into near-fistfights with Eisenhower partisans at the convention. Credentials fights also broke out in several states, with competing delegations each claiming to be the legitimate delegates from that state. To the chants of "We like Ike", Eisenhower narrowly won the nomination on the second ballot, after coming up nine votes short of a first ballot majority. I was glad to see 'Ike' win, believing that Democrats had become stale after twenty years in power at the White House.

Senator Richard Nixon helped Eisenhower by abandoning the favorite son candidate from his own state of California, Earl Warren, and rounding up crucial votes for 'Ike.' For this, Nixon was rewarded with the nomination for Vice President. Earl Warren was rewarded with the ultimate political consolation prize when he was named Chief Justice of the US Supreme Court a year later in September 1953.

This 1952 Presidential race started my practical education in politics as a young citizen. Following the Republican convention word for word was far more meaningful to me than the textbooks, newspapers, magazines and biographies that I read, or social studies classes in school. I owed no allegiance to any party, shifting my preferences on candidates, in turn, as I perceived them to be on the strength of their leadership qualities. This political campaign also cemented Nixon's notorious nickname, 'Tricky Dick' into posterity. He had earned this nickname in the 1950 Senatorial race when a Democratic ad blared "look at Tricky Dick's Republican record."

To cope with the summer heat in my stuffy Seagate room, away from the cooling influence of the beachside breezes two blocks away, I improvised a makeshift air conditioner. It was a wire cage stuffed halfway with ice cubes suspended over a bowl. A half-arc circulating fan blew air through the cage, which was cooled from the ice cubes within. Mom complained about the cost of buying extra ice each week, but Dad pleaded for me against Mom's argument, citing my infected toe as a reason, and we bought two bags of ice per week delivered to our rooms for the rest of the summer.

Our Seagate cottage had a private bathroom, without bathtubs. The showers were enclosed tin sheds in the backyard, one for each family. Weekday afternoons were the quietest time to shower, since families were at the beach and most fathers were working in the city.

One scorching early July afternoon, I was engrossed in the Republican convention speeches on the radio, when I heard giggling and splashing sounds from the tin showers. Mom and Dad were still at the beach, but Carol and Mark had come back earlier full of sand and silliness.

They had received the typical family 'no nakedness' lecture about modesty in front of others from Mom during their kindergarten year. It was repeated by me to them in a little more specific detail the next year. Now they were nine, and old enough to understand the concept of modesty (*supposedly!*).

I went outside to the shower shed and heard them laughing inside. The flimsy lock gave way to my pushing, and I walked into the spectacle of Carol and Mark both stark naked and splashing each other. I was shocked nearly speechless. In a moment I recovered my voice and tried not to yell, which could have attracted further attention, although no one was nearby at the time. "Out of there, both of you. MARCH!" Draped in towels and quickly drying, they meekly picked up their clothes, got dressed and trotted back to our bungalow. It was a long ten yards for them. Their heads hung in dismay, as they contemplated their misdeed and possible punishments.

I confronted them inside. "Mom and Dad taught you that boys and girls are not supposed to go playing around naked. You are old enough to know the meaning of modesty. I will give you a break this time and not tell Mom and Dad. But you must promise me not to do it again." They promised, and as far as I know, they never did it again.

After a week of being mostly off my feet, I returned to the clinic at Kings County Hospital and the doctor upgraded me for limited physical activity and walking, but no swimming or beach visits for at least another month.

The wooden planked Boardwalk began at West 37th Street and continued for four miles east past Coney Island and Ocean Parkway into Brighton Beach. I could not walk more than a few blocks at first, so I began traveling on the local Brooklyn bus going along Surf Avenue into the heart of Coney Island.

Coney Island

Coney Island is a two and a half mile long strip of beach-bordered land centered on the Boardwalk and its parallel city street Surf Avenue. In the summer of 1952, a short two block walk from our family bungalow in Sea Gate took me to the Sea Gate gatehouse entrance and 37th Avenue for the eastbound bus ride into Central Coney Island.

I had some money saved up and used it for my solo excursions into Coney Island. While boarding the bus, I could see the Parachute Jump Ride, a half mile away, thrusting its spidery structure skywards into the salty beachfront air. Twelve cantilevered arms sprouted from the top, from which the ride seats were suspended. One arm remained empty. The nickname for the Parachute Jump ride was 'the Eiffel Tower of Brooklyn'.

The Parachute Jump was originally built for the 1939 New York World's Fair in Flushing Meadows. The World's Fair Guidebook described the ride as follows:

"Eleven gaily-colored parachutes operated from the top of a 262-foot tower, enabling visitors to experience the thrills of "bailing out" without hazard or discomfort. Each 32-foot parachute has a double seat suspended from it. When two passengers are seated, a cable pulls it to the summit of the tower. An automatic release starts the drop, and the passengers float gently to the ground. Vertical guide wires prevent swaying, a metal ring keeps the chute open at all times, and rubber shock absorbers eliminate the landing impact."

Parachute Jump, Coney Island, NY

When the World's Fair ended in 1940, the Parachute Jump was disassembled, moved to Coney Island and then reassembled next to the Boardwalk between West 16th and West 19th Streets. The vertical drop took less than twenty seconds. Adults paid forty cents and children paid a quarter to experience it.

The structure is designated as a National Landmark, but it now serves as an active navigation beacon for airplanes. In its heyday, up to a half-million riders a year experienced the Parachute Jump, but I never could summon up the nerve to try it myself. It has remained closed permanently since 1964.

Across the street from the Jump was George C. Tilyou's Steeplechase Park, oldest of the Coney Island amusement parks, founded in 1897. The entrance archway was topped with an exaggerated facial lipstick grin of the clownish Steeplechase funny face, sometimes shown with green hair. This 'funny face', reminding some of the evil Joker from Batman comics, appeared throughout the park as the Steeplechase theme image.

The Steeplechase 'funny face'

The window-paned sides of the Steeplechase building stretched out for several city blocks, surrounded by an eight-track mechanical pony race ride. The 'ponies' were mounted on individual 'roller coaster' tracks with one or two riders, each one secured by seat belts. An initial twenty-two foot upslope track, similar to a cabled 'ski lift', provided the starting momentum for the ponies. At the top of the 'lift', they were propelled downwards on a 15% slope and then continued by gravity force around the racetrack encircling the Steeplechase building. The track continued with a series of humps, each of successively lessening height to maintain speed over the one-third mile course around the perimeter of the aptly-named Pavilion of Fun. The speed of the ponies could be steered slightly by the rider leaning forward or backwards, and to the right or left. I achieved the fastest results in my riding experience by leaning forward on the downhill stretches, and leaning to the inside (left) on the banked track turns.

After the Steeplechase race ended, dismounting riders were pointed towards the Pavilion of Fun in the Insanitorium and Blowhole Theater area. Backtracking provided no escape for customers, since it led to a maze which returned riders to the

Comedy Lane stage by another path. The only exit was through the Blowhole Theater, in which a set of compressed-air jets would blow off hats and lift ladies dresses up as they tried to scamper by.

Wary women (who had been through the Blowhole Theater before) wore slacks, but there were always some newcomer ladies with full skirts to be blown high for the entertainment of a mostly male spectator gallery alongside the Lane. The clown ringmaster of the Blowhole Theater used electric buzzers and Slapsticks to mildly swat customers. Slapsticks are two paddles joined on one side which make a loud sound when whacked on customers. It was all in good fun and caused no injury.

I went through the Blowhole Theater a few times during the summer—it was the only way to reach the Steeplechase pony race. Another ride that I wisely looked at, but avoided entering was the Human Pool Table. Still recovering from my injured toe earlier in the season, I was not about to risk being hurt again by stepping onto the spinning Pool Table. It was a giant-sized surface imbedded with 24 large rotating disks. Adjacent disks rotated in opposite directions. Players tried to cross its flat surface, but lost their footing and tumbled as they spun across the Table disks and bumped into each other.

In that 1952 memorable summer, I sometimes got off the Coney Island bus at Steeplechase to spend the afternoon. Other times, my trips continued eastwards towards the Stillwell Avenue train terminal. I often stopped for a hot dog with mustard and sauerkraut or a hamburger with onions and ketchup at Nathan's, and washed it down with a root beer. Nearby, on 22nd Avenue, was a stop at *Shatzkin's* for a Cherry Cheese or Kasha Knish for a quarter.

Scattered along Surf Avenue were Pitch-Ball booths offering rag doll and other prizes for knocking over three wooden bottles, arcades for shooting down tin ducks, baseball tosses, rubber ball rolling into playing card holes and other tourist lures. With only average success at the tin duck shooting game for small prizes, I avoided playing at the other booths, but just stopped and browsed around a bit if a particularly high scoring player happened to be in action.

Other street booths where I sometimes stopped to join the action were the Bumper Car rinks and Skee-Ball arcades along Surf Avenue. The steerable fiberglass Bumper Cars had pole mounted contacts to draw power from ceiling grids. The well-padded car bumpers and seat belts protected against hard bangs, while the often-ignored rules forbid head-on bumping and required same-direction driving. The objective of the ride was to bump other cars while avoiding being bumped. The bumper cars were appropriately nicknamed the 'Dodgems' and would sometimes cluster into mini-traffic jams which would be resolved by backing out of the jam—one car at a time. When Dad and Mom came along with us on his days off, Gloria and I would each ride the bumper cars separately. Her independence and aggressive driving made her a likely target for retaliatory bumping.

Skee-Ball arcades had become popular in Atlantic City and in Coney Island, among other resort areas, in the 1940s and '50s. The alleys were inclined lanes, about thirty feet long. The flat alley surface was similar to a bowling alley, with side rails mounted to keep the balls from rolling into adjacent lanes. Customers rolled the three-inch Masonite or heavy plastic balls up inclined slopes into a series of rings with holes of different point values. Points were accumulated with coupons which could be redeemed for gaudy toys and other prizes. The Skee-Ball parlors and bath houses along the western Boardwalk were next to other amusement arcades and mechanical rides. Gloria and Dad sometimes went on the less head-spinning rides and roller coasters together, but I avoided them because of their nausea-inducing potential. My family all joined in collecting Speedball coupons which were redeemed for a new phonograph at the end of the 1952 season.

It was a golden summer, which was only temporarily spoiled by my toe injury in the first few days at Seagate. I was further heartened by the prospect of Eisenhower's election to the Presidency that could bring the Korean War to a close. I was already considering the possibility of enlisting in the Air Force when I turned eighteen and would be eligible for the military draft. If Eisenhower was elected, and the Korean War ended, then I would not have to enter the military during a potential shooting war in Asia.

In the meantime, as autumn approached, I looked forward to entering DeWitt Clinton High School in the ninth grade. Clinton was founded in 1897 as an all-boys school. In its new building, on Mosholu Parkway, in the northern Bronx, it was in the 1930s the largest high school in the world, with several thousand students. It did not become co-ed until 1983.

DeWitt Clinton High School

*B*ack in the 1950s, New York City high schools were on a three-year-to-graduation path. The first year of high school was actually the tenth grade, continuing from the seventh through the ninth grades of junior high school.

DeWitt Clinton HS

When I entered De Witt Clinton in 1952, it was still an all-boys school. That did not matter to me since I was in the pre-dating phase of life and girls were of no special interest to me.

Clinton remained as the last local New York all-boys public high school for another thirty years, until 1983. The enrollment grew to about four thousand boys at its peak. Since there were no girls around for the boys to try to impress, typical teenage boy behavior was probably more 'locker room' macho style than would have occurred in a co-ed school.

DeWitt Clinton High was larger than a neighborhood school, so it drew students to its oaken doors, marbled hallways and 21-acre campus from all over the Bronx and Manhattan. Most of them traveled north to the Mosholu Parkway station, the next to the last northbound stop at Woodlawn on the Jerome Avenue elevated line. DeWitt Clinton High was nicknamed "the Castle on the Parkway", because it had a swimming pool and athletic facilities for over 30 student sports teams. On its looming campus, a squat gothic tower with a square pyramid green-tiled roof and a high arched window on each side commanded the parkway entrance to the three-story sandstone building.

Opening day of the school was Oct. 29, 1929—the day of the Great Crash on Wall Street. Over 2,000 people crowded into the auditorium that opening day to hear Mayor Jimmy Walker dedicate the new school to serve children from all walks of life. He declared that, "This temple of education will repay us even after we are gone, by training future generations to be good citizens." Unfortunately, flamboyant New York City Mayor Walker was hardly an example of a good citizen! He was removed from office under pressure from Governor Roosevelt in 1932 for taking bribes from businessmen seeking government contracts, publicly frequenting speakeasies (which others in public life visited more discreetly!) and consorting with showgirls.

I had no high ideals in mind when I chose Clinton High. I felt knowledgeable and interested in government and political affairs more than many adults and most teenagers that I knew in those days. Instead, my school choice was based on getting away from the West Bronx where I grew up and struggled to relate to other boys of my age in the neighborhood. The thought of having to potentially continue that struggle at Taft High gave me the chills. Many of the local boys and girls chose Taft because it was nearer, and because of the tribal feeling with their peers that lured them there—a feeling which I lacked.

A few days before school began, I received a package of forms and instructions for parents and students in the mail. It was an official-looking yellow manila clasp envelope marked 'For Incoming Students'. Included were a homeroom assignment and an appointment with a guidance counselor. The elective classes could be reassigned right after opening day, Tuesday, Sept. 2, 1952, if the student was qualified, and if the guidance counselor approved, and if a seat was available in the requested class.

On the first day of school at Clinton, some students were wandering the hallways, white-faced and confused. For the first time, they faced near-adult level situations in which they would make class choices that would affect their futures. Some of them looked like young immature boys. Others looked like grown men, but were still little boys on the inside. I met with my homeroom teacher for a brief orientation and then a session with the guidance counselor for class assignments.

The mandatory class list was basic and familiar to me from the school's mailed material. It included classes in Social Studies, English, and Science. I chose Earth Science because of its diversity. It covered Biology, Botany and Astronomy. I was knowledgeable about Astronomy, and looked forward to getting good grades in that course. Then I discussed the mandatory Gym class with the counselor, assuming that it would be mainly basketball and exercises with scheduled pool swimming sessions. Then I found out further details about the swimming conditions. Their rules for boys required nudity in the pool!

I thought the pool nudity was unfair to boys whose puberty was a little delayed. They were subjected to potential teasing from more genitally-developed teens. A generation later, around 1980, YMCAs and high school gym classes became integrated, so the male nudity swim problem at Clinton eventually ended long after my high school years.

I objected to the swimming nudity requirement on the grounds of male modesty and threatened a discrimination lawsuit, even though I had no support for this from my parents. They thought that I should just go along with it, but I had other backing. I knew several other boys who also raised the modesty issue, and refused to swim in the nude, and one of them was a lawyer's son. He told us that we had a right to protect our privacy. With a student mini-revolt brewing, Clinton High then compromised and I and other objecting boys were quietly permitted to skip the school pool sessions, and present an attendance letter from the public pool to the school principal. We also had to promise not to talk about it to others or to go to the newspapers about the issue. The school was obviously afraid of notorious publicity on this matter. The 1950s were a time of awakening civil rights consciousness. And some of the objecting boys were black. The swimming nudity avoidance secret was well-kept during my years at Clinton.

As I began my tenth grade class program in the early weeks of autumn, problems with the academic side of my school classes emerged. I enjoyed the American History class, and my extensive historical reading gave me an edge-up on the rest of the class. English Literature was a little more challenging, but I succeeded there as well.

In Earth Science, I was initially impressed with our elderly teacher, Dr. Rampolsky. Few local high school teachers then had doctorates, and he shared with us that he had been a research scientist, and showed us some botanical research that he had published in his field. I wondered: *teaching high school must be quite a comedown for him in professional status. Did he lose his research grant?* He never spoke of it again.

The first few weeks of Dr. Rampolsky's class were interesting, as the class delved into the basic structures of plant and animal life. Then the curriculum veered into Earth Science. The teaching problem began with the sub-topic of Astronomy. It soon became obvious to me that Dr. Rampolsky was not well informed on this subject.

Dr. Rampolsky told the class, with a straight face: "The planets orbit the Sun in circular orbits." My hand shot up. "Excuse me, but while Copernicus established the heliocentric theory of our planetary system four centuries ago, Kepler's applications of physics and math to astronomy proved that planetary orbits are ellipses, not circles."

The class looked shocked. Murmurs arose, then shushed in anticipation of Dr. Rampolsky's response. They were unused to seeing a teacher challenged so directly by a student on a scholastic point. The startled professor quickly recovered his poise. Sarcastically, he sneered at me, "Perhaps Mr. Bernie Seiden here would care to enlighten us further with HIS scientific knowledge!"

Cocksure that I would be unprepared to teach, and would stumble and humiliate myself, he gestured me to the front of the room. "Professor Seiden, if you please," he smirked. Some students smirked too, in gleeful anticipation of what they thought would be my forthcoming scholastic humiliation. I took a deep breath and began:

"There are three basic laws by which Kepler describes planetary motion. These laws were later amended by Newton and subsequently superseded by Einstein, but remain as a rough approximation of explaining solar planetary motion in modern science. The first law is that planets follow elliptical orbits, with the sun as one of the two focal points of the orbit." I then moved to the blackboard to demonstrate the ellipse.

"The second law is that the planet moves faster when closer to the sun along its orbital path around the sun and slower when it is at a more distant orbital point. The third law is a complex mathematical formula which calculates the relationship between the distance of planets from the sun and their orbital periods. Thank you." I chalked up the blackboard with an illustration of the planetary orbits and returned to my seat.

Dr. Rampolsky appeared somewhat flustered and retreated into presenting the next topic, where he was on safer ground—climate on our own Earth planet. After the class ended, I was approached in the hallway by several students with praise for my impromptu lecture and a proposal.

'Hey, Bernie," one of the boys said. "You can teach better than that guy up there. Why don't you take over the class? You can show us all that astronomy stuff!" The rest of the class agreed. A little adult voice inside my head said, *"Don't do it. You will get into trouble."*

But then my inner child voice whispered back,

"Go ahead. You can do it. It will be fun. If you get caught, you can talk your way out of it." I mischievously agreed with the child voice within, and my fellow students made plans to stage a coup and take control of the class next day to teach an astronomy course for as long as I could hold the floor against resistance. We all agreed to come in early the next morning and lock the door against the teacher. I also warned them not to discuss our secret plan with anyone else.

Surprisingly, no teacher or student in the hallway noticed the unusual activity of the entire Earth Science class arriving ten minutes before the period started! We swiftly bolted the classroom door and secured it with a braced chair.

I began speaking ad lib, with only an occasional glance at my outlined lecture notes. A wild thought flashed across my mind. *I'm so glad there are no girls in this class. They might giggle and distract me and the guys if they were here now.*

Some of the students began taking notes. It was interesting to see that some of those in class who paid the least attention to Dr. Rampolsky were now 'all ears' to listen to my astronomy lecture.

Clearing my throat, I began with a brief review of the main characteristics of the solar planets, then took a question from the class. "Why are the planets all nearly round?" I responded, "That's a good question! The short answer is that not all planets are nearly round. Planetoids are objects in the solar system that are too small to be considered as planets and too large to be rocks.

At this point, Dr. Rampolsky appeared at the door and started pounding. I calmly continued. "Only larger planetoids—at least 300 miles in diameter—have sufficient internal gravity and rotational force to be pulled by these forces into a roughly spherical shape. In our solar system, Ceres is the only asteroid large enough to be rounded. The smaller ones are irregular in shape and wobble as they rotate."

The pounding paused, and then a second face appeared at the glassed window—the Principal. Now they both continued pounding away at the door. I excused myself to the class and went over to the door, but did not open it. Without raising my voice, I said through the glass door panel, "You are disturbing my class. Please stop it and behave yourselves." In stupefied silence for a moment, the Principal found his voice again and blared forth at me. "Stop this classroom act right now and open the door, or I will call the police. You are suspended until further notice, effective immediately!"

I shrugged, gathered up my things, and opened the door. "Please mail me my homework assignments." I walked out as the class murmured confusedly behind me. One boy whispered as I passed by, "I'll get the homework to you." I nodded my thanks, but did not answer aloud to avoid making potential trouble for him.

I knew that going home early would arouse suspicions by Mom, so I went to the public library for the day. I decided to wait for Dad to come home from work that day, and to spring my suspension news on both of them after supper. Dad did not usually take part in a discussion of school for either me or my siblings. But if Mom verbally dragged him into it, he would join the parental dialogue.

I asked for Gloria and the twins to leave the dining table, so I could talk to Mom and Dad privately in low tones. My siblings obediently retreated to the bedroom. I began carefully. "Mom. Dad. Listen carefully to what I have to tell you about what happened at school today." I then told them the tale of my Rampolsky caper.

Mom frowned and began to raise her voice, momentarily forgetting that little ears in the next room picked up every spoken word. Dad asked, "Quiet for a moment, please. I have an idea." We listened. It was so rare for Dad to speak up like that! He continued. "Bernie, I know someone with influence who can put in a good word for you with the school. That's Mr. Carmine De Sapio, the big Manhattan Democratic party boss in Greenwich Village. I drive him to his office three times per week. He tips well and once told me, "if there is anything I can ever do locally for you, let me know." Dad paused momentarily. "Bernie, go see him, tell him you are my son. He will help you." I responded, "Sure, Dad. Give me his phone number. I will ask to meet with him." I did not share the prevailing middle class public scorn for political bosses and neither did Dad. He was flattered that such an important man could be friendly to him. De Sapio dispensed local political favors, job and school referrals and donated turkeys on Thanksgiving and Christmas to constituents on welfare.

The next morning, I called Mr. DeSapio's office and, after a brief hold on the phone, his secretary gave me a 5:30 p.m. appointment the next afternoon to meet with him at his apartment in Greenwich Village. Mom told me to dress up nicely, so I put on my Bar Mitzvah suit. It still fit me, but the sleeves of the jacket were a little short on my growing adolescent arms. Mom let out the jacket sleeves, and scolded me. "This does not mean that I forgive your school behavior. Good luck with Mr. De Sapio."

At twenty minutes past five, I appeared at Mr. DeSapio's 33 Washington Square West apartment building with a copy of my suspension notice. It was a seven-story, red-brick, solid-looking residence with a square, classic Greek-framed entrance supported by marble columns, and walls faced with black-edged casement windows. (Today that building flies the blue and white flag of New York University as its Lipton Hall residence.)

I knocked on the apartment door, and was admitted by Mr. De Sapio himself. His staff had left for the day. Cordially, he greeted me. "Come in, Bernie. Your Dad tells me you are having a little problem at school." He gestured me to a chair in the living room. "Tell me about it."

While relating the lockout story, I saw a little smile curling up the corners of his mouth, as if recalling some old indiscretions of his own youthful days. *But he had surmounted them and went on to Fordham University and Brooklyn Law School, so he could not have been too much of a bad boy!*

He asked me, "how long did you keep the door locked?" I told him, "It was only about ten minutes." I quickly added, "I made my point, then I surrendered the classroom to the Principal. Ten minutes, that's all I took."

He then asked a critical question. "How are you getting along with your other teachers? How are your grades?" I replied, "It's early in the semester, but I have no problems with my other teachers, and my first test grades of the term are all good." As an afterthought, I added, "Oh, by the way, according to Section 3204 of the New York State Education Law, it requires teaching of a subject by a competent teacher. Dr. Rampolsky is not competent to teach Astronomy."

I reached into my book bag and presented Mr. De Sapio with a copy of the state Education Law. He peered at me in surprise through his dark-tinted glasses. "Hmmm. You may have a point there. But that doesn't excuse you from not making your protest through official channels if you wanted to make an issue of it. If I can get your suspension reduced, do I have your word as a man that there will be no further bad behavior incidents from you at Clinton?"

Eagerly, I declared, "I promise!" "Call my office tomorrow afternoon," he said. We shook hands, and I departed to take the subway home. I left Mr. DeSapio with a 'feel-good' glow. *He had called me a man!*

Wow! I was still a teenager and it was the first time, other than the symbolic 'today I am a man' speech at my Bar Mitzvah, when I was 13 years old, that anyone called me a man. It made me feel very proud and grownup.

I did not want to hang around the house during school hours, so the next morning I went to my studying sanctuary—

the Highbridge Public Library branch. I dutifully did my smuggled homework assignment there. No questions were asked about why I was at the public library during school hours. The library staff was too busy to notice.

I did not worry about any possible truancy officers accosting me, since they knew that truants usually went to places of entertainment or shopping, not to libraries.

Then, the next morning I received a telegram from the Board of Education that notified me that my thirty day suspension was reduced to ten days if I waived a hearing and did not pursue Article 3204 charges against Dr. Rampolsky.

I mailed back my acceptance, called Mr. De Sapio's office to thank him for his efforts on my behalf, and continued my schoolwork at home for the next week, interspersed with trips to the library and downtown to the Hayden Planetarium.

I returned to class when my suspension ended and I did not brag or discuss it with any other Clinton students or teachers. My grades were good, and later in the school year I received a 99 on the American History Regents test. Then I disputed the one point that I missed while aiming for a perfect score on the test. It involved naming the key turning point in the Civil War. The textbook answer was 'Gettysburg' I answered 'Vicksburg' and disputed the standard textbook answer.

Keeping my promise not to resort again to classroom seizure tactics, I submitted a well-reasoned rebuttal defending my one-point answer to the Board of Regents. I wrote that "the successful siege and capture of Vicksburg gave the Union control of the Mississippi River as a supply line and tightened their military encirclement of the Confederacy." In a response letter, the Regents admitted that the designation of Gettysburg as a Civil War turning point was disputable and they gave me the final point to make a perfect 100 on the Regents exam.

Early in the morning of Friday, Oct. 23, 1953, at about 5:45 a.m., an empty ten-car northbound train crashed into another empty stopped train on the center track of the Jerome Avenue line. The collision happened just south of the Mosholu Park station one block away from DeWitt Clinton High. The northbound motorman was killed as his cab crumpled into a V-shape, and rained debris down onto the street below. The other motorman was not injured.

Train service on the Jerome Avenue line was suspended that morning, and I went to Clinton High by the Concourse line, which terminated at 205th Street, several blocks further away from the school than the Jerome Avenue train, which I usually took to school. As I walked past Jerome Avenue, skirting the crash scene by one block, I saw the awful sight of twisted and crumpled subway train cars and I thought to myself: *Wow! Good thing the train was empty except for the motorman. I am sorry for him too, of course. If the train wreck had happened a couple of hours later, I would have been on that train, with multiple casualties aboard and in the street. Dozens maybe, or more dead if it had happened near 8:00 AM—school time.*

Many teachers allowed their classes a brief viewing time at the school windows facing the el line if the students promised to resume their studies afterwards. In my brief time at the window, I saw that the clearance of the trains had already started with cables and ropes attached to pull the cars back to the track. Meanwhile, two blocks of glass and other debris were being swept up from the streets below. The train line was restored to full service by the following morning, and the school returned to its normal routine. The rest of the school year passed quietly. And then I prepared to enter the eleventh grade as a junior.

Train wreck on Jerome Ave. Elevated line. October 23, 1953

40

Transfer to Theodore Roosevelt Evening High School

In April, 1954, I passed a milestone in the journey to adulthood and independence from my parents—my sixteenth birthday. I was now eligible for working papers and an after-school job, working as a stock boy, pushing clothing carts and racks. I worked on the 2 p.m. to 6 p.m. day shift in Alexander's Department Store on Fordham Road at seventy-five cents per hour. Without substantial money of my own, other than pocket money, I had to depend on Mom for clothes and other purchases, and submit to her imposed tastes.

Meanwhile, the shadow of the continuing national military draft loomed over my future. Although an armistice was signed in the Korean War on July 23, both United Nations and Communist armies remained fully mobilized. They confronted each other across the demilitarized zone border, hostile and armed to the teeth, and there was no long term assurance that fighting would not break out again in Korea. There were periodic shooting incidents between the two hostile sides. I started to think again about enlisting.

Meanwhile, I resolved to continue my education on an adult level at night school to replace the juvenile level in my life at daytime high school. My decision to enlist was a secret, kept away from my family and school until a time came to implement it.

After several visits to the Bronx recruiting booth at Grand Concourse and Fordham Road, I chose to join the Air Force. It seemed cleaner and less subject to ground combat action and risk than the other services. Being in the Navy could involve long deployments at sea and weathering ocean storms. I ruled out joining the Coast Guard for similar reasons—the potential for involvement in dangerous bad weather rescues at sea. The Marines were too gung-ho and the Army was too involved in ground combat, and I doubted that my physical condition and toughness would stand up under the strain of such rigorous service.

The educational opportunities for college correspondence and on-campus courses in the military towards a degree were strong and available at government expense. Many of the military occupational fields could prepare for solid, well-paying civilian jobs after the enlistment period ended. Enlistees, particularly in peacetime service, could choose their military career fields. I chose Airborne Meteorology. It seemed to be a glamorous future adventure to fly as a crewman into the eye of hurricanes.

As my senior year at Clinton began, I felt a certain malaise —*am I a boy or a man?* Mom treated me as a boy, but Dad was neutral on this point. He meekly deferred to Mom's bossy parental style.

Realizing that money was the magic ingredient to becoming an adult, I made an appointment with the guidance counselor to discuss leaving day school and completing senior year in night school. In two weeks, I had a new full-time job waiting for me to start, after arranging to drop out of Clinton High and continue my education at Roosevelt Evening High School.

But first there was an exit interview with the school guidance counselor. Mr. Johnson leaned back in his swivel chair and studied my papers. "Hmmm. Bernie, have you thought out the consequences of dropping out? You know, lack of graduation can harm your future job prospects. Only the lowest level jobs will hire high school dropouts."

"But, Mr. Johnson," I exclaimed. "I am not dropping out of school. I just got a new full-time job yesterday, starting in two weeks, and I am enrolling in Roosevelt Evening High. I have every intention of finishing up the credits for my academic diploma and graduation."

Mr. Johnson frowned slightly and declared, "I know that you are continuing your education in night school. However, the Board of Education still requires you to take a trade school class despite your academic continuance towards a diploma. So I have to enroll you in a plumbing class—two hours once a week at Samuel Gompers High in the East Morrisania section of the Bronx."

He looked a little embarrassed. "I know that trade school is not your thing, but rules are rules and we have to follow them. Would it really do you any harm to learn how to fix a leaky pipe? Someday you may own a home and that knowledge will come in handy."

"Yeah, I replied. "I anticipated your sticking Gompers High on me and I looked it up. It is a school for blue collar laboring types, not me! Half of the incoming classes there are in the lowest third academically in the city. What kind of a learning environment is that for me? I would be dragged down by them!"

Mr. Johnson shrugged. "Just behave yourself and try to show

some interest in the plumbing business, and you will be out of it soon. When you turn seventeen, you can drop it on your own without compulsory attendance." I grudgingly accepted.

Shortly after the school term began, I transferred into the evening session at Theodore Roosevelt High on Fordham Road and started a full-time job as a helper in a millinery factory in the Garment District. I worked on the steam presser, kept the floor tidy of clothing scraps, and pushed hatbox racks to wholesalers and corporate retail buyers in the Seventh Avenue Garment District between 37th and 45th Streets.

All that kept this garment shop job from becoming a complete drudgery were the lunch hours. Dennis, the boss's son, was our manager. He was a young man in his early twenties who fancied himself to be a fencer. He was on the Columbia University college fencing team, had tried out but failed to make the Olympic fencing squad, and he sought to recruit some of my co-workers in the garment shop as fencers.

Some of the others volunteered for the fencing sessions as a way of currying favor with the boss and his son. I got involved because of a genuine interest in the thrust and parry skills of this sport, and in the historical battles that occupied Europe and Asia for 3,000 years that were won by sword-wielding soldiers. So on most lunch hours during the week, we gathered around in an open area of the factory loft, and donned equipment and masks for instruction in swordsmanship. Then we engaged in a series of short demonstrations and matches which were enjoyable and exciting. I knew that I would never be a serious fencer, but I did develop some proficiency in the sport and enjoyed the skill and interplay of the competition to score a touché.

Then, things went a little too far and there was an injury in the shop. One afternoon, about two months after I began working there, a metal millinery dummy head block crashed down on Dennis. The floor vibration from our sword thrusts and lunges had caused it to topple off a shelf onto his head. It knocked him down, but he remained semi-conscious.

His lips turned blue, and he mumbled, "I'm OK, I'm OK." But he was not okay, and his father called for an ambulance. It was back to work for us, in a subdued mood for the rest of the day, as we each prayed for Dennis in our own way. It was a mild concussion, and he was out from the job for only a few days.

When Dennis returned, his father decreed that there would be no more lunchtime fencing sessions. A few months later, I left the blue collar labor world to enter the white collar world of office work.

I commuted to Roosevelt Evening High by the Third Avenue El to the Fordham Road station, then running in its final year before demolition began. The city promises of a Second Avenue subway to replace it were postponed repeatedly, then suspended indefinitely during the fiscal crisis years of the mid-1970s. After my high school days in the '50s the Bronx section of the Third Avenue el continued to run for another twenty years.

Evening high school was a transformative experience. I joined the adult senior year class at the night session of Roosevelt High, two blocks east of the old Third Avenue elevated line on the south side of Fordham Road. I commuted there straight after work, first stopping for a brief dinner in the Fordham Road neighborhood. After class, I went home by bus.

Roosevelt was a smaller school than giant DeWitt Clinton. I soon adjusted to the adult atmosphere of the night school and appreciated the relative seriousness of these older students. At sixteen years of age, I was the youngest student in my class.

The other students, including many immigrants, were mostly

in their thirties and up, working to earn their high school diplomas just as I was doing in night classes. There was no parental or school pressure for them to be there—just their own drive and ambition to continue their education.

Some students had families to support and worked hard during the day to make a living. Then they sat for classes and did homework, setting a good example for their children, and they somehow found time for their family life as well.

I made one new friend, Ralph Pereira. He was a Brazilian deckhand on the Staten Island ferry and was striving towards American citizenship. He was old enough to be my father but treated me as an equal adult, and we established an easygoing camaraderie. Ralph admitted to me that his Americanized daughter, born in the United States and attending the day session of Roosevelt High, sometimes helped him with his homework. Coming from a macho Latin culture, it was not easy on Ralph's masculine ego to seek help from a grown daughter in his schoolwork.

I moved on to a new job at a wholesale auto parts supplier in the Bronx as their bookkeeper at $90 per week. This was a step up on the salary scale, and I would now be earning more than my Dad for the first time. So I exchanged my 'blue collar' for a 'white collar' and began to get used to wearing a shirt and tie to the office every day. It was a one-person office and I kept contact with the main office downtown by phone each day. My responsibility was to maintain the company 'books', verify the invoices and handle the payroll and inventory records. I was glad to have a shorter commute to school and work. I was also glad to be working in an office by myself, and be insulated from office politics. I was treated as a 'boss' and respected by the workers there, even though I exercised no authority over them.

My thinking began to shift towards an adult emotional level.

I was actually making a living wage now and could support myself. In the meantime, the Korean War had locked down into an armistice, and I felt less pressure about being drafted into the service. I thought: *better to enjoy life now as a young man in the Bronx, then worry about joining the military afterwards to beat the Draft.*

41

Discovering Girls

I had little social contact with teenage girls in my Clinton High School years, other than brief chatting with some of Gloria's friends from Taft High. They were, for the most part, vulgar and slutty. They wore tight sweaters and I'd heard them converse in trashy talk about boys. I resented that these girls, all a year or two older than Gloria, had lured my sister into smoking. I was well aware of the dangers of cigarettes from reading library books and magazine articles on smoking. The tobacco marketing blitz of the 1940s and '50s was generated by admired movie stars smoking on screen. Tobacco advertising was aimed at young smokers to hook them for life. Among the lures for younger smokers were chocolate Lucky Strike candy, that was packaged to resemble real cigarettes. Many succumbed to the bait, but some informed adults and youngsters resisted the lure and the pseudo-glamour of smoking as being 'cool' and 'sophisticated.'

My pleas for Gloria to stop smoking fell on deaf ears. "All my friends are doing it" was her response. "All your friends will have no lungs left, be coughing their guts out and dying of lung cancer or emphysema by the time they are in their fifties," was my tart reply.

I particularly remember Gloria's best friend Joanie. She was big, bold, brassy, and 'brassiere-y' with prominent breasts jutting out and filling up her tight pink sweater. She was sixteen and thus age-eligible to pair off with me— Gloria's big brother. I was usually a young gentleman in behavior with young women, but emotions of early sexuality stirred my loins and one time I slyly touched Joanie's breasts, accidentally on purpose, while brushing past her in our foyer. She reacted indignantly, screeched and slapped me hard. I apologized instantly. But Joanie's bold appearance and often slutty behavior was almost her undoing. One fine summer day, soon after the 'touching' incident, she came running to our apartment, crying and disheveled, with her blouse torn. Gloria ran to answer the door in instant concern. "Migod, Joanie! What happened to you?" she cried. I heard the commotion and followed Gloria to the door.

Joanie blurted out to us in near-hysteria, "Two boys jumped me. It happened around the corner on Nelson Avenue." Joanie did not object to my supportive presence. She blurted out a tale of being followed down the street and waylaid by two local toughs who ripped her sweater and blouse while trying to maul her. She broke away from them and ran to our place. Gloria comforted her while I called the police in a rush of concern for my sister's friend. Gone away was Joanie's anger at my touching her breast a few days earlier. I patted her hand in a friendly, non-sexual way and she calmed down. I was relieved that Carol and Mark were not yet home from school to see this upsetting scene. The police came and drove Joanie around the neighborhood to try to spot the culprits, but they had disappeared. With no names and no witnesses to the incident, they were never caught.

In the weeks following, Joanie began to dress more conservatively, and I vowed to myself never to sexually touch a girl again, unless it was by mutual consent. Gloria did not take the high moral ground with me over the Joanie incident, and she kept trying to 'fix me up' with Naomi or one of her other girlfriends. Finally, just to appease her, a few weeks later I asked Naomi, for a Saturday night date to see a movie at the nearby Zenith Theater on 170th Street, just west of Jerome Avenue—a short bus ride away from where she lived near the NYU Hall of Fame campus. She was a medium-built brunette with a happy-go-lucky attitude and a sunny disposition. She was rumored to be boy-crazy and could converse intelligently on events of the day, unlike most of Gloria's other girlfriends.

We took the Macombs Road bus downhill about ten blocks to 170th Street and walked to the Zenith. She took a little friendly initiative and slipped her hand into mine as we strolled along. I was sure that Naomi had heard of the incident between me and Joanie, and wrongly assumed I would get a little 'fresh' with her when the timing was right. After the movie, we took the bus home and walked to her apartment door. I wanted to reach out and kiss her good night, but did not dare. At her door, Naomi half-turned towards me expectantly. Summoning up my nerve, I gave her a half-hearted peck on her right cheek. Without warning, Naomi threw her arms around me and gave me a deep kiss with her tongue curling around in my mouth. Shocked, I pulled away from her and ran off in confusion. I caught the short bus ride home in a state of swirling dismay. As innocent as I then was in experience with the opposite sex, I did not then know that girls could behave like that! Especially on a first date!

It was still early, and Gloria was waiting for me expectantly in the living room. She shut off the television and began to question me. "How was it, Bernie? How did things go with Naomi?

Did you 'make it' with her up on the roof of her apartment house?"

"Well, it was like this." I confided what happened, and said, "I was surprised, not afraid about what happened—that's why I ran away. "Oh, Bernie," Gloria responded. "Don't be such a square! Everyone kisses like that nowadays, unless you are ancient—over thirty or something. And every boy I know has had sex with Naomi on the roof!" I laughed at her definition of 'a square' and that broke the tension in the room. "No, Gloria," I said. "I am not a 'square'. Just unprepared for heavy kissing. I hardly know her, after all. I am no prude! Just unready, that's all. When I have sex with a girl," I continued, "it should be with some mutual feeling between us, not just because everyone else does it with her." Pausing, I finished my brotherly lecture with some affection, "Gloria, I appreciate your helping me get into the dating scene, but I think it would be better if I find my own dates away from your friends. They are okay, but girls do talk about their experiences with each other, and I am uncomfortable with that kind of gossip."

Gloria pouted. "Boys talk to each other, too. Actually they brag and tell experiences that they wish they had, not actually what happened." *Gloria, you are right*, I thought. But I would not admit this out loud. "Let's not make a gender war out of this."

Several months passed before I tried again to date a girl. I had met her at a singles dance at the Concourse Y. There was no connection with Gloria's friends at the 'Y'. None of her friends ever went there, to the best of my knowledge. Presumably, the 'Y' was too 'square' for their liking!

Bronx "Y" on Grand Concourse

Sometimes, when Gloria was between boyfriends, I would escort her to the 'Y', then discreetly fade away to avoid spoiling any social connection that she might make there. Also, I practiced my own social skills in meeting girls after I chaperoned Gloria's boy connections. Sometimes, she failed to connect with anyone at the 'Y', and then I took her home. The Concourse 'Y' is where Gloria met Donald, my future brother-in-law, several months later.

Gloria was fifteen years old and Donald was twenty-three when they met and started dating. Ruggedly handsome and dark-haired, he was only about five foot six tall, shorter than most of the high school guys she had dated before. He was bulky, built like a tank, but with no body fat—it was all muscle! A picture of him on the sports wall of the 'Y' in tights with his emblazoned Title Belt proclaimed him as a past welterweight wrestling champion of the Bronx. Other girls were impressed by his rippling muscles, but Don only had eyes for Gloria from when they first met.

I was a little hesitant about approving Don as a potential boyfriend for Gloria. Not that she needed my official approval, but the age of consent was then seventeen in New York State, and Mom and Dad could have stopped the relationship if I had informed them of it. So that gave me leverage to check on their budding romance.

Gloria and Don both accepted my protective role as older brother to 'keep an eye on them'. Don confided his background to me. I tried not to be shocked when he told me that he had served five years in jail for an armed robbery. Prison was where he had learned to wrestle, and also finished up the required courses for his high school diploma. When he was released, he was hired as a grocery clerk in Olinsky's Supermarket on University Avenue.

Don worked hard at Olinsky's and impressed his bosses, who were aware of his criminal record. One day, I secretly observed him at work there. He could toss a pair of 80-pound grocery sacks onto a truck, one under each arm. But he was not a stereotype muscle man. Good with figures, and in handling customers and junior employees, he was promoted to assistant manager shortly before he met Gloria and became a manager a few months later. In those days, it was a rare employer that would even hire a felon, especially for a responsible job including cash register operations.

Seeing that he has 'gone straight', I told him that I approved of his dating Gloria, but warned him that with any misbehavior, I would report him to his parole officer. He promised me he would be 'good', declared his love for Gloria, and apparently kept his word about that.

In retrospect, I am sure that they were having sex at that time, but my sense of privacy prevailed and I did not inquire about that. They had my brotherly blessing to keep company with each other. Mom and Dad knew nothing about what was going on between Gloria and Don. I did not tell them anything about their relationship because Gloria had confided in me and made me promise not to tell anyone.

Meanwhile, I acclimated myself to the new adult student environment at Roosevelt Evening High. The women students there were mostly ten or more years older than I was and that was an impregnable barrier to socializing in those days. I did sometimes meet new girls at the 'Y' for casual dates, but no serious relationship emerged from these encounters. However, Gloria and Don were getting seriously involved with each other over the next several months.

42

Wedding Bells Ring for Gloria

Gloria and her new boyfriend Don were young and impulsive. They rapidly became entwined in a whirlwind romance after their first encounter. Was this love at first sight? I was not sure. Gloria was very immature and I did not think that she was ready for a committed relationship with a man. They were dating several times a week—and they barely knew each other! *Or so I thought!*

She was very anxious to escape from parental controls, which gave me some pause for thought. *Was she really in love or mainly looking to flee from home with whoever would take her?*

Before I could think further about their ongoing romance, fate intervened. On a balmy late September weekday evening, about three months after they first met, the telephone rang. If it was Gloria, I knew she would remain silent if Mom or Dad picked up the phone, so I answered the call.

"Hello?"

"Bernie, it's me," she whispered. ""Is Mom or Dad around?"

"No. They went to a movie about an hour ago. I am home with the twins."

"Okay. Then I can talk freely." A pause, then she gathered in a deep breath.

"Don and I are in Maryland."

"You are where?" I screeched, "What are you doing there?" I asked reflexively.

I was afraid of what her answer would be.

Gloria declared, "We are waiting two days to get married. Don't try to stop us."

I responded, "No I won't. But Mom will have a fit when I tell her. Do you understand that I have to tell her now?"

"Yes, tell her, but she better not try to interfere! I'll kill her if she annuls the marriage. I am not a kid anymore and I won't let her spoil my life!"

"Okay. I cannot say that I approve of this, but I will try to make peace for you with the understanding that what is done is done. I assume you will be staying in Don's place in the Bronx?"

"Yes," she replied. "But we will be looking for a bigger apartment next week."

For the first time in this conversation, I could hear Gloria relax a little. "Okay, Bernie," she declared. "I trust you. Do the best you can with Mom."

My mind raced. *How did they get a license with Gloria still underage? Don must have gotten a former criminal buddy to forge a birth certificate for Gloria.*

"Gloria, where are you? Give me a phone number where I can reach you. I won't tell her where you are, but I need to know so I can help you." She gave me the motel number, and said she and Don would be driving back to New York Tuesday because he had to be back at work on Wednesday.

Now came the hard part—telling Mom what happened, and

persuading her and Dad to accept the marriage. I knew they would be home in another hour or so, so I had time to think things over. *Gloria was underage, but did Mom really want to have the marriage annulled and throw Don back in jail on a statutory rape charge?* I was gambling that I could talk her out of doing it, for Gloria's sake.

I agonized over dealing with the elopement issue. *Was it really in Gloria's best interest for our parents to let the marriage stand?* I considered the alternatives. This was my first adult family decision. *I better not blow it!*

Two hours later, Mom and Dad came home from the movies. I greeted them in the most casual way that my mental state could muster at that moment.

"Mom … Dad …." Slowly with emphasis. "Gloria and Don eloped to Maryland to get married." You could have heard a pin drop. Dad gulped. Mom just stared, trying to find her voice. "That can't be so. You must be joking."

"Sorry, Mom. This is for real. I mean it."

There was silence in the air for the moment. A crow cawing in the tree at the curb mocked at us. *Were the birds getting the last laugh here?*

Her face contorted with rage. "You knew about this, didn't you?"

"No, I did not," I retorted. "Gloria and Don must have planned it and sneaked around to get packed and ready. Don has a good job and some money saved, I guess. They did not need my help for this elopement getaway." Dad interjected feebly. "Rose, maybe we should give them a chance to work this out."

"No way!" Mom sneered indignantly. "I will have him thrown back in jail where he belongs. Gloria is underage. She is a minor. She does not know what she is doing. I will get the marriage annulled. I am calling the cops right now."

"Mom, stop it!" I argued, struggling not to yell back at her.

"Listen to me now. If you do this, Gloria will hate you forever. They seem to love each other. He has been going straight, is reformed from his criminal past and has been holding a good job since he got out of jail."

Then, in a strained voice, I noted, "Moishe's Dairy knows he did time for a robbery, yet they made him an assistant manager and they trust him with the cash register, so I think you can trust him with your daughter." Trying not to sound argumentative, I declared, "She is my sister and I trust him with her. I will have a good talk with them when they get home."

Dad hesitated, then chimed in. "I vote for giving them a chance." That did it. Mom withdrew her hand from the phone. Still seething, she retorted,

"Then it is on your necks if anything goes wrong."

Don took an extra day off before going back to work. The couple arrived at his apartment late Tuesday afternoon. By coincidence, Don lived a block down the hill from my parents on Macombs Road. The sun was shining, and I put aside whatever misgivings still lingered and came to their door to greet them with a hearty handshake for Don and hugs for them both.

"Congratulations," I exclaimed. "I wish you guys all the best."

Don responded, "Thanks, Bernie." He gripped my right arm lightly. "I swear to you that I will take good care of her. I promise. I promise."

His sincerity was disarming. I gave him the benefit of the doubt for the moment. Smilingly, I said, "Let's go to see Mom and Dad now. Don't forget to call her Mom." The three of us then trekked back to our apartment and knocked. Dad answered the door. That made the situation a little easier. Mom retreated to the bedroom.

Upfront, Don declared, "Hi Dad. I've got your daughter."

Jokingly, Dad asked "Are you holding her for ransom?"

"Nah, I'm going to keep her. We are married!" In the most tense life situations, Dad could always manage a joke or two to ease the tension.

Mom chose this moment to stroll out of the bedroom to meet us, but she was still frowning. Gloria did not make a move towards her. Mom coolly greeted them and did not respond when Don said, "Hi, Mom." But at least, she did not reject him openly. Gloria became uneasy, so I spoke to her quietly on the side and persuaded her to observe a truce with Mom. No apologies, no accusations. Then we left our parents at their door with good luck wishes and went back to Don's apartment.

Gloria and Don settled down in his bachelor pad and soon began to look for a larger apartment. They did not say it, but it seemed obvious to me that they wanted to be further away from my parents to avoid any potential meddling by Mom in their affairs.

A few weeks later, Gloria and Don had their first big argument—about money. Gloria wanted to redo Don's apartment to restyle it for a married couple. Don did not want to spend the dollars, since they were planning to move shortly. Her argument was that they needed furniture and dishes now, so why wait until they could move?

About a month later, I arrived at their apartment door to visit. The door had been left unlocked. I heard her screaming at him, and was about to leave when the screaming stopped. Alarmed, I rushed into the kitchen—fearing the worst. It was bad enough, but it was not the worst! Mighty Don was holding her overhead with one hand and shaking her.

Omigod! What had I done? Did I put my sister into the hands of King Kong? She was out of breath and crying. For the moment I was transfixed with horror, then I grabbed a kitchen chair and smashed it across Don's back. Not even a flinch from him! It was as futile as slapping a Sherman tank with a bare hand. He slowly put Gloria down and turned to me calmly. "She is okay. I didn't hurt her." I trembled. *Would he break me in half? Would he throw me out the window?* Fortunately, he did neither.

Still grasping the chair leg, I snarled at him. "If you touch her again, I will smash this over your head!" Turning to my shaken sister, I said, "Get dressed. You are coming home—NOW!" Gloria trembled. "No, Bernie. It's all right. Don and I will work this out ourselves." Doubtfully, I went along with her request. *At least, he did not hit her!* Turning at the door as I left, I insisted, "I want you both to go for marriage counseling!" They reluctantly agreed. The following week, Don and Gloria went into therapy sessions at Bronx House and I breathed a sigh of relief—temporarily.

About three weeks later, they found a nice three-room apartment with kitchenette and foyer in the Pelham Parkway area near Bronx House. Gloria bought new curtains and some furniture, and they settled down into married housekeeping in their little 'nest.' All seemed well at first, but they were both volatile, and further flare-up problems remained and erupted during the rest of their five-year troubled marriage.

Gloria, born Jewish, did not practice her faith, and Don, born and raised a Catholic, did not practice his faith either. Gloria did not communicate with Mom, but she kept in touch with Dad and me. I hoped that she would eventually get over her anger at Mom, but she did not. This feud continued to fester, casting a shadow over her family relationship with both Mom and Dad.

Meanwhile, now that I was freed from my self-imposed guardianship of newly-married Gloria, my social life moved into higher gear. Don and Gloria continued their counseling sessions at Bronx House. At the Bronx YW-YMHA on the Grand Concourse, two blocks south of East 168th Street, I sought to meet compatible girls to socialize with and date. Restlessly, I entered the Bronx and Manhattan young singles scene, browsing and sometimes joining other young singles groups and events. I met several young ladies, but no more than casual temporary dating interest developed there.

Mom waited up for me when I came home from Saturday night dates and scolded me for getting home late. I sensed that the time was approaching for me to spread my wings and fly away from the parental home. I made plans to join the Air Force as a better alternative to being drafted into the Army.

A few weeks later, I celebrated my 18th birthday. Gloria and Don invited me to their new Pelham Parkway apartment for a small party. At my request, they also invited Mom and Dad.

At last, I thought. *There will be peace in my family again. Things are going well for us now. Mom and Dad will accept Don as their son-in-law, I am working on a nice job and earning a living, Gloria is married and away from further conflict with Mom. Under Carol's tutelage, Mike is doing better in school, and Carol has overcome her disappointment at only getting a partial scholarship at Juilliard.* Instead, Carol accepted a free after-school music scholarship at Bronx House. I sighed and mused. *It's too bad that Mom's being on the 'outs' with her sisters and brothers, together with her own stubborn pride, interfered with her asking relatives for financial help for Carol's musical education.*

43

The Crippling Car Crash

My eighteenth birthday party at Don and Gloria's went smoothly. Gloria greeted Mom somewhat coldly. They did not hug or kiss, as she did with Dad. I expected that and pretended not to notice. The birthday candles were lit and I received a nice shirt and tie combo from Gloria and Don. Mom and Dad gave me a gift certificate for *Barnes and Noble* bookstores. The twins did not come, because Gloria said their apartment was too small to also entertain them. At age thirteen, they were old enough to stay home alone for the evening.

Hopeful that the party might start a thawing process in the relationship between Gloria and Mom, my parents and I said our goodbyes to Gloria and Don at around 10:00 p.m. Dad drove us home in his old Chevy. Mom sat next to him in the front, and I sat in the back. There were no seatbelts in the car. *(Seatbelts were not commonly available until late in the 1950s).*

Heading westward on Pelham Parkway, we stopped in the left lane next to the wide center divider for a traffic light near the Esplanade. Suddenly, looming large in the rear view mirror, there were two blazing headlights. For a few seconds, Dad's car and the parkway, and the headlights of a speeding car behind us that ran the red light, were the center of our focused universe.

We all screamed, and I braced for an impact. A tremendous metallic crunch as our Chevy's rear end crumpled, was followed a split-second later by a second crash, as the impact shoved our wrecked car into an elm tree along the center divider. The tree impact cracked the windshield, and a shard of glass slashed across my chin, but caused only a deep scratch. Another inch to the left would have cut my throat like a knife. The other car's main impact was on the left rear side of our Chevy rear, thus sparing me serious injury in the right-side rear seat. I managed to push the partly-crumpled rear door open and checked on my parents. I quickly turned off the engine and silently prayed there would be no fire.

Mom was less fortunate. The glass slashed her chest and right arm, and she was bruised and thrown around in the car. Hysterical and screaming, she was unable to free herself from our wrecked car. I could not calm her down, so I squeezed her hand and told her that help was on the way.

I could not reach Dad, but spoke to him through the shattered car window. His legs were splayed up over the steering wheel, and he was in severe pain. He moaned a little with clenched teeth and asked me, "How's Mom doing?"

"She is OK. Shaken up and cut with glass, but not too bad. I can't move her, or get you out." I heard sirens wailing. "That's the police and firemen. They will get you and Mom into an ambulance to Jacobi Hospital. We are only a few blocks away from there."

I gave him a quick kiss, then backed off as the rescuers went to work to remove my parents from the car safely. It took about fifteen minutes of hydraulic spreading with prying tools and popping two doors off their hinges to free them from the car. I held Mom's hand, called out to Dad and gave them what reassurances that I could. They took Mom into the ambulance on a stretcher, but Dad was transported in a sling because of multiple injuries. He was hurt quite severely.

Sirens blaring and lights flashing, the ambulance sped us off to Jacobi Hospital. Dad was immediately x-rayed and seen by a doctor. Mom got a sedative, and then was stitched up. A few minutes later, I received two stitches in my chin and a pain-easing antibiotic in order to do the paperwork to admit my parents to the hospital.

Then, while Mom and I waited in the emergency room, I made some quick phone calls. First call was to Gloria. "Hello, I have some bad news. We were in a big car crash on Pelham Parkway after we left your place. Dad was hurt very badly, Mom was cut by flying glass, and I had some minor cuts and bruises. Come with Don right away to Jacobi Hospital. Don't ask me now what happened. Get here fast and I will tell you."

Gloria responded quickly and they were there in a half-hour. I then called Carol and Mark on the phone and told them I would be getting home late. I lied a little and said that Mom and Dad were busy and could not talk on the phone now. With the adult family assembled in the emergency room office, the resident doctor briefed us on our parents' condition.

"Your father is in serious condition but is expected to survive. He will be hospitalized for at least several months with a compound fractured pelvis, four broken ribs, a broken arm, and lacerations. Your mother has multiple lacerations and will be hospitalized for at least a week or two. After they go home, they will need follow-up nursing care. Bernie, you have some cuts and bruises that were stitched up in the emergency room." He paused and introduced Mrs. Fields, a hospital social worker who was seated next to him. She was a slightly plump, motherly-looking gray-haired lady with a kindly face framed by large glasses. She asked me, "what are your plans to take care of your brother and sister?"

I responded. "I am eighteen and earning a living as a bookkeeper. My siblings are thirteen. I can cook meals. I will assume responsibility for them with some help from the family." Gloria said quickly, "We will help. I will come over twice a week to cook dinner." I hugged her. "Thanks, Gloria. I do have one special request for you meanwhile." I whispered in her ear. "Please, please, do not get into any arguments with Mom. Bite your tongue. We know how difficult she can be at times. You will be making it much harder for me to maintain the household if you get into any fights with her. It would also aggravate Dad and me. Promise?" Gloria nodded her head in agreement.

On the way back to Macombs Road in a taxicab, my head was buzzing with plans and arrangements. All of a sudden, my world was turned upside down. I was sure that I could manage the apartment after working on my day job. Carol would be a help, but she was also busy getting ready to start her after-school musical education at Bronx House.

Carol could take a school bus to Bronx House Music School, which was located near Gloria and Don's apartment. On her music school night, she could have dinner with Gloria and Don, then Don would drive her home. I fixed dinner for myself and Mark after work. *On and on...*, my thoughts raced. I jotted down some notes on a pocket pad; and in about twenty minutes, the cab pulled up to the walk-in door of the Macombs Road apartment.

The twins were watching television when I walked in alone. "Where's Mom and Dad?" Mark asked. I told them what had happened, and they were stilled by the realization that things would change in this household. From being a third, 'surrogate parent', I would now assume actual parental responsibility for weeks and possibly months to come. My plans to join the military would be put on hold for at least a year.

Mom came home in two weeks, and was assisted by a home-aid nurse coming over twice a week while she continued to recover. Dad's boss at his taxi garage referred us to a high-profile lawyer to pursue our case against the other driver. I gradually ceded my parental responsibilities back to Mom and returned to only being a big brother to Mark and Carol.

Some semblance of normal routine returned to the Seiden household. Two weeks later, Carol was enrolled on a music scholarship at Bronx House. Mom had recovered enough to sign the papers, relieving me of the necessity of seeking a guardianship of Carol to sign her into the Bronx House School of Music.

Mom was subdued when she came home from the hospital but gradually returned to her old feisty self. I took driving lessons and earned my license within a few weeks.

After school, Mark became a neighborhood repairman for radios and televisions and contributed to the household income. When I tried to claim Carol and Mark as dependents on my tax return, the IRS objected because I only supported them for the latter six months after the accident in that calendar year. After I explained the situation to them, a compromise was reached and I was allowed to claim one dependent—Carol.

As the following weeks and months rolled by, Aunt Irma came over to help out about twice a month. I figuratively held my breath and crossed my fingers when Aunt Irma visited; but fortunately, no quarreling erupted between her and Mom. Likewise, Gloria helped out a little; but she was now expecting her first child, which limited her availability. Meanwhile, a hostile truce prevailed between daughter and mother. (This was a type of truce in which both sides remained verbally armed and ready to strike but avoided full family hostilities.)

Carol thrived in the collegial atmosphere of Bronx House, and her skills as a pianist rapidly blossomed into a near-professional level of proficiency. I eagerly awaited her performance debut in the annual Bronx House student recital and stood guard by the living room door when she practiced to prevent distractions. There was a first year student recital also, but Carol was selected to play in the advanced students recital the following week.

44

Carol's Music: Triumph & Finale

When Carol first began to play the piano, Mom had bought an old, somewhat scratched Horace Waters upright from Uncle Rudy. Its cherry mahogany finish clashed with the frayed green slipcovers of the living room couch. I wanted the piano to look nice for Carol, so I polished out the scratches.

There was a streak of musical talent on the maternal side of my family. Mom had never taken formal piano lessons, but learned to play with help from Rudy. She played mainly popular music to entertain family and friends. Before the big car accident, Mom had applied for a music scholarship for Carol at Bronx House Community Center, and Carol was accepted as an after-school student with a school bus to transport her there and home twice a week.

Bronx House, at 990 Pelham Parkway South, is still a settlement house today, with many gym, swimming and summer camp activities. It has been a mid-Bronx community center since 1911. The parkway is lined with stately American elms and wide center island green spaces, with a bicycle path winding along its 2 ½ mile tree-canopied length. A subdued red brick three story windowless façade formed the right wing of the Bronx House building, across from the entrance canopy separating it from the East wing of the Dance school.

The performing arts division of Bronx House provided low-cost and scholarship music and dance education to children and adults as an alternative to private music schools. Students unable to afford to buy an instrument could borrow instruments from Bronx House for home practice.

Carol's first year at Bronx House went by quickly. She developed her own personalized piano performing style with small synchronized head nods to keep time. In her first student recital, several hundred friends and family of the young music students were there to applaud for their performing children.

The program consisted of typical classical pieces for intermediate or beginner pianists. Some students played with early glimmerings of blossoming skill, others stumbled through their pieces while their teachers winced in the first row. Then Carol, the calmest of all present, stepped forward to center stage and seated herself in one graceful sweep at the Steinway concert grand piano. She had been saved on the program for the Recital Grand Finale, pert and pretty in a pale blue chiffon dress with a white corsage.

I was breathless with anticipation. No easy Mozart minuet or Clementi Sonatina was stacked on her music stand. She had chosen to perform the Liszt *"Hungarian Rhapsody #2"*, arranged for solo piano.

As the opening arpeggios of Liszt reverberated throughout the hall, the audience first looked startled, then thrilled. Was this really a second-year music student? Carol played on lyrically with a professional fluid grace, and the audience was enraptured.

A standing ovation greeted the closing chords of the Liszt piece, and she followed it with a Chopin etude. The house reverberated with bravos and cheers, as she blushingly took her bows. The audience called for an encore, a rare event for a Bronx House student recital. *(Carol had briefly transformed Bronx House into a 'Carnegie Hall'.)*

I was proud—so proud that day to be Carol's big brother. I will never forget that first Bronx House recital. Never. Or my memories of her onstage debut.

Although Carol's behavior and moral standards were above reproach, Mom's paranoia went into orbit after Gloria's elopement. She constantly checked on Carol, lecturing the poor girl stridently, and warning her not to follow in her sister's footsteps and run off with a boy. But Carol was unusually level-headed for a young teenager and had no such ideas. She had a few boyfriends from time-to-time, whom she met secretly after school. She quietly introduced me to each boy she was seeing, and it seemed to me that they were nice and respectable young fellows. She pledged me to secrecy, because Mom did not want her to date at all—even after school in the afternoon! I told Mom it was unfair to punish Carol for her sister's elopement and marriage, but it was like talking to a stone wall. So I soon gave up trying to stop Mom from harassing her.

Early in the fall term, three copies of a letter arrived from the Board of Education. Coincidentally, I had just stopped off early for dinner at Mom's place after work that day. One copy each was addressed to Mom and Dad and to Carol! Mom turned pale when she saw this official envelope and asked me to open it for her. In a reassuring manner, I began to read it:

Dear Mr. & Mrs. Seiden:

> *It is with the greatest pleasure that I wish to inform you of the results of the first tabulation of academic scores in the current semester for the entire school encompassing the tenth through the twelfth grades. Your daughter, Carol Seiden, has reached the level of highest scholastic standing— ranked first out of 2,138 students at William Howard Taft High School with the equivalent of a straight 'A plus' average. On behalf of the Board of Education of the City of New York, I offer my heartiest congratulations for this notable academic achievement, and best wishes for continuing scholastic success.*

Mom looked slightly stunned, then in a diffident manner, she commented to me, "That's great news. I hope she keeps up the good work and that this does not go to her head." Meantime, visions of Carol's future danced in my head. *Carol at Harvard ... or Yale?... Phi Beta Kappa ... graduating Summa cum laude ...*

"Mom, is that all you have to say?" I exclaimed. *I could not believe her cool response!* "Give me the letter. I will show it to Carol myself when she gets home!" And so I did. I greeted her right at the door. "Carol, we received a letter from the Board of Education about your academic ranking today." I grinned and hugged her. "Congratulations. You are ranked as the number one student in the entire school!"

She responded warmly. "That's a wonderful honor to live up to."

"I want to take you out to celebrate!"

"You mean like a date?"

"Yes, like a date!"

"Mom does not let me go out on dates."

"This is different." I winked. "I think she can trust ME to go out with you." We both laughed.

And so it happened. That Saturday night, I wore my best suit, and Carol wore her recital dress. She had never experienced a concert or opera in Manhattan's splendid symphonic halls before.

We went downtown to Manhattan by taxicab to City Center. As the terracotta high-domed Moorish-revival style performing arts center loomed into mid-block view, Carol declared, "You are the best big brother a girl ever had." I blushed and said, "We are here," and gallantly opened the taxi door for her.

Carol was amazed by the embroidered scroll-work framed doors and stage proscenium of City Center. We took our seats in the second balcony as the curtain rose and the orchestra struck up the soft bravura and skipping cadences of the overture to Giacomo Rossini's *"La Cenerentola"* (Cinderella).

After the performance, we went into Schrafft's on 57th Street and Third Avenue for ice cream sundaes and hot chocolate. Carol looked so beautiful and grown-up as I took her home that magic night. We arrived shortly after 1:00 a.m.

Mom was waiting up in the living room, and greeted us in a subdued manner.

"Did you have a nice time?"

Carol responded. "Yes, we did."

I kissed Carol good night on the cheek and went home to my new furnished room near the Grand Concourse. I had just moved in a few weeks earlier. That was the way I remember her —my baby sister almost all grown up now at fourteen.

A week passed, then another one. There was a telephone call to me. The ring tone itself seemed urgent before I even picked up the receiver. It was Carol. She was crying in a melancholy way that was most unlike her normal cheerful self.

"What's the matter, my sweet little sister?" I asked tenderly. I had not called her that in years. She replied, "I must come and see you right away. It's urgent. I am taking a bus and I will be there in a half hour."

I met her at the bus stop, and we walked together back to my apartment. She refrained from any discussion until we arrived there.

"It's Mom. I can't take her anymore. She follows me home after school from the bus stop, lurking across the streets and hiding behind cars as I pass. She yells and threatens me constantly at home, and says "You are just like your sister. I will not let you wind up like her. I cannot focus on my schoolwork, with her breathing down my neck."

I said softly, "you need to get away from there for awhile"

Despairingly, she answered. "Mom would never allow that."

"Maybe we can force the issue. I could try to seek custody of you. It would be an extended visit, at first. I would be happy to have you here. There would be some rules, of course, but I will not breathe down your neck. You are a responsible young lady".

She asked hopefully, "You would do that for me?"

"Yes, I would. But first there are some legal issues that I have to research about this situation, then I must consult a lawyer."

I paused. "It will take about a week. Then I will go to Mom and Dad and see if I can move you over to my place for an extended visit without a fight. Meanwhile, try to avoid her as much as possible."

Carol's voice brightened considerably. "Okay," she said." I guess I can take it for one more week."

I hugged her and wished her well. *This was my little sister, and I felt fiercely protective towards her.*

I went to the Fordham library to study family law and took notes to discuss with a lawyer. But which lawyer? I began making some calls in the next few days, which had no result. I needed some professional source to help me to help Carol.

Meanwhile, unknown to me, the next day, Carol suffered a brief fainting spell at home. Mom rushed her across the street to Dr. Weinberg. He diagnosed her as having some mild complications after the onset of her menstrual periods which had started irregularly a few months earlier. The doctor sent her home and prescribed bed rest for a few days.

The next day was a Friday. Mark had just come home from school and looked in on Carol at around 4:00 p.m. She was stretched out on the couch in the living room watching television. Mom had just left the apartment a few moments earlier to go shopping and was walking along Macombs Road towards the University Avenue stores.

Mark cried out, "Carol? Carol??? CAROL!! Are you okay?" He sensed immediately that she was not okay. She started to sit up, then fell back and mumbled something unintelligibly. Mark tried to arouse her but could not. Alarmed, he ran outside to intercept Mom, catching her midway up the block. "Mom, something is wrong with Carol. I cannot wake her up. Come home NOW!"

Mom ran back to the apartment. Moments later, a piercing wail arose from the walk-in apartment as Mom saw Carol lying there. She instinctively sensed that her daughter was dead and descended into crying hysteria. Mark sprinted to Dr. Weinberg's medical office across the street and burst in. Dr. Weinberg told his nurse to cancel remaining appointments that day and rushed across the street to the apartment. The doctor, after examining Carol, with a stricken look on his face, tried to comfort Mark and Mom as best he could, but they were inconsolable.

Meanwhile, the nurse called the police, to report the sudden death. There was chaos. Confusion. Hysteria. An ambulance arrived and the attending doctor aboard officially pronounced Carol dead. Dad arrived home from work a few minutes later and nearly collapsed at the sight of Carol's still body on the living room couch, a sheet covering her face.

A policeman stood guard at my parent's walk-in apartment entrance as stunned friends, family and neighbors began to gather near the door. Gloria phoned me and said to come home immediately but did not say why—just that it was an emergency. I heard the crying and screaming in the background on the phone and immediately hopped into a taxicab to head for Macombs Road.

Heading down Macombs Road from the north side, I saw the people gathered near my parents' door. A policeman guarded the entrance. They were at a respectful distance from the door itself. Then, emerging from the taxicab, I saw something which I had never seen before—Dad emerged from the apartment in tears. I had never seen him cry. We hugged. He whispered, "It is Carol. She is dead."

My world spun around my shoulders, and I suddenly felt the heaviness of tragic gloom descend over me. Carol? CAROL?! My baby sister? **OMIGOD!!"**

Dazed, I stumbled into the living room. A blanket was pulled up over her stilled form. Just the top of her head showed out a little over the hemmed edge.

I SCREAMED! I ran into my former bedroom, sobbing. I fell to my knees by the old chest of drawers in the corner.

"God, please give her back to us. Please. Please!" I cried and begged, then cried some more. After a few minutes, I managed to compose myself. My high school and my boyhood were suddenly gone. Adulthood and mourning was my new reality. Later, an autopsy disclosed that her death was caused by a rare cerebral pneumonia, striking suddenly with symptoms similar to a massive stroke.

The Bronx itself faded into the background as I faced the painful present. Carol was gone, the bright promise of her musical future snuffed out at age fourteen. All my past efforts to nurture her were now wiped out. My merry childhood misadventures seemed to be empty pranks from the past as I faced the grownup Cold War world of the approaching 1960s—no longer the growing-up nickel trolley ride world of a Bronx Brat who was a third parent to three younger siblings. I postponed planned military enlistment until Dad would be recovered and back at work to support the family.

Perhaps, because of my redeeming relationship with them in their formative years, I was not such a Bronx Brat, after all.

45

Fond Memory

The memory of Carol lives on in the heart of all who knew her. A plaque at Lincoln Center carries her name forward into musical eternity.

"In Memoriam" painting by my wife: Claire Leder.
Carol is seated at right by the piano, next to sister Gloria.

Epilogue

Twelve days before Carol died, unbeknownst to Bernie or his parents, she sent the handwritten and heartfelt letter below to Uncle Dave and Aunt Margaret. It was her final legacy—to try to bring estranged uncles and aunts together again with her parents. Tragically, she succeeded. The aunts and uncles did come together again, hugged and kissed at the funeral and vowed that they would be alienated from each other no more. But this reconciliation only happened at Carol's funeral. Once … only once …

Dear Uncle Dave and Aunt Margaret:

I would have sent you a New Year's card, but I felt that a card couldn't contain my suitable words. My fondest wish for the New Year is that you have a most wonderful one & that we will be together once again under a lasting peaceful environment.

Being a young lady of fourteen now, as well as a new

aunt, I realize that an aunt and uncle's relationship with their nieces and nephews are almost as nice as the "Parent-Children" relationships. I don't know if my attitude is shared or if I am ever thought about by you, but I hope by this letter that you can judge me as I am—caring.

My thoughts, ever since our family separation, have been of you many-a-time. I think of you on top of all other aunts and uncles of mine, for you are "tops" in my book. My brother Mark shares my opinion although he is not a writing "bug".

Whatever the unfortunate circumstances are that brought about these improper family relationships, I'm sure can be settled in due time. Besides the pressure has died down for after all it's been quite a few years. I'm signing off with a sincere hope for an ideal family relationship in the near future.

With all my love,
   Your niece,
   Carol

Note: This letter was returned by Uncle Dave to Bernie's parents at Carol's funeral. They tucked it away in a dresser drawer. Bernie never saw it until about twenty five years later after his parents died. He had undertaken the sad duty of disposing of the furniture and effects from their apartment, and came across this letter.

Acknowledgments

Claire Leder,
My wife, a retired high school/college teacher and museum-exhibited artist; for loving, and patient encouragement of the author, and for her skilled and diligent assistance in editing it.

David Billings (In Memoriam)
My father, who taught me loving kindness to others, and chivalry towards women.

Rose Billings (In Memoriam)
My mother, who meant well and gave much of herself to her children.

Mary Ruke,
A dear friend to myself and my wife. She has been like a sister to us.

* * *

Dr. Alan Hartman,
Chief Cardiac Surgeon, Northwell Hospital, Manhasset, NY, whose skills saved my life in 2017, and made it possible for me to reach my 80th birthday and write this book.

Emblem Health HIP/VIP,
The great medical support team at Emblem Health HIP/VIP, Lake Success Medical Center, Lake Success, NY.

Dr. Avni Thakore,
My Cardiologist, and her dedicated staff at Catholic Health Services, St. Francis Hospital Heart Center, East Hills, NY.

I also thank Nicole Noonan, NP at the St. Francis Center for her caring medical skills and comforting presence to me as a patient.
And finally, I especially thank Northwell Hospital itself for their dedicated medical staff.

www.ingramcontent.com/pod-product-compliance
Lightning Source LLC
Chambersburg PA
CBHW030145100526
44592CB00009B/130